Advocating for children

'To rescue our children we will have to let them save us from the power we embody: we will have to trust the very differences that they forever personify.'

June Jordan, Keynote address to Child Welfare League of America, 1978

Advocating for Children

International Perspectives on Children's Rights

Edited by

Anne B. Smith, Megan Gollop,
Kate Marshall and Karen Nairn

Children's Issues Centre,
University of Otago

University of Otago Press

Published by University of Otago Press
56 Union Street/PO Box 56, Dunedin, New Zealand
Fax: 64 3 479 8385
email: university.press@stonebow.otago.ac.nz

First published 2000

ISBN 1 877133 90 6

Printed by PrintLink Ltd, Wellington, New Zealand

Contents

Acknowledgements

The editors gratefully acknowledge financial assistance from the following organisations, which assisted with funding speakers to come to the conference *Children's Rights: National and International Perspectives*: the British Council, the Ministry of Foreign Affairs and Trade, the New Zealand Law Foundation and the Social Policy Agency. We would also like to thank Childwatch International for deciding to hold their meeting of Key Institutions in Dunedin, which helped to make the conference and this book into truly international events. The book would not have been possible without the ideas and support of Rachael Brinsdon and Michael Gaffney.

About the authors

Nicola Atwool is a lecturer in the Department of Community and Family Studies at the University of Otago, Dunedin, New Zealand. She has professional qualifications in social work and child psychotherapy. Nicola has previously worked as a social worker, senior social worker, social work trainer and child psychotherapist with the New Zealand Children, Young Persons and Their Families Service. She has a particular interest in work with children and adolescents. Her research interests are focused on attachment, the impact of trauma and the social construction of childhood.

Anne Bray is the director of the Donald Beasley Institute, an independent national research institute on intellectual disability in Dunedin, New Zealand. Anne has been involved for over thirty years in advocating, teaching and researching in the rights of children with disabilities to inclusion, participation and achievement.

Katherine Covell, a psychologist, and **R. Brian Howe**, a political scientist, are the founders and co-directors of the Children's Rights Centre at the University College of Cape Breton, Sydney, Nova Scotia, Canada. Bringing their perspectives together, they have published widely on children's rights issues and co-teach courses on children's rights. Katherine and Brian are the architects of the first children's rights curriculum to be adopted by an education department in Canada.

Professor James Garbarino is co-director of the Family Life Development Center at Cornell University and Professor of Human Development in Ithaca, New York. From 1985-1994 he served as President of the Erikson Institute for Advanced Study in Child Development. He is the author or editor of seventeen books, among them *Raising Children in a Socially Toxic Environment* (1995) and most recently *Lost Boys: Why Our Sons Turn Violent and How We Can Save Them* (1999). He was the first recipient of the C. Henry Kempe Award in the United States from the National Conference on Child Abuse and Neglect, in 1985. He has conducted field work on the development of children and youth in war zones – including Kuwait and Iraq in the wake of the Gulf War. His work on children in war zones is reported in his 1991 book *No Place to be a Child: Growing Up in a War Zone*. Currently he is focusing on the developmental pathways that lead to lethal youth violence, and has served as an expert witness in youth homicide trials. Of special interest in his current work is the role of spiritual development and human rights education in the rehabilitation of violent youthful offenders, a project entitled *From Boot Camp to Monastery*.

Sue Gates is an educational psychologist and lecturer at the Dunedin College of Education, Dunedin, New Zealand. She is also undertaking a doctorate at the Bioethics Research Centre, University of Otago, Dunedin. Sue worked for ten years as the National Advocate for IHC, which involved extensive national advocacy on behalf of children with disabilities, particularly within education.

Mark Henaghan is a Professor of Law at the University of Otago, Dunedin, New Zealand. Mark specialises in family law with a particular interest in the law as it applies to children. Mark was a member of the New Zealand Committee for Children which advocated for the establishment of the Commissioner for Children's Office in New Zealand. Mark is an editor of *Butterworths Family Law Service*, *Butterworths Family Law in New Zealand*, and *Butterworths New Zealand Family Law Journal*. Mark is also a member of New Zealand Law Society Committees which are assessing the application of the United Nations Convention on the Rights of the Child to current New Zealand law. Mark has written over a hundred articles on the law as it relates to children. He has also been involved in writing the leading texts on family law in New Zealand, *Family Law Policy in New Zealand* and *Family Law in New Zealand*.

Cindy Kiro is a senior lecturer in the Department of Social Policy and Social Work, Massey University (at Albany) in Auckland, New Zealand. Her iwi is Ngapuhi and her hapu Ngati-Hine and Te Rangiweweha. Her background and experience includes an MBA (Executive), certificates in social work and epidemiology; and experience as a social worker, community volunteer working with Maori women and children, health and child advocate, and environmental advocate (former executive director and member of the International Board of Greenpeace) and manager. She is completing a PhD (supported by a Health Research Council fellowship) on the impact of social policy changes on children and young people, particularly Maori tamariki and rangatahi. She is interested in the relationship between health policy and broader social policy, particularly as it impacts on vulnerable populations such as Maori. She has recently co-authored a paper (with Alison Blaiklock, Will Low, Michael Belgrave, Ian Hassall and Eileen Davenport) for the Innocenti Development Centre in Italy called 'When the Invisible Hand Rocks the Cradle'.

Aiono Dr Fanaafi Le Tagaloa was the first woman to obtain her doctorate (from the University of London, in Education Philosophy and Applied Linguistics) in Samoa. She is a chief in her own right and has been a torch-bearer in Samoan society, having been Director of Education, Professor of Samoan Language and Culture and Vice-Chancellor at the University of Samoa, and a Member of Parliament for Western Samoa. She is currently the president of a private tertiary institution of higher learning called Le Amoso. She has been a consultant in many countries and has published widely on language and cultural issues. She is a strong advocate of the rights of people everywhere (especially children) to have access to an education in their mother tongue.

Robert Ludbrook is a lawyer who has worked as an advocate for children in England, Australia and New Zealand. From 1983 to 1985 Robert worked with the Children's Legal Centre in London. In 1987 he founded the Youth Law Project, the first specialist youth legal advocacy group in New Zealand. In 1993 Robert was founding director of the National Children's and Youth Law Centre, based in Sydney. In 1996/97 Robert worked with the Office of the Commissioner for Children. Robert is the author of six books including *A New Zealand Guide to Children and the Law* and has written numerous guides, booklets and fact sheets on aspects of law and policy affecting children and young people.

Dr Berry Mayall is a reader in Childhood Studies and assistant-director of the Social Science Research Unit, Institute of Education, University of London. She is also the co-convenor of the Childhood Research and Policy Centre. She has carried out many research studies on the daily lives of children and their parents and carers, in the context of social policies and practices affecting children's well-being. She has a particular interest in children's health experiences in relation to health services and educational institutions. She is a leading figure in the field of the Sociology of Childhood which emphasises children as social actors who are active participants in society and co-constructors of the social order. She has published many books and articles in this area, including *Children's Childhoods, Observed and Experienced* and *Children, Health and the Social Order.*

Professor Gary Melton is the director of the Institute on Family and Neighborhood Life at Clemson University in South Carolina, USA. Gary is well known for his work on children's rights and child and family policy in his own country and internationally. He is the president of Childwatch International, a global child research network, and past president of the American Psychology-Law Society. He has more than 250 publications on such topics as paediatric AIDS, forensic mental health services, the use of social science in legal reform, and child protection policies. He has had a major influence on policy for children in the United States, especially in social services and legal areas, and was the principal architect of the child protection strategy proposed by the US Advisory Board on Child Abuse and Neglect.

Per Miljeteig holds a masters degree of psychology, specialising in developmental and social psychology, from the University of Oslo, Norway. Per has been the director of Childwatch International since its start in 1993. He also works as a consultant for the World Bank child labour programme and serves as Technical Advisor to the Norweigian Ministry of Foreign Affairs. Per has also more recently worked for the Ministry of Children and Family Affairs, Norway and the UNICEF headquarters in New York. Per also participated in drafting the UN Convention on Rights as a representative of the Norweigian Government.

Professor Irene Rizzini is from the Department of Social Policy at the Rio de Janeiro State University and is director of the Research Program for Children, Youth and the Family in Brazil. She serves as the vice-president of the Advisory Board of Childwatch International, the global child research network based in Norway. She is widely known for her work on concepts of childhood, child labour and children who have experienced violence, poverty and homelessness. She is the author and editor of a number of books including *Children in Brazil Today: Disinherited from Society: Street Children in Latin America* (1995); *Children and Youth in the World of Work* (1996); and *The Lost Century: The Historical Roots of Public Policies on Children in Brazil* (1997).

Professor Anne B. Smith convened the Children's Rights Conference and is director of the Children's Issues Centre at the University of Otago in Dunedin, New Zealand. She is an applied developmental psychologist with a particular interest in social development and in ecological and sociocultural influences on children's development. Anne's past research has been in the field of early childhood education and care. More recently she has been influenced by the new field of the sociology of childhood and has incorporated children's own constructions of their experiences into a broad range of research studies.

Pauline Tapp has taught and written about the area of child and family law for over twenty years, and is currently an associate professor in the Faculty of Law at the University of Auckland, Auckland, New Zealand. She is a member of the NGO Coalition, Action for Children in Aotearoa, which presented the alternative report on New Zealand's compliance with the United Nations Convention on the Rights of the Child to the Committee on the Rights of the Child in 1996. She was involved, as a consultant to government and a member of the National Advisory Committee on the Prevention of Child Abuse, in the development of

New Zealand's child protection legislation and is the author of one of the leading legal texts on the topic. Her recent work has explored children's autonomy rights.

Pat Tuohy is the chief adviser in child and youth health with the Ministry of Health, New Zealand. His responsibilities include co-ordination and leadership of child and youth health with respect to the Ministry of Health, the Health Funding Authority and health service providers. Pat is a specialist paediatrician with particular interests in community child health, SIDS (sudden infant death syndrome) and developmental and behavioural paediatrics. Since completing a medical degree at the University of Otago in 1979, Pat has undertaken postgraduate training in Paediatrics and worked as a general paediatrician. Pat joined the New Zealand Plunket Society in 1991 as its regional paediatrician based in Wellington (NZ) and was later appointed to the position of director of Child Health Policy in the Plunket National Office and in 1995 to the role of National Paediatrician.

Beth Wood has a professional background in social work, nursing and policy work related to children's issues. Beth is currently working as a policy analyst/ health promotion advisor for the New Zealand Plunket Society National Office, Wellington, New Zealand. Beth is interested in the issue of children's rights generally, with a particular interest in the prevention of child abuse.

• Introduction •

Children's rights: An overview

ANNE B. SMITH

In July 1999, the Children's Issues Centre held a child and family policy conference on the theme of *Children's Rights: National and International Perspectives* at the University of Otago. The conference participants represented an interdisciplinary forum of professionals working either directly or indirectly with children – they included lawyers, teachers, health professionals, social workers, police, researchers, policy officials and students. The conference was preceded by a meeting of Childwatch International, a network of directors of child research organisations supported by the Norwegian government. The involvement of the Childwatch researchers helped to give the conference a strong international flavour with delegates coming from Australia, Brazil, Canada, China, the Cook Islands, England, Fiji, Israel, Japan, Jamaica, Kenya, Norway, Russia, Samoa, Senegal, Sri Lanka, Thailand, the United States and Venezuela. For many of those who attended, the conference was an enriching and enabling experience. Not only was it an opportunity for people in New Zealand to discuss their concerns about children's rights in this country, but it brought together a group with a variety of concerns from all over the world. This book provides a permanent record of this excellent conference.[1]

The conference involved much discussion and many papers about the United Nations Convention on the Rights of the Child (UNCROC), and the importance of developing a working awareness of the contents of the convention and applying it in daily practice and policies for children was emphasised. James Garbarino described the convention in his keynote address as 'an attempt to aid us in transcending individual and collective limitations on behalf of some universal commitment to the subjective value of children.'

The Children's Issues Centre was motivated to organise this conference by its wish to make a contribution towards meeting New Zealand's obligations in relation to UNCROC. Article 42 of UNCROC says that the principles and provisions of the Convention should be made widely known. We very much hope that the conference and its publications will help to disseminate some essential information about UNCROC and issues of children's rights more generally, not only to the group who participated in the conference, but to a wider audience.[2] UNCROC consists of fifty-four articles. The articles have been divided into three main types of rights by Lansdown (1994, p. 36):

- **Provision rights** – rights to minimum standards of family life and access to parental care, health, education, social security, physical care, play, recreation, culture and leisure. The conference included many papers on provision rights, and covered such issues as rights for children with parents in prison to have contact with their parents, the rights of children with disabilities to have access to education, and the rights of children to a healthy toxin free environment, rights to appropriate mental health services and to access to an appropriate standard of living.
- **Protection rights** – including the right to be safe from discrimination, physical and sexual abuse, exploitation, substance abuse, injustice and conflict. A number of papers addressed issues of protection – protection from childhood injury, family violence, physical punishment, exploitation through child pornography, and the right to be safe going to and from school.
- **Participation rights** – civil and political rights such as the right to a name and identity, to be consulted and to taken into account, to physical integrity, to information, to freedom of speech and opinion and to challenge decisions made on their behalf. There were many papers on participation rights (children's right to be heard and their views respected and taken into account) in the family and criminal court, after trauma and abuse, and in violent families. Also children and young people's right to be given information is an issue covered in several papers.

Children and children's rights have been argued about for centuries. 'Rights are entitlements, valuable commodities', which we 'do not have to grovel or beg to get', according to Freeman (1996, p. 70). Children's rights are not generally greeted with huge enthusiasm in New Zealand or further afield, and few politicians give children's rights any prominence. The media coverage of children's rights is not balanced. There are plenty of horror stories about children, but few of these give any prominence to the idea that children have rights and a great deal to contribute to society. The notion of children having rights tends to be interpreted as being permissive and giving them too much power and control, while at the same time taking power and control away from parents or others in authority over children. Yet as is shown by many papers at the conference, the rights of children and young people in New Zealand are very much at risk, and there is an ever increasing need for everyone to be vigilant about them. Child advocacy involves taking a proactive approach towards recognising the rights of all children, and responding by changing systems, policies and individuals, to ensure that they are given the opportunity to reach their potential and improve the processes which affect their daily lives. It is not about undermining the role of parents and families, nor is it about denying children their childhood.

Many of the papers in this book underline the importance of highlighting children's rights. Children are suffering from poverty and its associated environmental hazards, they are committing suicide at unprecedented rates, lacking in access to quality health care, not being adequately protected against abuse or neglect, and they do not have equal access to high quality education (from early childhood through to tertiary education). There is every reason to believe that provision of services and access to services is not equally available to children regardless of their socioeconomic status or ethnicity. These statements are true for New Zealand but also on a global level as is highlighted by Irene Rizzini's paper. Cindy Kiro outlines some of the public health and socioeconomic issues for Maori. We have no reason for the smugness (especially at the governmental level) that children are doing fairly well in New Zealand, which is documented so carefully by Robert Ludbrook's paper about New Zealand's ratification of the Convention.

The trends in New Zealand are mirrored in many other industrial societies. Rizzini documents the often worsening conditions of childhood throughout the world, but especially in developing countries and for those at the bottom of the income scale. Coming together with so many international colleagues, however, has not only heightened understanding of issues for children in other countries, but also allowed us to learn of positive practices which can help us move forward. One really useful instance of this is described in Covell and Howe's paper on the incorporation of children's rights into the primary school curriculum in Nova Scotia, Canada.

Coming from a background of advocating for better environments for children as a researcher in child development has helped me to advocate for children over the years. Yet recently I have become more aware that there are also legal and ethical grounds (as well as research knowledge) on which to argue for changes to policy in favour of children. I think that this is something that everyone interested in the well-being of children should be aware of, and should make more use of. Legal and ethical arguments are provided by domestic legislation and international treaties such as the United Nations Convention on the Rights of the Child. This book includes a combination of research-based information and legal/ethical arguments in favour of children's rights.

Policies, programmes and legislation can be measured against the UNCROC in terms of their impact on children. This process is only just beginning in New Zealand. According to Michael Freeman:

> It [the UNCROC] can be used in a number of ways: to make children aware of their rights, to put pressure on the legislature, on governments and policy makers, to measure practices and policies against, to make the case for child impact statements, to be used in committee discussion and commissions of inquiry, and as an advocacy tool. As such it can be used by ministries, by institutions, such as the Commissioner for Children and, most importantly, in litigation, by lawyers arguing cases and by Judges by reasoning their judgements (Freeman, 1996, p. 84).

Starkly revealed by the conference was a major concern that children are not respected as human beings who have an important contribution to make in society, and that their voices are rarely listened to. Child advocacy is very much needed, but as much as possible it must be carried out with humility, without seeking personal glory or one's own political ends, and in partnership with children. Adults for centuries have made assumptions about what is best for children, but recently we have come to question this perspective, and to argue that to be an effective child advocate it is necessary to listen to children's voices and be sensitive to children's perspectives. Melton (1987) argues that if children are involved in setting the agenda for child advocacy, there is much less danger that it will be dominated by adult ideology. Listening to children and viewing the world from their perspective is possible even with very young children.

Article 12 of the Convention, which says that children should have the right to have their voices heard in decisions which affect them, was given a lot of attention at the conference. Agencies and organisations were asking themselves how they could involve children and young people, encourage them, and give them opportunities to express their views within groups and institutions in society. Several of the keynote speakers highlighted this theme – Gary Melton, Berry Mayall, Pauline Tapp and Mark Henaghan particularly.

Another major theme of the conference was the centrality of cultural context in human development and in the consideration of children's rights. James Garbarino believes that cultures are 'collective solutions to social and human situations' and that they must inevitably be incomplete in achieving this. He argued that cultures need to adapt to changing ecologies or else they can become maladaptive. Several keynote speakers highlighted Treaty of Waitangi and other cultural issues, including Cindy Kiro talking about the impact of social and economic change on Maori, Riripeti Haretuku on attempts to reduce rates of cot death in Maori families, and Aiono Dr Fanaafi Le Tagaloa who highlighted the importance of children's rights in a Samoan context. Papers given by indigenous people outlined the importance of indigenous retention of control and initiative in addressing concerns for children and families, within the value system of the indigenous culture.

An important part of the conference was the inclusion of a Youth Forum and a Children's Forum, organised by Sue Willoughby, the Community Advisor – Youth from the Dunedin City Council. Below is a summary provided by seven primary school children from George Street School in Dunedin (mostly ten and eleven year olds) who participated in the Children's Forum at the conference. These children had some very important things to say, and their statements reinforced our feeling that children's views should be respected and listened to, and their views taken into account when making decisions.

The late Commissioner for Children, Laurie O'Reilly, was a strong promoter of the idea of children's rights. Laurie spoke and wrote extensively on this topic and we

REPORT FROM THE CHILDREN'S FORUM

Seven of us met yesterday with Sue Willoughby to talk about Articles 12 and 13 of the United Nations Convention of the Rights of the Child. The most important information we came up with in our discussion is:

- *we are people as well.*
- *we are all different, with different maturity levels.*
- *we are children, but we do have rights.*
- *we can make responsible decisions if we are given a chance.*
- *it is okay for us to make the wrong decision sometimes, even if we know all the information.*
- *please listen to us instead of ignoring us, and take notice of what we have to say.*
- *expect an opinion from us, and ask for it.*
- *give us the space to ask for information when we need to.*
- *give us time to think before we have to answer.*
- *we need to practise asking for information.*
- *we need to practise being given information.*
- *you may not want to hear what we have to say, but we have the right to say it.*
- *Lastly, we need adults to guide us towards making good decisions, but we also need you to let us practise making the wrong decisions as well. Thank you for listening.*

The seven children involved in the Children's Forum were: Amber Ashley, Kauia Moriarty, Georgia Birnie, Karl Radermacher, Andrew Musk, Sajith Herath-Mudiyanselage and Emily Wallace. Amber, Kauia and Georgia reported back to the plenary session at the end of the conference.

all remember with affection and gratitude his contribution to changing attitudes in this area. Laurie pointed out that children's rights are not just something to be used to argue with governments about, but they affect many different levels of society. He posed four basic questions about our responsibility for children's rights as set out in the UNCROC and I think that they are questions which we can usefully ask ourselves in the aftermath of the July conference (O'Reilly, 1997, p. 2):

- What commitment am I prepared to make to the Convention?
- What commitment is my organisation/employer prepared to make?
- What commitment are my representatives prepared to make?
- What is the current level of social and political commitment to children in New Zealand?

This conference was the first opportunity for many of us in New Zealand to reflect on our own approach and commitment to children's rights in the context of a national and international group of colleagues. It is important, though, that the commitment is an ongoing one, and that advocates for children have a louder voice in New Zealand and internationally. As Irene Rizzini points out, the world has never before had such an array of scientific and technological resources available to address issues which affect children, yet children suffer increasingly from the effects of inequalities. In my view, we can be most effective as advocates when we respect and listen to children's views and perspectives, when we have a good understanding of the personal stories of children and families, when we have a strong basis of argument in research knowledge, and when we use legal and ethical arguments to best effect. We can be more effective if we move in a coherent and consistent direction together. I hope that this book will enable all of those who read it, to respond to the plea made by Laurie O'Reilly for people, institutions and societies to take more responsibility for children's rights.

References

Freeman, M.D.A. (1996). The importance of a children's rights perspective in litigation. *Butterworths Family Law Journal, December*, 165-96.

Lansdown, G. (1994). Children's rights. In B. Mayall (Ed.), *Children's childhoods: Observed and experienced.* London: The Falmer Press, pp. 33-44.

Melton, G. (1987), Children, politics and morality: The ethics of child advocacy. *Journal of Clinical Psychology, 16* (4), 357-67.

O'Reilly, L. (1997). Editorial. *Children: A newsletter from the Office of the Comissioner for Children*, 23, 1-2.

United Nations Convention on the Rights of the Child. Adopted by the United Nations General Assembly, 20 November 1989, ratified by New Zealand 1993.

Notes

1 The Children's Issues Centre Conference 'Children's Rights: National and International Perspectives' took place in Dunedin at the University of Otago from 7–9 July 1999.

2 Not all of the conference papers could be included in this book, because of length restrictions. However, all of the papers presented which were provided to us in an appropriate form are available from the Children's Issues Centre, University of Otago, Box 56, Dunedin, New Zealand. Phone 64 3 479 5038; Fax 64 3 479 5039.

· *1* ·

Trauma and children's rights[1]

NICOLA ATWOOL

Introduction

Article 39 of the United Nations Convention on the Rights of the Child states that:

> State parties shall take all appropriate measures to promote physical and psychological recovery and social reintegration of a child victim of: any form of neglect, exploitation, or abuse; torture or any other form of cruel, inhuman or degrading treatment or punishment; or armed conflicts. Such recovery and reintegration shall take place in an environment which fosters the health, self-respect and dignity of the child.

The rights contained within the Convention fall into four categories: survival, development, protection, and participation. 'Developed' countries like New Zealand pride themselves on maintaining high standards for children in comparison with other countries. There is a tendency to believe that many of the Articles refer specifically to children whose lives are threatened by war, famine and disease. However, trauma also threatens children's survival and development and it is for these reasons that they need to be protected.

Participation rights as outlined in Article 12 of the Convention grant children the right to have their views taken into account in decision-making processes. This presents a major challenge throughout the adult world. I have worked as a social worker and child psychotherapist in a care and protection agency and continue to work with a small number of children since moving into an academic position. Through my practice I have met many children exposed to trauma. In my experience we fall short of meeting the rights outlined in Article 39. A major factor is the invisibility of children. In this paper I will begin by discussing the definition of trauma and then describe the processes by which traumatised children become invisible and their voices silenced. I will propose an alternative way of understanding the impact of trauma and outline the changes necessary to ensure that the rights of traumatised children are respected.

Definition of trauma

There are a number of definitions of what constitutes trauma and these share a common theme of trauma as an overwhelming event or series of events which renders the individual helpless. Some emphasise the overwhelming of defensive capacities (Goodwin, 1993) while others emphasise the helplessness experienced in the face of intolerable danger, anxiety and instinctual arousal (Eth & Pynoos, 1985, cited in Armsworth & Holaday, 1993). Terr (1991) has combined these two elements in her definition: '… the mental result of one sudden, external blow or a series of blows, rendering the young person temporarily helpless and breaking past ordinary coping and defensive operations' (p. 11).

Children may be exposed to one or more of the following: abuse (physical, sexual, and/or emotional); neglect; parental separation; multiple changes of address, school, household structure; living with parent(s) with substance addictions or psychiatric disorders; natural disasters; accidents; serious illness in themselves, parents or siblings; death of a friend or family member; bullying; witnessing violence at home or in the community; exposure to violence through the media. There is room for a wide range of opinion as to how these constitute trauma. Research on stress and coping indicates that individual children differ in the extent to which they experience these events as traumatic (Cairns, 1996; Monahon, 1997; Rutter & Rutter, 1993). I have taken a broad definition of trauma which recognises that all of the above events have the potential to have a traumatic impact on children's lives and I argue that paying attention to the child's voice is the most appropriate way to address issues of individual variation.

The invisibility of the traumatised child

When children are exposed to risk and trauma their voices are frequently not heard. First and foremost they are dependent on the significant adults in their lives to recognise that they have experienced such exposure. Children are dependent on adults for access to resources, and parental recognition of their experience is a prerequisite for obtaining support to cope with trauma. Even more important, the child is dependent on external validation of their experience if they are to avoid the most common pitfall – the assumption of personal responsibility for the events which have impacted on them. There are many reasons why this external validation may not occur: the parent(s) may not know what has happened to the child; the parent(s) may choose to cope with events by denying that they occurred or denying that the event has any importance; when there is a conflict of interests (for example when parents are separating or a parent is the source of the trauma), the parent may suppress or avoid considering the child's perspective. Even when parents recognise that the child has been exposed to trauma they may block the child from having access to support. Sometimes parents actively resist intervention fearing that their child – and themselves – will be retraumatised in the process (Schwarz & Perry, 1994).

The emphasis on the overwhelming nature of events in defining trauma may also contribute to children's invisibility. This definition implies that the impact of the trauma would be obvious, that the child's behaviour and emotional response would alert adults to the gravity of the situation. Therefore if these signals are not present, it is possible to conclude that the child must be coping. Lenore Terr (1990) draws attention to the resistance which parents experience in acknowledging that their child may be affected by trauma. In her work with the parents of children involved in the Chowchilla kidnapping she discovered that many did not want to think of their children as suffering any negative consequences and accentuated the evidence that their children were coping.[2] Herman (1992) emphasises the extent to which children's dependence on parents leads them to adapt to abuse within the home in ways which preserve the relationship with the parents in spite of the abuse. It is therefore possible for a child's exposure to trauma to remain invisible. This is the most powerful way in which the child's voice is silenced.

However, even when parents recognise that something is wrong, they may not be aware that the child is reacting to trauma. When children are referred to professionals, it is usually as a result of their behaviour. Parents seeking help are likely to be referred to a mental health service or a social work service. The range of professionals offering such services includes psychologists, psychiatrists, psychotherapists, counsellors, and social workers. Each discipline has its own system for assessing and categorising the child and/or the family and the response of the professional is shaped by this process. The primary source of information is usually the parent(s) or caregiver(s). Information may also be sought from the school, family doctor or other agencies which have contact with the family. The child is not necessarily consulted (Smith, 1996) and when they are, doubt may be cast on the validity of their account (Hall, 1996). Glaser (1996) documents the vulnerability of the child in mental health settings and points out that there may be a lot of conversation about the child but little, if any, consideration of either the child's view or what impact being talked about might have on the child. In these ways the child becomes invisible, or at best is seen indistinctly through a series of adult filters, despite being the focus for concern.

Invisibility as an outcome of the social construction of childhood

A closer examination of the theories which inform our understanding of the impact of trauma on children's lives reveals that this tendency to overlook the child may have its origin in the very knowledge that informs practice. Psychology, psychiatry, psychoanalysis and psychotherapy have all made significant contributions to the development of explanations and models of intervention. These explanations, often backed up by empirical research, become powerful forces in defining children's experience as they assume the authority of objective 'truth'. Alice Miller (1985, 1987a, 1987b, 1991a, 1991b) has written extensively on the subject of childhood trauma and has been critical of the role psychoanalysis has played in negating the impact of external events. Her concerns are echoed by others who have remained within the sphere of psychoanalysis. Jean Goodwin (1993), in the introduction to *Rediscovering Childhood Trauma*, notes that extreme polarisation between trauma theory and psychodynamic theory has produced clinicians who have solid grounding in only one of the two perspectives.

Within psychiatry Lenore Terr has drawn attention to the impact of trauma as a distinct diagnostic category for children. Her work has identified specific consequences for single event trauma and for multiple or long-standing trauma (Terr, 1991). These consequences are long term and are not identical to those found in adults. Prior to the inclusion of Post Traumatic Stress Disorder (PTSD) as a diagnostic category for children there was no means of recognising that 'problem' behaviour could have its origins in trauma. Although the identification of PTSD has opened the way to wider recognition of the impact of trauma in children's lives, the possibility that trauma will be overlooked remains. Professionals specialising in this field make the point that the symptoms associated with PTSD can be overlooked and misinterpreted (Brooks & Siegel, 1996; Monahon, 1997).

Much of the theory which informs practice is based on the notion that objective meaning exists and can be defined and categorised. In relation to children the lack of attention paid to external events by psychoanalytic theory is an example of the way in which meaning has been defined in a specific way. In this example the internal world was privileged and meaning defined in terms of intrapsychic processes. The language of psychoanalysis became a system by which experience was defined in particular ways. This illustrates the process by which socially constructed meaning becomes embodied in discourse. Within discourse certain social meanings are given primacy. Objectivity and rationality have been privileged in modern Western society. In addition prevailing discourses within the Western world are based on binary oppositions, for example normal/abnormal, mature/immature, rational/irrational. These binary oppositions signify implicitly both an unequal distribution of power (with one pole of the binary accorded a positive valuation and the other a negative valuation) and an exclusionary element whereby one pole of the binary is defined in contradistinction to the other. For example, normal is normal because it is not abnormal. The psychoanalytic emphasis on the internal world represents an inversion of these binary oppositions. However, this inversion relegates trauma to the private, internal world thus reinforcing the isolation of traumatised children and allocating them an inferior position, relative to those with 'expert' knowledge and the power to define their experience in particular ways.

Within both critical psychology and sociology attention has been drawn to the way in which childhood is socially constructed (Prout & James, 1990; Mayall, 1996; Stainton Rogers & Stainton Rogers, 1992). Developmental psychology plays a central role in this construction and underpins all of the theories and models of trauma. Central to this theory is the notion of stage-by-stage progression from a state of immaturity to a state of maturity. Trauma is seen as interrupting this progression. Developmental psychology also forms the basis for understanding not only what is normal but that which is abnormal. Prout and James (1990) outline the way in which this account was imported into sociological theories of socialisation.

In deconstructing the discourse of developmental psychology, attention is drawn to the way in which children are allocated an inferior and passive position on the basis of their immaturity and irrationality (Burman, 1994; Stainton Rogers & Stainton Rogers, 1992). Children's invisibility and silence can be seen as the inevitable outcome of this binary process. This positioning is what makes it easy to discount children in situations where the only other witness to their trauma is an adult perpetrator. Implicit within this positioning is the assumption that adults know best and this provides the mechanism by which parents minimise the impact of trauma on a child or ignore trauma in the child's life. Furthermore such a positioning relegates children to a minor role in their own experience as adults are generally considered to be the most reliable informants when children are referred to professionals.

This way of viewing the world also places on adults the burden of responsibility for having answers when something goes wrong in children's lives. Trauma, especially trauma inflicted by other human beings, challenges our beliefs and assumptions about people and society. One of the ways of responding to this is to minimise the impact and protect ourselves from the horror that is some children's lives (Cleaver, 1998). This response is most clearly seen in society's attitude to children who commit serious crime. Children who have murdered other children may be subject to adult justice, and public reaction is concentrated on how to punish these crimes. Very little attention is directed to exploring what events in these children's lives may have created this situation and what we might learn from this (Morrison, 1998; Sereny, 1998).

Another reaction is to focus on how we can 'fix' children who have experienced trauma. We need to believe that the damage can be put right. This is a false promise which also creates the risk that if the child does not respond to intervention the fault lies in them. Perry (1997a) maintains that severe abuse and neglect during the early years compromises brain development. He argues that children are malleable and not resilient and points to the pervasive impact of early trauma on emotional, physical and cognitive development, attachment, and behaviour (Perry, 1997a, 1997b). The extent to which children are affected by severe trauma may be far greater than we have appreciated and the question of whether the physiological and neurological impact can be overcome when the child is older remains unanswered.

Recognition of the impact of trauma on children is relatively recent and in some instances still does not occur. I have located the reasons for this in the social construction of childhood and the dominant discourses which maintain the positioning of adults as superior and children as inferior. What is missing from the analysis thus far is the child's view of trauma.

Children's experience of trauma

Case studies provided by practitioners are one of the primary sources of information about childhood trauma. These come from two sources: children in therapy (Terr, 1990; Monahon, 1997); and retrospective accounts of childhood experience presented by adults in therapy (Briere, 1992; Herman, 1992; Miller, 1985, 1987a; Terr, 1990). Two other sources of information provide insight into childhood experience: retrospective reconstructions provided through interviews with adults who have experienced trauma (Sanford, 1991; Sereny, 1998) and autobiographical accounts (Fraser, 1987; Johnson, 1995). All of these accounts bear witness to the profound impact of trauma on children's lives. Trauma in adulthood threatens our established patterns of coping and challenges previously held beliefs. Trauma in childhood may become a central focus around which the child's growing takes place, shaping and possibly distorting their perception of themselves, the significant adults in their life and their view of the world. The impact of relatively minor trauma can be profound, as this story illustrates:

> Once upon a time there was a little girl. She lived with her parents, older sister and younger brother. She had a special friend who used to come and help her feed the hens. It was a secret. Her special friend played games with her. The little girl knew these were naughty games and she did not tell anyone. The little girl became afraid that if her mother and father found out about these games they would not love her.
>
> Long after the friend had stopped coming to visit she continued to believe this. Years later when she was twelve the little girl became very ill. Her illness meant that she was at home with her mother and during the time when no one knew what was wrong with her, the little girl told her mother what had happened. She told her mother that she didn't know if it had really happened or if she had dreamed it. The girl was able to describe her 'friend' and the mother recognised this person and knew that it was not a dream. By this time the little girl had lived most of her life believing that if anyone found out they would not love her. This did not happen, but years later as an adult the grown-up little girl realised that she had continued to live her life believing that if anyone really knew her, they would not love her.

Many of the issues identified earlier are illustrated in this example. At the time that the child experienced trauma her parents did not know what was happening to the child. Some would argue that the absence of behavioural change disqualifies this experience as traumatic. However, the fact that the child chose to keep this matter a secret, and her reasons for doing so, indicate that high levels of fear and anxiety were experienced. These levels of fear and anxiety prevented her from accessing her usual support systems within the family and undermined the security of her attachment. The disclosure at a later time of crisis is further evidence of the intensity of these feelings. Although this trauma is relatively minor it was sufficient to produce a belief that continued into adulthood. One of the consequences of this belief was that the child tried very hard to be good and the adult continued this pattern. It is possible that this compliance was a factor in the trauma not being recognised and that this is a not uncommon response in children who encounter trauma.

Many of the illustrations contained in Lenore Terr's book *Too Scared to Cry* (1990) are testimony to the enduring and individual effects of trauma. Although all of the children involved in the Chowchilla bus kidnapping shared the same experience, the consequences for each were different. I would argue that the difference is based in the unique meaning which this experience took on for each child. This meaning was constructed through the complex interaction of several variables: their previous experience; their personality; their role during the traumatic incident(s); the reaction of family; the reaction of the wider community; and the child's response to the portrayal of the incident by the media.

When I work with children they rarely deal with specific incidents in an overt manner. Rather recurring issues, themes and concerns can be identified in their play, in their drawings and in their talking. This material relates to broad issues such as trust, conflict, self-esteem and self-perception. I have come to the conclusion that trauma is not experienced by children as a stand-alone incident or series of incidents. All of what children experience becomes interwoven and underpins their self-concept, their worldview, their feelings and their behaviour. What children bring to therapy is the sum total of their lives, not discrete issues or problems. Furthermore they bring their unique subjective experience which may or may not coincide with the perception of the significant adults in their lives. Not only is the child acted upon by external events, they are also engaged in the process of interpreting these events and incorporating them into their world view. The issues identified in the example of one child's story, and questions arising from my work with children, have led to a search for a less disjointed formulation which places the child centre stage in their life.

An alternative construction

Central to postmodern theory is the idea of the subject and subjectivity. Weedon (1987) states: '"Subjectivity" is used to refer to the conscious and unconscious thoughts and emotions of the individual, her sense of herself and her ways of understanding her relation to the world' (p. 32). Furthermore she argues that this subjectivity is not 'fixed and coherent' but is 'precarious, contradictory and in process' (p. 33). This conceptualisation of subjectivity has particular importance when applied to children who have experienced trauma as it allows for the possibility of multiple and conflicting interpretations of events and their meanings for the child. Applying postmodern theory to the understanding of the impact of trauma on children's lives suggests that a useful starting point is the child and the subjective meaning(s) which they attach to their experience. Such an approach also acknowledges the child as the central actor in their own story. The child is not simply acted upon by the traumatic event and the response of parents and professionals, the child is active in the process of making sense of their experience. Furthermore, when the trauma is on-going the child is active in managing this. Portrayal of the child as the innocent and passive victim of abuse fails to acknowledge the energy and inventiveness that is necessary to survive such experiences (Kitzinger, 1990). We have much to learn from children but our assumptions of expertise on the basis of adult status and professional training may prevent us from acknowledging the contribution that children can make to our understanding and the development of appropriate responses.

Implications for parents, practitioners and policy-makers

This brings us back to the issue of children's rights. If professional practice with children exposed to risk and trauma is to be consistent with the Convention, it is important that Articles 12 and 39 are central to any model of intervention. Although Article 12 is qualified on the basis of age and maturity, we have to ask ourselves who we are seeking to protect when we exclude children from consultation about their experience. Clearly, children who have not yet acquired language present a particular challenge. However, even in these circumstances the child has the capacity to communicate (Pugh & Selleck, 1996) and intervention must be based on what we can learn from them as well as on the information provided by the parents. It is difficult to see how the child's health, self-respect and dignity can be fostered unless their participation is central to the recovery process.

In all work with children, it is important to be alert to the possibility that trauma has been experienced. If children are to have a voice, all adults who come into contact with children need to have an understanding of the impact of trauma and be willing to consider the possibility that children with challenging behaviour may be children who have experienced or are experiencing trauma. When children are referred, close attention to the family history may reveal events that have been experienced by the child as traumatic. However, the process of history-taking needs to provide an opportunity for the story of the family and the child to be told rather than a perfunctory check of predetermined categories or milestones. Opportunities to explore the possibility that the child or family may have secrets also need to be offered.

However, if the child who has been exposed to trauma is to have a voice, we need to be prepared to listen. There is ample evidence that adults are not good at this (Butler & Williamson, 1994; Cousins, 1996; Lansdown, 1994; Lewis, 1996). Ross (1996) challenges the view that 'professional people' have any preordained ability to communicate with children and points out the difference between hearing and listening. If our strategies of intervention are to be child focused they must provide opportunities for the child to communicate. Such an approach requires time, patience and an appropriate environment. Children are not likely to respond to an interview format and may well remain silent in the face of a barrage of direct questions. They are most likely to respond in an environment which offers the opportunity to play and to draw. Additional training may be necessary to ensure that professionals have the confidence and skills necessary to communicate with children.

It is also essential when working with parents that the importance of listening to children and the need to make space to ensure that this happens is emphasised. Part of the professional role is to model appropriate communication. When practitioners talk with parents about their child in front of him/her, without involving the child, adult superiority is reinforced and by implication a message is conveyed to the child that he/she is not important. This is not helpful to either parents or child and is likely to reinforce feelings of powerlessness and unworthiness which accompany trauma.

Recovery following trauma takes time and the child revisits and reworks their understanding as they grow. There is a risk that professionals, anxious to assure parents that children will recover, inadvertently mislead them into believing that the effects of trauma will be minor and short term. Parents may look to 'experts' to put things right. At best, therapy or counselling can only supplement the twenty-four-hour a day care that parents provide. The real work takes place in the home. It is important that parents are supported and given practical strategies that they can use.

Practitioners need to be willing to question the theories, experiences, attitudes and values which they bring to this work and the ways in which these shape responses to children. It is possible that the need to appear expert may get in the way of working effectively with parents and children. Practitioners must be willing to explore the wide range of therapeutic responses which may be necessary to work effectively with children who have experienced trauma. Perry (1993, 1997a) argues that cognitive-behavioural strategies, which form the basis for many intervention models, are inadequate when children have experienced early trauma. He makes a strong case for early intervention, and he has been involved in the development of creative therapeutic strategies based on collaboration between clinicians and artists. These programmes utilise massage, rhythm, movement, music, dance, art therapy, play therapy, nature discovery, storytelling, and drama (Miranda, Arthur, Milan, Mahoney, & Perry, 1998). Such programmes are resource intensive and are likely to be rejected on these grounds.

In New Zealand such programmes are not available and many parents and children simply cope without assistance. Practitioners and parents need to combine to advocate for the resources necessary to facilitate children's recovery following exposure to trauma. In the present climate this is very difficult. Our Care and Protection Service is under-resourced and only the most serious cases are investigated. There are waiting lists at many of the services providing counselling or therapy and most intervention is short-term only. Free services are particularly difficult to access and Accident Compensation assistance with the cost of counselling is restricted to sexual abuse. In rural areas families may have to travel long distances to access services.

Children's invisibility is particularly pronounced at the level of society where policy is made. Policy related to mental health, social service provision and education must place a higher priority on children's rights to quality intervention. The Commissioner for Children has recently noted that children make up 30 per cent of the population but receive only 9 per cent of the funding for mental health services ('Fewer Mental Health Services,' 1999). Article 39 of the UN Convention stipulates children's entitlement to recovery and social reintegration. For this to happen change needs to occur on all levels: adults must be willing to listen to children and to take appropriate action, professionals have to be willing to critically evaluate the knowledge and strategies which underpin their practice and a range of services must be available to assist children and their families. None of this can be achieved in a climate of New Right economic policy, which places primary responsibility on families without ensuring that appropriate services are in place to ensure that families can exercise this responsibility.

Conclusion

Life is not the same following a traumatic experience. In saying this I do not subscribe to the pessimistic view that the traumatised child is condemned to a less than satisfactory existence as victim or perpetrator of further abuse. If we regard children as participants in the construction of meaning and engage with them on this basis there is much that can be done to facilitate an understanding of their experience. In so doing we allow them to continue with the business of living. This process is all the more effective when parents are willing to engage with their children on the same basis. Practitioners have a responsibility to model this way of relating to children and policy-makers have to give children the priority they are entitled to.

For any who doubt that children have the capacity to come to terms with their experience, I recommend a book entitled *A Rock and a Hard Place*. This is an autobiographical account of childhood abuse written by a fourteen-year-old after he discovered that he had AIDS as a consequence of his abuse. By this time he had run away from his family and had found people who cared for him. I would like to leave the last word to him:

> Yes, I love being my age and saying I wrote a book. But more than that, I love knowing that I did have a say in the world, that my thoughts were considered, if just for a little while, by people I don't even know about. A reporter tried to discredit me

by theorizing that I didn't exist and insinuating that someone my age could not write my book. I was so hurt that I wanted to give up. It was my faith in the people who I love – and who love me – that prevented me from deciding it was time to die. I won't go into what the reporter said and what was not true about it, but I will say it is a shame that a child can still be silenced or made to regret having the courage to tell a difficult truth. When this happened to me, I spent night after night wanting to slap myself for telling the secret – that those adults were right and I was wrong. I thought back to those nightmarish times and remembered being told that no one would ever believe me. The truth was, as my new dad pointed out, that people ultimately believe me. People *were* on my side, and they were offended at the thought that someone *wouldn't* believe me. We could populate a country with people who have stories similar to my own. Children are basically powerless beings who have to trust in their parent's mercy. ... No adult was around to act on our behalf until it was too late and the damage was already done. In our cases there had to be an uproar before those who could do something finally did. ... Unfortunately, until people stop turning away, until children can confidently look up to adults and rely upon them for help, my story will remain just one of many. (Johnson, 1995, pp. 213–14).

References

Armsworth, M., & Holaday, M. (1993). The effects of psychological trauma on children and adolescents. *Journal of Counselling and Development*, *72*, 49-56.

Briere, J.N. (1992). *Child abuse trauma*. Newbury Park, CA: Sage.

Brooks, B., & Siegel, P.M. (1996). *The scared child*. New York: John Wiley & Sons.

Burman, E. (1994). *Deconstructing developmental psychology*. London: Routledge.

Butler, I., & Williamson, H. (1994). *Children speak*. Harlow, Essex: Longman.

Cairns, E. (1996). *Children and political violence*. Oxford: Blackwell.

Cleaver, L. (1998). A personal account of lessons about the relationship between violent hope, hopeful violence and the development of therapeutic imagination: The legacy of Bruno Bettleheim. *Smith College of Studies in Social Work*, *68*, 347-62.

Cousins, J. (1996). Empowerment and autonomy from babyhood: The perspective of 'Early Years' research. In M. John (Ed.), *Children in charge: The child's right to a fair hearing*. London: Jessica Kingsley, pp. 191-203.

Fewer mental health services for young. (1999, June 18). *The Otago Daily Times*.

Fraser, S. (1987). *My father's house: A memoir of incest and healing*. New York: Harper & Row.

Glaser, D. (1996). The voice of the child in mental health practice. In R. Davie, G. Upton, & V. Varma (Eds), *The voice of the child: A handbook for professionals*. London: The Falmer Press, pp. 78-90.

Goodwin, J.M. (1993). *Rediscovering childhood trauma*. Washington DC: American Psychiatric Press.

Hall, N. (1996). Eliciting children's views: The contribution of psychologists. In R. Davie, G. Upton, & V. Varma (Eds), *The voice of the child: A handbook for professionals*. London: The Falmer Press, pp. 61-77.

Herman, J.L. (1992). *Trauma and recovery*. London: Harper Collins.

Johnson, A.G. (1995). *A rock and a hard place*. London: Warner Books.

Kitzinger, J. (1990). Who are you kidding? Children, power, and the struggle against sexual abuse. In A. James & A. Prout (Eds), *Constructing and reconstructing childhood:*

Contemporary issues in the sociological study of childhood. London: The Falmer Press, pp. 157-83.

Lansdown, G. (1994). Children's rights. In B. Mayall (Ed.), *Children's childhoods: Observed and experienced.* London: The Falmer Press, pp. 33-44.

Lewis, J. (1996). Children teaching adults to listen to them. In M. John (Ed.), *Children in charge: The child's right to a fair hearing.* London: Jessica Kingsley, pp. 209-18.

Mayall, B. (1996). *Children, health and the social order*. Buckingham: Open University Press.

Miller, A. (1985). *Thou shalt not be aware*. London: Pluto Press.

Miller, A. (1987a). *The drama of being a child*. London: Virago.

Miller, A. (1987b). *For your own good*. London: Virago.

Miller, A. (1991a). *Banished knowledge.* London: Virago.

Miller, A. (1991b). *The untouched key*. London: Virago.

Miranda, L., Arthur, A., Milan, T., Mahoney, O., & Perry, B. (1998). The art of healing: the CIVITAS healing project. *Early Childhood Connections, Journal of Music- and Movement-Based Learning*, August 1998.

Monahon, C. (1997). *Children and trauma*. San Francisco: Jossey-Bass.

Morrison, B. (1998). On childhood and violence. *British Journal of Psychotherapy*, *14*, 420-44.

Perry, B. (1993). Medicine and psychotherapy. Neurodevelopment and the neurophysiology of trauma II: Clinical work along the alarm-fear-terror continuum. *The Advisor, 6* (2), 14-20.

Perry, B. (1997a). Incubated in terror: Neurodevelopmental factors in the 'Cycle of Violence'. In J.D. Osofsky (Ed.), *Children in a violent society.* New York: Guilford, pp. 124-49.

Perry, B. (1997b). Memories of fear. In J. Goodwin & R. Attias (Eds), *Images of the body in trauma*. New York: Basic Books.

Prout, A., & James, A. (1990). A new paradigm for the sociology of childhood? Provenance, promise and problems. In A. James & A. Prout (Eds), *Constructing and reconstructing childhood: Contemporary issues in the sociological study of childhood.* London: The Falmer Press, pp. 7-35.

Pugh, G., & Selleck, D.R. (1996). Listening to and communicating with young children. In R. Davie, G. Upton, & V. Varma (Eds), *The voice of the child: A handbook for professionals.* London: The Falmer Press, pp. 120-36.

Ross, E. (1996). Learning to listen to children. In R. Davie, G. Upton, & V. Varma (Eds), *The voice of the child: A handbook for professionals.* London: The Falmer Press, pp. 91-106.

Rutter, M., & Rutter, M. (1993). *Developing minds. Challenge and continuity across the life span.* New York: Basic Books.

Sanford, L. (1991). *Strong at the broken places.* London: Virago.

Schwarz, E., & Perry, B. (1994). The post-traumatic response in children and adolescents. *Psychiatric Clinics of North America*, *17*, 311-26.

Sereny, G. (1998). *Cries unheard. The story of Mary Bell*. London: Macmillan.

Smith, P. (1996). Social work perspective. In R. Davie, G. Upton, & V. Varma (Eds), *The voice of the child: A handbook for professionals.* London: The Falmer Press, pp. 49-60.

Stainton Rogers, R., & Stainton Rogers, W. (1992). *Stories of childhood*. Toronto: University of Toronto Press.

Terr, L. (1979). Children of Chowchilla. *Psychoanalytic Study of the Child, 34*, 547-623.

Terr, L. (1983). Chowchilla revisited: The effects of psychic trauma four years after a school-bus kidnapping. *American Journal of Psychiatry*, *140*, 1543-50.

Terr, L. (1990). *Too scared to cry*. New York: Basic Books.

Terr, L. (1991). Childhood traumas: An outline and overview. *American Journal of Psychiatry*, *148*, 10-20.
Weedon, C. (1987). *Feminist practice and poststructural theory*. Oxford: Basil Blackwell.

Notes

1 A version of this paper appears in Smith, A.B., Taylor, N.J., Gollop, M.M. (Eds). 2000. *Children's voices: Research, policy and practice.* Auckland: Pearson Education.

2 In 1976, 26 children and one adult, from the small rural community of Chowchilla, were kidnapped when travelling home from school. They were placed in a container which was buried underground and eventually dug their way out. Lenore Terr worked with the children and their families during 1977 and completed a follow-up study four years later (Terr, 1979, 1983, 1990).

Children with disabilities: Equal rights or different rights?

Anne Bray and Sue Gates

Abstract

*The United Nations Convention on the Rights of the Child is the only international human rights treaty which specifically identifies disability as a basis for non-discrimination (Article 2) and as a special focus for attention (Article 23). The purpose of this paper is to identify and examine the dilemma of difference. Children with disabilities must be included in the community of **all** children, enjoying equal rights and non-discrimination. At the same time, some children with disabilities need additional or special resources to enable the achievement of those rights. However, different treatment may lead to stigmatisation and negative outcomes for children with disabilities.*

*This paper will argue that a greater focus on the similar needs of **all** children and equality of rights is more effective in achieving the goals of the Convention for children with disabilities than a special focus on their different characteristics. The discussion will use education as an illustration, drawing on research data from national and international studies, and local examples. The role of national educational policies in New Zealand education will be examined, and the gap between policy and practice described, in terms of the experiences of children with disabilities and their parents. Implications will be drawn for international and national policies and practices to ensure the inclusion of the rights of **all** children.*

Introduction

The core of the universal human rights system consists of the United Nations Charter and its three instruments composing the so-called International Bill of Rights. These three instruments are the Universal Declaration of Human Rights of 1948, and the two principal covenants that became effective in 1976 – the International Covenant on Civil and Political Rights (ICCPR), and the International Covenant on Economic, Social and Cultural Rights (ICESCR).

The principle of universality requires that the 'inalienable rights' set out in these treaties apply to all human beings without distinction. Thus children are included in all international human rights treaties and conventions. Nevertheless, the United Nations recognises that some groups of people are particularly vulnerable to abuse of human rights – women, people of less powerful races or ethnic groups, and children – and has developed special treaties, declarations, or special mention within declarations or conventions.

What is surprising is that no treaty or convention has been passed to protect the vulnerability of people with disabilities, given the gross abuses perpetuated against them in the Holocaust (Hume, 1991; Sobsey, Donnellan & Wolbring, 1994), when more than 200,000 people with disabilities were killed. Neither was 'disability' explicitly mentioned in any of the major international human rights treaties as a prohibited ground for distinction in a person's entitlement to the rights specified. 'Other status' has, however, been interpreted as including 'disability'. The United Nations General Assembly repeatedly failed to pass a proposed international convention on the elimination of all forms of discrimination against persons with disabilities. Apparently, many representatives believed that such rights were unnecessary as they were already guaranteed by existing human rights covenants (United Nations, 1994). The United Nations has, however, passed various declarations regarding the rights of people with disabilities, and undertaken various programmes of action to promote their rights.

The United Nations Convention on the Rights of the Child, which came into force in 1990 and was ratified in New Zealand in 1993, is the first and only United Nations Convention to identify disability as a prohibited ground for discrimination (Article 2, Section 1). This Convention also sets out in some detail the special obligations of States with regard to the rights of children with disabilities as a distinct group (Article 23). The United Nations Convention on the Rights of the Child is therefore unique, and deserves particular attention.

Are the rights of children with disabilities better protected by receiving special attention, rather than simply emphasising similarity in rights entitlement and the importance of non-discrimination?

This chapter will examine this 'dilemma of difference'. As described by Minow (1990):

> ... when does treating people differently emphasize their differences and stigmatize or hinder them on that basis? And when does treating people the same become insensitive to their difference and likely to stigmatize or hinder them on *that* basis? (p. 20) [emphasis added]

Educational rights in law

As a focus for illustrating this dilemma, we will focus on the key area of children's rights to education. Within the Convention, the following articles are relevant: Article 2, which protects children with disabilities against all forms of discrimination; Article 23 (sections 1 and 3), which focuses specifically on the rights of children with disabilities to effective access to education and to a full and decent life; and Articles 28 and 29, which set out the rights of all children to education and what that education should be directed towards.

The history of education for children with disabilities illustrates the necessity for a strong focus on non-discrimination in this most basic right – the right to education. In New Zealand this right was only given legislative status in 1990, when the Education Act 1989 came into force. (It may be no accident 1990 was also the year the Convention was passed, although at this stage it had not been ratified in New Zealand.) Before this, children with more severe disabilities were often denied any state-provided education. The Education Act 1989 guaranteed a right to free primary and secondary education for all children:

> … *every person* who is not a foreign student is entitled to free enrolment and free education *at any school* during the period beginning on the person's fifth birthday and ending on the first day of January after the person's nineteenth birthday (Section 3). [emphasis added]

Furthermore, the Act spelled out clearly that this right *included* children with disabilities – 'every person' did mean just that:

> … people who have special educational needs (whether because of disability or otherwise) have the *same rights* to enrol and receive education at state schools as people who do not (Section 8(1)). [emphasis added]

It is interesting to note that the statute clearly interpreted children with disabilities as only *part of* a wider group of children with 'special educational needs'.

The most important legislative provision is to assert the rights of *all* children, thus emphasising that children with disabilities are children first, and their rights, *as children*, are the most important consideration. If this primary right is not fully recognised, then any 'special' considerations may lead to separation from other children, stigmatisation, and even poorer services. Without this essential value base of equality, their perceived impairment will receive undue attention and their holistic needs as children will often be ignored or denied. For example, Hammarberg (1995) notes:

> The pattern already emerging from the discussions between the UN Committee and the reporting governments does indeed give cause for deep concern. Disabled children are discriminated against and too little is done to rectify this. … A trend in the richer countries seems to be to overemphasise the technical side of the support to the disabled child – *'the child in the child' tends to be forgotten* (p. 151). [emphasis added]

Discrimination in practice

Are New Zealand children still discriminated against in terms of equal rights to enrol and receive education? Their rights under the Education Act 1989 are also reinforced by the Human Rights Act 1993, particularly Section 21 (1)(h) and Section 57. Unfortunately the legal rights of children with disabilities to education are not always recognised or upheld at the school level. In 1996, the Human Rights Commission noted in a discussion paper concerns about 'the attitude of certain principals and Boards of Trustees towards enrolling students with disabilities at school and/or accommodating the children's needs within the school' (Human Rights Commission, 1996, p. 2). For example, they describe blatant discrimination in a written document from a school 'which stated that the school's acceptance of the child for enrolment was conditional upon:

- mainstreaming of the child being successful and her education would be discontinued if it were not
- her education not persistently interfering with or derogating from the learning rights of other children
- if the class teacher, other children or teacher-aide became stressed her enrolment would be terminated' (p. 2).

No other child's enrolment at this school had conditions placed upon it, and the Education Act 1989 sets out the clear rights of all children to enrolling and receiving education at any school. Such attitudes illustrate the frequent and fundamental problem: that children with disabilities are *not* seen as part of the population of *all* children. When laws, policies and provisions that affect children are being developed, it is critical that the needs of children with disabilities are carefully considered – not to exclude them but to ensure their *inclusion* is strengthened and catered for. Because of the continuing ignorance, stereotyping and even discrimination, their rights are still in danger of being conditional and their differences from other children over-emphasised.

The then Minister of Education, the Hon. Nick Smith, in a speech in 1999, provided two examples of these pervasive attitudes. First, he claimed that 'A central theme for over a century has been a core belief that every young New Zealander, regardless of wealth, status or location has the right to a quality education' (p. 2). As we have noted previously, this 'core belief' was only apparent in New Zealand (as shown in a legislated right) nine years ago. Dr Smith went on to question the rights of children with disabilities currently set out in the Education Act 1989:

> The notion of mainstreaming is now 10 years old. It is has had huge benefits but I feel the pendulum has swung too far. Some pupils I see being mainstreamed benefit little, and their needs are so great that I think it is unreasonable to expect the school to cope. I think the policy of parents being able to send their special needs children wherever they choose is too pure and needs revisiting. (Smith, 1999, p. 8).

The Hon. Nick Smith's statement illustrates Hammarberg's comment on richer countries' failure to attend to 'the child within the child'. Rights are not contingent on some measure of ability to benefit, and inclusion with one's peers is about more than academic achievement.

The same types of contradictions are illustrated in national educational policies in New Zealand. For example, Hulston (1999) shows how the New Zealand Curriculum Framework (1993) promotes an inclusive curriculum that promises to meet the needs of all students in New Zealand schools and to provide 'the tools to meet the learning needs of *all* students' (Hulston, 1999, p. 35). While these policy claims are consistent with a recognition of the equal rights of *all* students, they are inadequately understood or translated into the actual education that some students with disabilities experience.

In her research within an urban secondary school, Hulston found multiple examples of conflicting messages about the meaning and practice of an inclusive curriculum and the inclusion of students with disabilities. It appears that to many of the key personnel in the education system – politicians, policy-makers, principals, teachers, and support staff – *all* students does not really mean all students. Some students are clearly not considered as part of *all* students because of their 'special' educational needs. Thus, if they are not really part of the larger group, they are not treated as having the same rights.

There are two major justifications put forward to support exclusionary policies and practices for children with disabilities – parental choice and insufficient resources. The United Nations Convention on the Rights of the Child clearly promotes the importance of the child's parents and family to her or his well-being. However, it also puts the child's right to non-discrimination *above* his or her parents' 'political or other opinion' (Article 2).

From extensive interactions with parents of children with disabilities we believe that parents who choose segregated educational provisions for their children do so because of the failure (or perceived failure) of mainstream education to meet their children's educational needs in an effective and non-discriminatory way. The separate empire of special education developed over this century for largely the same reasons. For most parents, 'choice' has been a misnomer for the situation they felt placed in. For them, there was *no* choice in terms of having a range of acceptable alternatives to consider. This situation is similar to the pressures for earlier 'choices' forced on an older generation of parents who placed their children with intellectual disabilities in institutions. These parents were faced with discrimination and lack of support for the family and their child. The 'experts' of the day also pressured them to 'choose' an institution, by assuring them that the institution would provide the 'expert' care that their children required, which could not be provided anywhere else. We now know how their rights as children *and* their rights to special care failed to be met in those institutional settings. As Hulston (1999) points out:

> The rhetoric of a shift to an inclusive education system that allows for 'choice' of segregation or inclusion of students with disabilities is not only a philosophical contradiction but it also provides schools with conflicting messages in regard to the responsibilities of the class teacher for all of their students. This confusion can also potentially provide a context for the invisibility of 'special needs' students (p. 37).

But would the educational rights of children with disabilities be met by simply including them all within the current provisions provided for most other children?

A failure to recognise and meet the diversity of educational needs of *all* children will inevitably fail to make educational rights a reality for *some* children. This general principle holds true for all of society's children. The rights set out in the Convention apply to individual children and are met or denied to individual children.

If educational provisions do not meet the special educational needs experienced by some children with disabilities, then unlawful discrimination may still be taking place. The Human Rights Act 1993 also outlaws indirect discrimination against people with disabilities. Indirect discrimination can occur when providing the same services or provisions denies the student access to education. The issue of indirect discrimination is particularly relevant to issues of how resources are allocated and what 'special' resources are provided. The New Zealand government has recently put into place a major policy initiative relating particularly to the allocation of resources for 'special education'. The stated aim of the new policy is:

> ... to achieve, over the next decade, a world class inclusive education system that provides learning opportunities of equal quality to all students (Ministry of Education, 1996, p. 5).

The outcomes expected for children with special educational needs are that they will:

- achieve better learning outcomes;
- be welcome at their local school;
- benefit from early childhood centres and schools having more flexibility in provision of programmes;
- receive equitable levels of resourcing according to level of need, whatever their learning environment;
- have decisions on their resourcing needs made by those closest to them;
- be able to attend the type of facility of their family's choice, where there are enough enrolments (Ministry of Education, n.d.).

Unfortunately some of the outcomes of the current policy may be achieving the opposite of these positive aims. For example, the average amount of individual funding allocated per child under the Ongoing Resourcing Scheme (for the 1 per cent of children with the greatest special educational needs) is the same for children in both segregated and inclusive settings. Far from providing equity, this 'equal provision' is often inadequate to meet the needs of children in inclusive settings, but provides significant financial benefits to segregated, special schools in which the majority of pupils qualify for ORS funding. The incentives provided by the new policy promote segregation, rather than inclusion, of children with disabilities. Furthermore, the decision by government to limit this special individual entitlement to 1 per cent of the school population, appears to be based on simple dollar calculations rather than data on the actual number of children with high and on-going special educational needs. It is to be hoped that current research evaluating the implementation of the policy will provide critical information for future developments.

Once again, we find policy and practice relying on an emphasis on assumed differences between groups of children rather than on the continuum of the differing education needs of all children. The new policy appears to fail to promote changes to enable the education system to be more flexible and adaptable to the diversity of children's needs. Instead, complex regulations and administrative practices are developed to determine each child's eligibility to a predetermined range of 'special' resources, based on a focus on individual impairments rather than an assessment of the needs of *this* child in *this* setting.

A critical question which needs to be asked is: Do the special resources provided for this child with a disability promote the type of outcomes for this child that we want for *all* children? Or, do they increase this child's isolation from other children, limit her educational achievement unnecessarily, and teach all children that the equal rights espoused by the Convention do not really mean anything?

Two examples of special resources, and how they may be used, illustrate this issue. Both of these resources are the site of much dissatisfaction and disagreement in New Zealand over the eligibility of individual children to access the resource, and the adequacy of the amount of resource.

First, a traditional provision of 'special' education has been the involvement of health professionals in the education of children with physical impairments or conditions. Physiotherapists have been involved in the education of children with physical disabilities since the first special schools were established in 1950 (Caswell, 1996). Since this time, children with physical disabilities have been increasingly integrated into ordinary classes and schools, and the physiotherapy service has been faced with the challenges of providing itinerant services to an increasing number of individual students.

The critical question for this discussion is: Is the provision of physiotherapy to some children with disabilities in school settings enhancing the child's educational outcomes, in terms of the rights of all children to education (as set out in Articles 28 and 29)? At one level this is clearly a question which can only be answered by empirical research. There are important issues, however, which deserve reflection within a values and justice framework.

Firstly, a health professional's training and orientation is towards the treatment of specific impairments and conditions within a clinical context. Working in an educational setting, particularly within an ordinary classroom and school, to enhance the child's achievement of educational goals, requires a very different orientation and context. Caswell's (1996) research on the role of physiotherapists in New Zealand education raises serious questions about physiotherapists' preparation and skills to work within inclusive educational philosophies and settings. From the point of view of the child's right to education there are a number of questions to be examined. For example, is the time spent away from the school curriculum (i.e. out of the classroom with a physiotherapist) the most effective way of achieving educational and socialisation goals? If the goals are not educational but health-related, is it essential that they are undertaken during school time? If they are educational, they should be undertaken within the actual setting in which they are to be used, and should reflect the broad educational goals for all children of that age and culture.

The second example of 'special resources' that is the focus of much parent and school anxiety relates to the use of an extra adult to support the child with a disability in the classroom. In New Zealand these adults are called 'teacher aides', although it would probably be more accurate to call them 'child aides'. This special resource can be essential for some children's attendance at school, and can be of great value to a child's educational progress.

Unfortunately, the inappropriate use of teacher aides can also jeopardise the child's rights in a number of ways. The presence of an extra adult in close proximity to a child with a disability for all or most of the school day can stigmatise the child among her peers and set her apart as being not a part of the class community (Giangreco, Edelman, Luiselli & MacFarland, 1997).

Another danger of close adult attention is that the child learns to become over-dependent on an adult for all learning and classroom tasks. Finally, it is ironic that a person who is not a trained teacher, is often given the responsibility for curriculum adaptations and teaching of a child with special learning needs (Marks, Schrader & Levine (1999)). As an unknown person once quipped unkindly about special education, 'the trouble with special education is that it is not special and it is not education'. By over-reliance on teacher aides, schools and class teachers relinquish responsibility for the education of some of their children (i.e. those with a disability). Thus the focus on differences, and different ways of addressing these, can deny the child's rights to an education which develops 'the child's personality, talents and mental and physical abilities to their fullest potential' (Article 28, 5.1(a)), prepares 'the child for responsible life in a free society' (s.1(d)) and teaches 'respect for human rights and fundamental freedoms' (s.1(b)).

Our children cannot learn respect for diversity, equality and non-discrimination when they are separated from children with disabilities. And our children with disabilities cannot be socialised and learn to become responsible, self-determining adults if they do not learn and play amongst the diversity of children in our society.

The issue of special resources is also frequently used as an excuse for discrimination. While it is important to acknowledge that legislation in the area of human and consumer rights usually includes phrases such as 'reasonable' accommodations, or 'as far as possible', or 'within the resources available', the onus is on the person using these excuses to justify their validity. Too often they are used to discriminate and deny children's rights. Some examples of these excuses and their results include:

- children with disabilities being refused the right to attend school for the full school day;
- a parent being required to be available at any time, if called upon, to come to school and remove her child from school;
- a child not being allowed in the playground because of a lack of supervision;
- parents being required to pay for support for their child to attend school;
- children with disabilities being denied the right to be included in areas of the curriculum such as class trips and camps.

Conclusion

This paper has sought to focus attention on the issue of children's rights, particularly the rights of children with disabilities. As a focus for discussion we have looked at the rights of all children to education. We have pointed out how an undue emphasis on difference and special rights can inadvertently lead to injustice and inequality for children with disabilities.

While international human rights are essentially about the rights of individuals, they are also about the human values of community and visions of what sort of societies the world community, through the United Nations, wants to promote. Respect for diversity, participation of all citizens, and the outlawing of discrimination are some of these core values.

Educational rights are about more than education, more than equal educational opportunity. They are primarily about social justice for all. The most important word in international and national treaties and laws relating to children's rights is the word *all*. Because children with disabilities have often been excluded from 'all children', ensuring their rights as children are upheld requires broader changes than devising *special* resources for individual children.

In the area of educational rights, we need to move past the rhetoric to changing systems and practices. In a consideration of the issues of disability, education and the discourses of justice, Rizvi and Lingard (1996) state:

> ... reform for educational justice is complex, and requires attention not only to issues of the political economy of schooling – concerns of access and equity – but also to issues of the culture of schooling; that is, the way things are named and represented, the manner in which difference is treated and the ways in which values, significations and norms which govern life in schools are negotiated and established (pp. 24-25).

The rights of children with disabilities will be better protected if they receive more attention from groups concerned about children's rights rather than being seen as someone else's responsibility because of presumed special expertise.

All children are children first and foremost and the rights in the United Nations Convention on the Rights of the Child must be inclusive of all children. Ensuring the achievement of those rights may mean additional or different supports for some children. But we must be very careful that our attention to differences is not used as an excuse for discrimination. We must also ensure that our 'special' help promotes their rights as children and does not diminish their potential or increase their separation from other children.

References

Caswell, P.A. (1996). *The role of the physiotherapist in New Zealand special education: Present practice, future directions.* Unpublished master's thesis, University of Otago, Dunedin, New Zealand.

Giangreco, M.F., Edelman, S.W., Luiselli, T.E., & MacFarland, S.Z.C. (1997). Helping or hovering? Effects of instructional assistant proximity on students with disabilities. *Exceptional Children, 64*(1), 7-18.

Hammarberg, T. (1995). The rights of disabled children: The UN Convention on the Rights of the Child. In T. Degener & Y. Koster-Dreese (Eds), *Human rights and disabled persons: Essays and relevant human rights instruments.* Dordrecht, The Netherlands: Martinus Nijhoff Publishers, pp. 147-55.

Hulston, S. (1999). Framing the framework: Discourses of invisibility. *New Zealand Journal of Disability Studies, 6*, 35-58.

Human Rights Commission. (1996). *Human rights and special needs education: Discussion paper*. Auckland: Human Rights Commission.

Hume, J. (1991). The unremembered Holocaust. *New Zealand Disabled, 11*, 61-5.

Marks, S.U., Schrader, C., & Levine, M. (1999). Paraeducator experiences in inclusive settings: Helping, hovering, or holding their own? *Exceptional Children, 65*(3), 315-28.

Ministry of Education. (1996). *Special Education 2000.* Wellington: Ministry of Education.

Ministry of Education (n.d.). *Special Education 2000 – Getting it right, together.* Wellington: Ministry of Education.

Minow, M. (1990). *Making all the difference: Inclusion, exclusion, and American law.* Ithaca, USA: Cornell University Press.

Rizvi, F., & Lingard, B. (1996). Disability, education and the discourses of justice. In C. Christensen & R. Rizvi (Eds), *Disability and the dilemmas of education and justice.* Buckingham, UK: Open University Press, pp. 9-26.

Smith, N. (1999). *The education agenda priorities for '99.* Speech Notes prepared for Closing Address to Secondary Principals' Association of New Zealand Conference, Rotorua.

Sobsey, D., Donnellan, A., & Wolbring, G. (1994). Reflections on the Holocaust: Where did it begin and has it really ended? *Developmental Disabilities Bulletin, 22*(2), 121-35.

United Nations. (1994). *The standard rules on the equalization of opportunities for persons with disabilities.* New York: United Nations.

· 3 ·

Children's rights education: Implementing Article 42

KATHERINE COVELL AND R. BRIAN HOWE

Abstract

We describe our experiences, considerations and obstacles faced in promoting children's rights education in Canada. Our focus here is on the choice of age for introducing children's rights education, the means by which school district cooperation was gained, our approach to dealing with concerns about teacher resistance to new curricula (particularly that which some perceived to threaten their authority), and how the curricula were designed to promote student interest. The benefits of children's rights education are also described.

In signing and ratifying the United Nations Convention on the Rights of the Child, Canada, like other signatories, is obligated to educate children as well as adults about children's rights. Article 42 specifies that states parties are 'to make the principles and provisions of the Convention widely known, by appropriate and active means, to adults and children alike.' This obligation fits well with Canada's general policy objectives of promoting multiculturalism and equality rights, and with existing human rights legislation. Nonetheless, little has been done.

One obvious means to increase public awareness of the Convention is through education in Canadian schools. However, this has yet to be done in any serious or systematic way. In reviewing Canada's report in 1994, the UN Committee on the Rights of the Child suggested that Canada should make more effort to implement Article 42 by incorporating children's rights education into the school curricula (UN Committee, 1995). Since that report, only two school boards in Canada have included children's rights education in their curricula. In the Greater Victoria School Board, in British Columbia, children's rights education at the Grade 3 level is available for those teachers who wish to use it. In the Cape Breton Victoria Regional School Board, in Nova Scotia, children's rights education is an integral part of the social studies curriculum for all Grade 6 classes, and at this time is optional at the Grade 8 level. It seems likely that the UN Committee will once again fault Canada's record in its response to the 1999 report.

In our attempts to initiate children's rights education we have encountered a number of obstacles that may help explain why Canada continues to lack children's rights education. We explain these obstacles here, our means of addressing them, and the benefits of children's rights education. First, we briefly examine our experience of implementing children's rights education at the post-secondary level.

Children's rights education at university

Encouraged by student interest in contemporary issues of relevance and by university administrators' calls for interdisciplinary courses, we developed two senior undergraduate courses in children's rights. The courses, which are co-taught, combine the disciplines of law, political science and developmental psychology. They have proven popular with a variety of students. Class members include traditional university students, social workers, police officers, foster parents, teachers, and native counsellors. Class size grew from twenty-five students in the first year of offering to a current average of a hundred. Attendance has been exceptionally high, debate lively, and regardless of viewpoints the classes have been successful in spreading awareness of children's rights. In essence, providing children's rights education at the university level has been straightforward and fills Canada's obligation to some extent. But it is not enough.

Under the Convention, children – not just adults – are to be informed about their rights, and the most logical place to reach children is at school. We need to have children's rights education systematically incorporated in the Canadian school curriculum as noted by the UN Committee. There is an additional imperative here. We believe that children's rights education has the potential to play an important role in creating and maintaining a rights-respecting culture. But implementing children's rights education in schools has been significantly less straightforward. Our initial task was to decide:

- at what age we should introduce children's rights education into the classroom;
- how we would get cooperation from the provincial Department of Education;
- how we would gain teacher cooperation;
- how we would present the information to elicit the children's interest and have a positive impact on the development of their social concepts and social behaviours.

We discuss each in turn.

Appropriate age

There is evidence that even young children have some general understanding of the concept of rights (Helwig, 1997). Older children, however, starting around age eleven, become able to consider their own and another person's opinion and recognise that the other person can do the same. In addition, the child is able to assume the perspective of a third party and to anticipate how each person may react to the other's perspective (Selman, 1980). This improved role-taking ability allows an appreciation that rights can be in conflict, and that rights for one person subsume responsibilities toward others. As role-taking skills develop, so does children's sensitivity to the needs and feelings of others. Unlike in earlier childhood, direct experience with another's distress is no longer necessary to arouse empathy. Empathy now is achieved through information about another's distress (Hoffman, 1987). This more adult-like empathic responding should allow for an understanding of rights violations and, in turn, that rights must apply to all and must be protected. During this same developmental period is the early questioning about personal values (Erikson, 1968; Marcia, 1991), and about social and legal systems (Berman, 1997; Piaget, 1932). The impact of rights on a culture of respect, peace and tolerance can be understood. Our choice of Grade 6 (ages eleven to thirteen) as the introductory point for children's rights education was made primarily on the basis of the developmental changes described above. In addition we took into account the social changes in early adolescence that result in greater time spent with and greater dependence upon peers (Durkin, 1995). Successful social transitions at this age require effective problem-solving skills and peer support (Dunn, Putallaz, Sheppard & Lindstrom, 1987). Learning about rights was expected to facilitate both peer support and positive decision-making. These issues were a major motivator of the development of a follow-up children's rights curriculum designed for Grade 8 (ages thirteen to fifteen).

Gaining education department cooperation

In Canada, education is under provincial jurisdiction. This decentralisation means that implementing new curricula can be a slow and arduous process (Buckingham, 1996). It is necessary first to have cooperation from a local school district, then the province in which that district is based, and only then can there be serious attempts at widespread curriculum implementation. Since school boards are operating under the constant pressures of inadequate resources and ongoing directives for improved education, it is necessary also that school officials be convinced that any new curriculum will fit with existing priorities and be of obvious benefit to students.

We had no difficulty with the first step in the process: convincing our local school district officials that children's rights education was a worthy endeavour. Fortunately, they held attitudes supportive of children's rights, and were eager to cooperate. They provided us with six Grade 6 classrooms whose teachers agreed to undertake a one-year pilot test of the curriculum we had designed.

The details of this pilot study evaluation are presented elsewhere (Covell & Howe, 1999). In essence, the evaluation indicated that teaching children's rights at the Grade 6 level may have positive effects on the child's well-being, on teacher and peer relationships, and is likely to promote positive attitudes towards ethnic minority children. Moreover, feedback received from pilot study teachers and children was highly positive. Armed with our data we approached the provincial department of education. We met with cautious support.

At the provincial level, two concerns were raised that were practical and two that were substantive. The practical concerns were the result of our not having researched provincially approved curriculum presentation styles. To meet department standards we agreed to revise the curriculum to conform to a learning outcomes framework, and to be inclusive in language (for example, we had to replace phrases such as 'ask each child to *stand* at the front of the class' with 'allow each child a turn *to be* at the front of the class'). The substantive concerns centred on the necessity of the curriculum and the relative focus on rights versus responsibilities.

The necessity of the curriculum was questioned in light of existing anti-discrimination laws and the Canadian Charter of Rights. Given existing laws and education about these laws, we were asked why a curriculum would be needed. Our response was as follows. Existing laws and programmes are not always clear about what rights pertain to adults and what pertain to children. The Convention is important because it provides a systematic statement of the rights of children in particular and adds rights that did not previously exist in law. The Convention also requires that children become aware of their basic rights. Existing education programmes do not necessarily do this. We also stressed that adoption of the curriculum would make Nova Scotia a leader in filling Canada's obligation for children's rights education.

We had more difficulty with the issue of responsibilities. In fact, this has been a recurrent theme: Shouldn't we be teaching children their responsibilities? Don't children have too many rights now? Why would we encourage disregard for adult authority by actually telling children they have rights? These questions concerned members of the provincial department of education; teachers have raised them, and parents have raised them. We have been able to respond with reference to our own evaluation data as well as with reference to literature in educational psychology. Our data showed that those children who had received the children's rights curriculum, when compared with their peers who had not, had a broader and more accurate knowledge of rights in which the needs of all were expressed as more important than the wants of some. Children who learned about their rights under the Convention understood and valued rights to equality. In the words of one of the children, 'I learned that respect and equality are important for everyone.' In the words of one of the teachers, 'I have experienced the benefits of the 3Rs – rights, respect and responsibility'. Teaching about rights means learning about responsibilities. As Berman (1997) noted, when community issues are emphasised in a classroom, relationships are equalised, and competitiveness is replaced with a sense of collective responsibility. We certainly have seen this recently in the pilot testing of the Grade 8 curriculum: one class has initiated a breakfast programme, another has been working to help the homeless. The evidence was enough to persuade the provincial education officials. It has remained an issue with some teachers.

Gaining teacher cooperation

We have had no difficulty in gaining cooperation from teachers to pilot test the curricula at both the Grade 6 and Grade 8 levels. The issue is how to gain cooperation such that widespread implementation of the curricula is successful. The Nova Scotia Department of Education has now agreed to make the children's rights education an integral part of the social studies curricula for all Grade 6 classes in the province. The curriculum is being integrated into a new health and social studies curriculum that will be introduced across the province in September, 2000. It will also be available across the country to any other school district who wishes to adopt it. In the interim, the Cape Breton Victoria Regional School has adopted the children's rights curriculum for use in all its Grade 6 classes. The response of the teachers is increasingly positive as their experience with children's rights education grows.

Three fundamental concerns have been expressed. First, teachers recently had been concerned about new responsibilities in the context of larger classes, fewer resources, loss of support personnel and inclusion policies (Nova Scotia Teachers Union, 1996). Few were interested in adding a new area to their teaching. Second, a few teachers were concerned with the broadening of their teaching responsibilities and believed that 'sensitive topics' such as children's rights should be taught in the home rather than at school. Third, and perhaps most important, a significant minority of teachers have expressed concerns about the potential loss of authority in the classroom that they anticipate would follow children learning they have rights (c.f., Franklin, 1996; Covell & Howe, 1997).

To facilitate the acceptance of the curriculum, we designed it to fit into the existing health and social studies curriculum, for example matching Article 33 to the existing section of the health curriculum on drug prevention. We provided a choice of activities for each section, and we described preparation time and materials where necessary. For additional support we have a web site with links and further information. Also we held a workshop with the teachers at which time we also discussed the issue of responsibilities versus rights.

To lessen concerns about children running amok when being told they had rights, we presented the data from the Grade 6 pilot study, and we had pilot study teachers talk about their experiences with the curriculum. We talked also about the special role of teachers in spreading awareness of the Convention, and of Canada's educational obligations under international law. Not all were convinced. We distributed a questionnaire to the eighty Grade 6 teachers at the end of the year. Fifty-four returned them. Interestingly, their attitudes toward teaching children's rights did not vary with teacher qualifications, gender, or years of experience. The majority reported that they had found the workshop useful, the curriculum easy and somewhat enjoyable to use, and that the children were interested in the classes and responded well. Nonetheless a number (20 per cent) also expressed discomfort with teaching children's rights, mostly with regard to loss of their authority in the classroom. For example, 'Students quickly learn to take advantage of opportunity and gain control of the classroom. Giving them tools is not my idea of a solution.' It may be the design of the curriculum activities, in which children are encouraged to express their views, that underlies this concern. It may also be that some teachers' strong views precluded use of the curriculum. One teacher who commented favorably noted, 'Initially there was some concern of what children would do with these rights once they knew them. Obviously this was a lack of knowledge of what children's rights means.'

Overall, the responses were positive and in sharp contrast to the negative comments. Twenty-six per cent of the teachers expressed very strong support for the curriculum and for teaching children's rights. Since demographic variables failed to discriminate the two extreme positions, we will be investigating other potential sources such as a belief in authoritarian control (see Bickmore, 1999). It seems unlikely that teachers who are opposed to teaching children's rights will be effective in so doing. It is not enough, for example, to tell children they have participation rights without providing them.

Two other concerns have been noted by the six teachers who over the past year have been pilot testing the Grade 8 curriculum. Both concerns stem from the specifics of activities. Some teachers were uncomfortable facilitating discussion with their students on sensitive topics, such as sexuality, that are part of the curriculum. For some, discussing date rape or condom use (rights and sexuality) is more difficult than describing the position of the fallopian tube (the typical sex education class at this level). Perhaps of more importance, however, is the teacher's difficulty responding to parents' concerns – for example, when a mother calls upset that the child has learned that she has a right to maintain contact with her father (Article 9). Provision of teacher supports beyond information on a web site or in a handbook seems necessary to gaining widespread teacher cooperation. Determining the optimum delivery and type of supports, together with identification of teacher variables that predict reluctance to teach children's rights, may be essential to children's rights education in the classroom being meaningful.

Interesting the children

In designing the Grade 6 and Grade 8 curricula our goal was to impart the information in the Convention in a manner that was developmentally appropriate and that modelled the rights the children were being taught they had. In terms of the latter it was important to provide the children with opportunities to express their opinions (Articles 13 and 14), to work with friends (Article 15), and have their views heard (Article 12). In terms of the former we considered issues salient to the developmental needs of early adolescence.

There is significant evidence that some children appear to lose motivation for school during the early adolescent years; their grades decline, they skip classes and set out on a downward spiral path toward school failure and early school leaving (e.g. Eccles, Midgley & Adler, 1984; Simmons & Blyth, 1987). The problems seem to arise from a mismatch between children's developmental needs and the typical school environment (Eccles et al., 1993). In early adolescence, development is characterised by increases in the desire for independence and self-determination, increased opportunity for peer interaction, and by the capacity to engage in more abstract and hypothetical thinking (Simmons & Blyth, 1987). Students need an environment that allows for questioning ideas and exploring issues with peers; they also need to have their ideas listened to, respected and appreciated. These developmental needs mesh well with the Convention articles described above.

With these considerations in mind, we designed the two curricula to include a variety of group activities in which students are encouraged to role-play, question and discuss issues of interest to them. For example, in the Grade 6 curriculum one activity to learn about Article 14 (freedom of conscience) and Article 33 (protection from the use or sale of drugs), involved students alternating between playing a drug dealer trying to convince a young person to sell drugs, and the youth who is being pressured. A series of questions are included for the teacher to facilitate subsequent discussion. Examples from the Grade 8 curriculum include discussing the representation of rights and responsibilities in sexual activity (Articles 13, 16, 29, 34) in existing popular music, examining cases of children living on the streets (Articles 6, 9, 24, 27, 29), and designing advertisements for alcohol and tobacco that do not violate rights (Articles 3, 24, 27, 33). Teacher reports on children's responses to the curriculum activities have been unambiguous; we have been told that the children are really enjoying the activities and are asking for more children's rights education. It is noteworthy that a number of children have expressed a particular interest in learning more about how to exercise their rights during custody decisions and for post-divorce parental contact.

Benefits of children's rights education

We anticipated children's rights education would increase favourable human rights attitudes and behaviours. The positive impact was expected to result from both the curriculum activity style and content.

Leming (1992), in a review of contemporary issues curricula, concluded that attitude change is most likely when curricula are designed to involve peer interaction through group discussion and activities in which students are able to explore opinions and values in an egalitarian and open manner. Role-play exercises are a particularly effective way of exploring opinions and an effective means of promoting tolerance (Bickmore, 1999). Similarly, in an examination of the development of social consciousness and social responsibility, Berman (1997) noted that when children are encouraged to challenge opinions and to develop their own ideas, they develop an increased level of tolerance for dissent. In addition, tolerance and empathy are enhanced through teaching moral and political conflicts (Berman, 1997).

Preliminary data suggest children's rights education does have a facilitative effect on promoting tolerance and respect for others. Decoene and De Cock (1996) in their study in Bruges, Belgium, report a linkage between exposure of children to a children's rights education programme and increased support for the general values of rights, tolerance and multiculturalism. During the course of learning about their rights, the children asked questions about the rights of others, and raised issues concerning the values of diversity and tolerance. Their teachers noted increased behavioural acceptance of children with differences. In our evaluation of the impact of the Grade 6 pilot study, we compared attitudes of the 175 children (average age of twelve years) with a sociodemographically equivalent sample of 89 children (Covell & Howe, 1999). The comparison indicated that the children who had received the curriculum perceived greater levels of peer and teacher support and were more accepting of ethnic minority children. In the evaluation of the impact of the Grade 8 pilot study, the 89 adolescents who received the curriculum (average age fourteen years) showed greater support for rights for children in general and also showed greater support for rights for adults than did a comparison group of 91 Grade 8 children who did not have the curriculum. These latter included rights for ethnic minorities, native peoples, homosexuals, and people with disabilities. As such we hypothesise a contagion effect: when children learn they have rights, they become more aware of and more supportive of rights for others.

We must now examine what generalisations can be made from such beneficial impact. If we can provide evidence that inclusion of children's rights education in the school curricula is of value to the teacher, the classroom and even the community, as well as a legal obligation, we can expect more support. As the curriculum is implemented across the province of Nova Scotia, we will have the opportunity to assess the impact of teacher attitudes on the effectiveness of the curriculum, and whether the more rights-respecting attitudes engendered among the children are long lasting or are reflected in behaviour. We shall also monitor the response of other educational jurisdictions to Nova Scotia's lead in implementing Article 42 of the Convention. Through an existing arrangement among provincial departments of education, Nova Scotia will make the curricula available nationally. It is our hope that prior to Canada's 2004 report to the UN Committee, Article 42 will be implemented fully. We have made a start.

Acknowledgements

We gratefully acknowledge funding from Canadian Heritage to design and test the Grade 6 curriculum, and from Canadian Race Relations to design and evaluate the Grade 8 curriculum.

References

Berman, S. (1997). *Children's social consciousness and the development of social responsibility.* New York: State University of New York Press.

Bickmore, K. (1999). Teaching conflict and conflict resolution in school. In A. Raviv, L. Oppenheiner, & D. Bar-Tal (Eds), *How children understand war and peace.* San Francisco: Jossey Bass, pp. 233-59.

Buckingham, D. (1996). Teaching international law in high schools. *Education and Law Journal, 8*, 51-8.

Covell, K., & Howe, R.B. (1997). Toward children's rights education. In A. Richardson (Ed.), *Canadian Childhood in 1997.* Edmonton: Kanata Learning, pp. 270-6.

Covell, K., & Howe, R.B. (1999). The impact of children's rights education: A Canadian study. *The International Journal of Children's Rights, 7*, 171-83.

Decoene, J., & De Cock, R. (1996). The children's rights project in the primary school 'De Vrijdagmarkt' in Bruges. In E. Verhellen (Ed.), *Monitoring children's rights.* The Netherlands: Kluwer Law International, pp. 627-36.

Dunn, S., Putallaz, M., Sheppard, B., & Lindstrom, R. (1987). Social support and adjustment in gifted adolescents. *Journal of Educational Psychology, 79*, 467-73.

Durkin, K. (1995). *Developmental social psychology.* Cambridge, MA: Blackwell.

Eccles, J., Midgley, C., & Adler, T. (1984). Grade-related changes in the school environment: Effects on achievement motivation. In J.G. Nicholls (Ed.), *The development of achievement motivation.* Greenwich, CT: JAI Press, pp. 283-331.

Eccles, J.S., Midgley, C., Wigfield, A., Buchanan, C.M., Reuman, D., Flanagan, C., & MacIver, D. (1993). Development during adolescence: The impact of stage-environment fit on young adolescents' experiences in schools and families. *American Psychologist, 48*, 90-101.

Erikson, E. (1968). *Identity: Youth and crisis.* New York: Norton.

Franklin, B. (1996). Children's right to participate in decision making. In E. Verhellen (Ed.), *Monitoring children's rights.* The Netherlands: Kluwer Law International, pp. 317-26.

Helwig, C. (1997). The role of agent and social context in judgements of freedom of speech and religion. *Child Development, 68*, 484-95.

Hoffman, M. (1987). The contribution of empathy to justice and moral judgement. In N. Eisenberg & J. Strayer (Eds), *Empathy and its development.* New York: Cambridge University Press, pp. 47-80.

Leming, J.S. (1992). The influence of contemporary issues curricula on school-age youth. In G. Grant (Ed.), *Review of research in education.* Washington, DC: American Educational Research Association, Vol. 18, pp. 111-61.

Marcia, J. (1991). Identity and self-development. In R. Lerner, A.C. Petersen, & J. Brooks-Gunn (Eds), *Encyclopedia of adolescence.* New York: Garland, Vol. 1, pp. 529-33.

Nova Scotia Teachers' Union. (1996, September 2). Shattering the myth. *Cape Breton Post.*

Piaget, J. (1932). *The moral judgement of the child.* New York: Harcourt Brace Jovanovitch.

Selman, R. (1980). *The growth of interpersonal understanding.* New York: Academic Press.

Simmons, R.G., & Blyth, D.A. (1987). *Moving into adolescence: The impact of pubertal change and school context.* New York: Aldine de Gruyter.

UN Committee on the Rights of the Child. (1995). *Consideration of reports submitted by state parties under Article 44 of the Convention*: Canada UN CRC/C/15/Add.37, June 20, 1995.

Children's rights in the ecology of human development

JAMES GARBARINO

My paper is a natural complement to my long-time friend and colleague Gary Melton's presentation.[1] Like him, I see the UN Convention on the Rights of the Child as an intellectual work in progress. I too am trying to refine some of the ways we can move forward in thinking about parents and children and the political and social discourse about the rights of parents and children. And I take two texts for this 'sermon' about children's rights in the ecology of human development.

The first is from a German psychologist who moved to the United States, eventually ending up at Cornell University. His name is Kurt Lewin. Among other things, Kurt Lewin said, 'There is nothing so practical as a good theory'. Nothing so practical as a good theory – an expression which often strikes American audiences as being a *non sequitur* because we pride ourselves on being practical, and often think that theoretical is the opposite. So it's a particularly useful epigram for American audiences and, given that we bear some cultural connection, perhaps for New Zealand audiences as well. There is nothing so practical as a good theory, meaning that until we understand things really in depth and in the broadest deepest possible way, our practice, our actions and our policy are likely to be impoverished. I think that's also consistent with what Gary Melton was saying earlier today: we need to think deeply.

The other text comes from another famous figure, the liberator of India, Mahatma Gandhi. Among other important things, Gandhi once wrote, 'You must be the change you wish to see in the world.' The beginnings for social change and social policy lie in transforming the self, in transforming one's self, one's mind, one's heart, and one's spirit. We'll think about these texts as I go forward with this lecture.

The term 'human ecology' or an ecological perspective on development has many meanings, but where I come from intellectually at Cornell University, we attach a special significance to the term 'an ecological perspective'. In particular, what we refer to is the centrality of context in understanding human development, the recognition that rarely, if ever, is there a simple process of cause and effect in human development independent of context. If the question in human development is 'does x cause y?' the best scientific answer is always 'it depends'.

It depends on context. We'd be hard pressed to find exceptions to that principle.

There are many examples of the contextual nature of human development that span the gamut from intellectual to social development. For example, twenty years ago, a study asked the question 'are children born with a minor physical anomaly (usually indicating some neurological damage typically occurring as a result of insult during pregnancy) more likely to develop problems with aggression and violence as teenagers?' (see Mednick & Kandel, 1998). With the insight of the ecological perspective you already know the answer: 'It depends.' When such physiologically, biologically damaged children grew up in positive, warm and supportive families and communities, it turns out they were no more likely than physically normal children to develop problems with aggression. However, when they grew up in abusive families, they were four times as likely as physically normal children to develop problems with aggression as teenagers.

Similar results are found if we look at the role of genetic heritage in producing intellectual development. The classic studies concern genetically identical twins (see Bronfenbrenner & Mahoney, 1975). These studies are often offered up to us to say that genetic identical twins end up having IQs very similar regardless of whether or not they grow up together. The typical finding was that they grow up to have IQs that are highly correlated. However, an ecologically provoked reanalysis of those data asks the question: 'How similar are their IQs, not if they're separated or not, but if they are separated and put in similar families and communities or dissimilar families and communities?' For example, are they put two in middle class families or two in low income families, or is one in middle class and one in low income? When the data is reanalysed that way, the finding was that when identical twins are separated and put in dissimilar environments, the correlation in their IQs was .29. When they were separated and put in similar environments, the correlation was .89. So if we ask the question: 'Do genetically identical twins grow up to be similar in their intellectual development?' the answer is, 'It depends.' This ('it depends') recurs whether the issue is evaluating programmes or understanding professional development.

In the United States there's a lot of interest today in what are called mentoring programmes, and the question is: 'Do mentoring programmes work?' You already know the answer: 'It depends.' It turns out if children are in mentoring programmes for less than two and a half years, it has no effect or even a negative effect on their development. Only when they're in the programmes for two and a half years or more (the studies are showing) do you see the desired outcomes. After a lecture somebody once asked: 'Are people who were sexually abused as children better or worse as professionals dealing with child sexual abuse?' and I was able to answer with great confidence, 'Yes, they're better or they're worse!' It depends upon what else happened in their development. We take that as a beginning point, this ecological perspective, and we find that it applies to many issues that have relevance to children's rights.

One way of rendering some of Gary Melton's analyses this morning is to say if the question is: 'Are children competent to decide?', the answer is: 'It depends.' It depends a great deal on what the issue is and how effective the adults are in creating a situation in which children can be competent, because the competency of children is quite variable across context, particularly across styles of adult interaction. This ecological perspective becomes a fundamental challenge when we seek to talk about children's rights because certainly the rhetoric of children's rights conveys a kind of universality. It's very difficult to think of how you could speak of rights in context. What would it mean to speak of rights in context? Do children have rights? If we answer 'it depends', it makes the concept of children's rights almost a kind of oxymoron because the concept of rights in our conventional way of thinking suggests universality or transcontextual validity. Part of the reason why the ecological perspective challenges the concept of children's rights is because it testifies to the importance of context in normalising experience. Anyone who has transcultural or multicultural experience certainly has some familiarity with the fact that many experiences which are perceived and experienced as deviant in one setting, are perceived and experienced as normal in another, and the power of context to normalise things psychologically is really extraordinary.

I thought of this a number of years ago when visiting Sudan. My family and I had been involved in one of the international programmes where you 'adopt' a child and send money to their family and their community through an agency. Many people do this and in Sudan there was a significant programme involving thousands of partners from both European and North American countries. I did the audacious thing of actually going to Sudan to visit the child that we had 'adopted'. It was a girl. Visiting her brought home the issue of genital mutilation, which as many of you know is very widespread in Sudan, affecting in many places more than 90 per cent of girls. In childhood, girls are subjected to a procedure which involves the cutting off of the exterior genitalia and the sewing up of the vaginal opening to the size of a pinhole. This issue is, to a Western sensibility, an obvious and grotesque violation of human rights, a form of oppression, a form of torture. The empirical data show that it's a cause of primary sterility, a significant cause of serious infection and frequent death.

Nonetheless, in the Sudanese context, it is experienced as normalised and indeed it is so normalised that for a girl *not* to go through the procedure means that she's likely to experience ostracism, and even a sense of personal devaluation because she asks herself 'Why am I not as good as the other girls in my community?' An ecological perspective leaves us to think about this power of the context to normalise. Certainly it must somehow be taken into account. But, how do we do it? How do we use our ecological science to begin to approach issues like this, or indeed any other issue, which from one culture to another seems like a travesty? I think the way we begin is to understand that when we speak about cultural differences, we need to understand that there is not one kind of cultural difference, but at least three kinds of cultural difference. And to understand these three kinds of cultural differences requires us to push ourselves far beyond where we're usually willing to go intellectually (and perhaps philosophically) and certainly emotionally.

Perhaps as a kind of transitional preparation to go there, we can recall a parable – a parable I like to call the parable of the lamp post. The parable of the lamp post is useful in pointing out that technique and conventional conceptualisation may not be enough to solve difficult problems. In the parable of the lamp post, a friend of ours – let's call him Joe – is on his way home one night from a meeting. As he walks down a dark street, he comes upon his friend George on his hands and knees on the street under a lamp post. Joe stops and says, 'George, what's the matter?' George says, 'Oh, Joe I've lost my car keys and I can't go home until I find them. I live thirty-five kilometres away.' 'Well,' says Joe, 'let me help you.' So he gets on his hands and knees and begins to search around under the lamp post.

Some time passes and they haven't found the car keys. So Joe says, 'Well George, maybe we need a more systematic approach to this problem. Maybe we need a public health approach.' So from his pocket he pulls a piece of chalk and there under the lamp post on the street he draws a grid and he labels the boxes A through Z and 1 through 26. And they begin to search systematically, box A1, box A2, box A3, box A4. On and on this goes, they get to box Z26, but they haven't found the car keys. 'Well,' says Joe, 'no, no, no, that's the wrong paradigm. Perhaps we need a more behaviourist approach to this problem.' So from his other pocket he pulls a bag of M & Ms, candies. He says, 'George, I'm going to feed you these candies to get your behaviour under control' and soon he has George moving left and right and back and forth and up and down and it's a magnificent tour de force of behaviourist technology.

However, they haven't found the car keys. 'Well,' Joe says, 'no, no, no, no, no. What we need is a more psychoanalytic approach to this problem.' So he begins to ask George about early experiences of loss in his life. Soon George is getting real insights into his early experience when his mother went in the hospital, when he lost his teddy bear and how these losses reverberate with the loss of the car keys and he's feeling like the insights are just coming fresh and fast. But they haven't found the car keys. Joe says, 'No, no, no, no. What we need is a kind of multidisciplinary humanistic approach to this problem.' So from his bag he pulls a book on the history of the key in western civilisation and they discuss the key as a symbol and Ingmar Bergman's films and how Woody Allen brought that symbolism to the twentieth century. It's just fascinating. But they haven't found the car keys.

Joe says, 'No, no, no, no. What we need is a campaign to find the keys.' So from his bag he pulls out a banner that says 'Find the Keys', T-shirts that say

'Find the Keys', and little key shaped ribbons and they link arms and they chant, 'Find the keys, find the keys', and they take pictures to have in their offices of the Find the Keys Campaign and years later remember the great Find the Keys Campaign and they feel so satisfied with themselves. But they haven't found the keys. Finally Joe says, 'Look George, I think we need a really radical approach. Now where exactly were you when you dropped the keys?' George says, 'Oh, I was about 150 metres up the road when I dropped the keys.' So Joe of course says, 'Well, George, why are we looking here?' George replies, 'Oh well, the light is much better here!'

Now this is a parable we need, particularly in dealing with things like children's rights, where it's so tempting and easy so long as you have agreeable people around to look where the light is good. But no matter how good our technique is and how effective our rhetoric is, if the keys really lie up the road somewhere in the dark, we'll never find them unless we're willing to go there. And that's in essence my belief that we need to go beyond a simple unidimensional idea of children's rights, and cultural differences, to look at a more complex and, if you will, challenging sense of cultural differences.

The first kind of cultural difference I think we need to understand is when there are cultural differences simply in style, which have no particular substance or significance for development. For example, if you go into a Muslim place of worship, the way you show respect is by taking off your shoes and keeping your hat on. If you go into most Christian places of worship, at least in the English-speaking world, the way you show respect is by taking your hat off and keeping your shoes on. Certainly a significant cultural difference. Do we think it has any particular significance for development? Probably not. Language is certainly highly cultural and highly variable and yet, with relatively few exceptions, it probably doesn't have a lot of significance for development. It's an imperfect example because the classic linguistic studies of the Worfian hypothesis (Worf, 1956) indicate that language indeed may be connected to culture and perception. However, on a larger, more simplistic scale, Noam Chomsky (1957) argued that all languages are basically equivalent, and any group who can learn a language is basically as intellectually competent as any other group that learns a language. Language is basically interchangeable, in a sense, a manner of style, and whether you speak French or Spanish or English or German or Russian, you're speaking a language.

Of course which language you speak may have tremendous implications in context. And indeed that's characteristic of cultural differences in style. While they may have no intrinsic significance for development, they often have enormous contextual significance for development, because if you violate the norm, no matter how arbitrary it is, it may well have significant consequences. I remember years ago I worked at a summer camp for children and each week we'd have children of different ages come in. One week the group of children who were aged twelve to fourteen came, and the first thing we would do at the camp was have the children come to the lake and do their swimming test. Well, a child came down to do the swimming test who the staff had assigned to a girl's cabin. Yet this child showed up at the swimming dock, wearing what appeared to be a boy's bathing suit. I remember the staff were really intrigued and more than intrigued, compelled to figure out: was this a girl without the top of her bathing suit or had they mistakenly put a boy in the girl's cabin?

It emerged eventually that indeed it was a girl, but that her parents thought that the social convention of having a top on her bathing suit was purely conventional. In an absolute sense they're perfectly correct. Nonetheless, in context, the deviant behaviour of this girl had real psychological consequences and she was subjected to all kinds of humiliation by the other children because she was violating this convention. A difference in style with no intrinsic significance for development, in context had a lot of significance.

That's one kind of cultural difference, and identifying those differences is very important, because any notion of a just society would certainly recognise that if we identify those kind of cultural differences, we are almost inevitably obligated to respect them. That is when there are group differences of that sort which cultural differences must be: it's hard to imagine one person creating a culture. One person can only create style or psychosis. It takes a group to create culture. But there's a second kind of cultural difference, where cultures differ not just in style but in goal, where the cultures differ in what kind of human being they're seeking to create. A compelling example of major significance in many societies around the world, and certainly for the world as a whole, is the question of whether cultures seek to create individualists or collectivists. This is certainly one of the fundamental differences among cultures.

Some years ago a colleague of mine, an anthropologist, Jill Korban, was working in Hawaii with native Hawaiian mothers. After she had worked with these mothers over a long period and gained their confidence, they finally posed for her a troubling question. They said, 'Jill, we understand that among the non-Hawaiian population mothers require their infants to sleep in a separate room at night. This is so abusive, this is so horrible, such emotional torture. How could these mothers do this?' For them, the only appropriate place for an infant to sleep was in the bed with its parents, whereas in North American culture infants are 'supposed' to sleep alone. In fact some years ago, the American Psychiatric Association had a taskforce to decide at what age it was pathological to have the child sleep with the parent. You can imagine the difficulty a Hawaiian psychiatrist would have had being on such a panel.

What sense can we make of that difference? Is that simply a difference of style, like language? I would maintain that no, it's not simply a difference of style; it's a difference of goal. Hawaiians are seeking to create a different kind of person, a person for whom connection and interconnectity and interdependence is a central feature of personality and identity. North Americans on the other hand are seeking to create autonomous individuals and so the culture reflects the ultimate goal. The Hawaiian culture says, you are with us. The North American culture says, you have to grow up to be a rugged individual, you have to learn to stand on your own two feet; even when you're a baby and you can't even sit up, you have to learn to stand on your own two feet, and so you sleep by yourself.

If we try to translate this to the question of children's rights, the question would be: Does the child have a right to have these cultural differences and goals respected? This certainly becomes a political challenge in many situations. And in fact, the whole concept of child abuse in a multicultural setting can be nothing other than political decisions about which goals for human development are acceptable and which are not. A common example of this challenge occurs in many multicultural settings. I know it occurs in Hawaii, for example. If certain cultures (because of their goals), produce children who are ineffective in school, does the maintenance of that culture become a form of educational neglect?

In the United States educational neglect is a major category of child protective intervention and some of it may be understood as cultures that are not well suited to producing students who can perform in academic settings, at least academic settings as defined by Western models, Western European models and North American models. Is it possible to find a way to change the context so that the culture becomes more functional? Hawaii offers an example, something called the Kamahamea Early Education Project (see Tharp & Gallimore, 1988) in which an attempt was made to change the culture of the school context to make it more consistent with the native Hawaiian collective orientation. A strategy for teachers to use collective teaching and collective rewards was developed as a way to make the context more consistent and congruent with the culture from which these children came.

One might say that part of the impetus behind the UN Convention on the Rights of the Child would be to challenge and provoke and perhaps even require that everything possible be done in changing contexts to make them consistent with varieties of cultures. So long as that was technically feasible, it might well be seen as a coming to fruition of the spirit of the UN Convention to say that every child has a right to have every effort made to ensure that the major contexts of his/her society are arranged to permit him/her to be successful, and if it requires collectivising educational strategies then that is implicit as a goal, I would say, of children's right to their culture.

Those are two kinds of cultural differences. There's a third kind, however, that perhaps is even more challenging because it goes beyond this need for political accommodation and goes to an even more profound sort of difficulty. That is when cultures are 'wrong', when cultures are in error. It may seem like a kind of anthropological anathema to suggest that a culture could be in error, but I think it's a sensible concept. How could a culture be in error? A culture could be in error if it draws inadequate or inaccurate conclusions about some fundamental features of human development. Let's remember that cultures are basically collective solutions to social and human situations. Therefore, cultures must inevitably be incomplete at this.

If cultures develop and respond to specific settings, specific contexts, historical, geological, geographical contexts, then by definition they must be incomplete because there are other possible ways to live. If traditional cultures develop in response to a hunter/gather kind of economy and there are other kinds of economies, those cultures must be incomplete. If new technologies transform the nature of social environments and even physical environments, cultures must by definition be incomplete at best, which is why we have terms like culture lag, to show that when cultures are slow to adapt to changing ecologies, they may become maladaptive or unadaptive. That much ought to be clear. But can a culture be in error? I think a culture can be in error when it forms an inaccurate conclusion about human behaviour.

I'll give you an example. The work of Emmy Werner on resilience (Werner, 1982) has reached several conclusions which challenge culture. One of her conclusions is that across a variety of cultural and ethnic groups a number of studies document the empirical fact that androgeny contributes to resilience. Androgeny is the combining in one human being of traditionally feminine and traditionally masculine attributes. Many cultures, one might even say most cultures, have some degree of sex typing in them – of gender sex typing – identifying certain characteristics as being characteristically feminine and characteristically masculine. And of course in many cultures this is tied up in differences of status, power and prestige. Emmy Werner says that the research indicates gender sex typing is a maladaptive pattern. One way for individuals to increase their resilience is to become more androgenous.

If a child has a right to maximise their resilience (and it certainly seems a plausible case could be made, philosophically or ethically, that a child has a right to maximal resilience) then the implication would be a child has a right to androgeny. A child has a right to be able to transcend traditional masculine/feminine gender sex typing and incorporate both. Werner's view, which makes a lot of sense, is that to be sex typed is to approach challenges with one hand tied behind your back and obviously having two hands is more adaptive. If this is true, then we could make a case that cultures which rigidly promote and insist upon gender stereotyping are in a sense in error, because they contradict the research showing that androgeny is superior to gender sex type.

There are other examples we could think of. I remember some years ago being in a seminar and the researcher was saying, 'We have studies that show that the most effective way to increase desirable behaviour in a child is to respond to and reinforce that behaviour and to attempt to extinguish their negative behaviour.' Someone in the audience said, 'In my culture we don't believe in that. We believe you should ignore their positive behaviour and only respond to the negative behaviour.' The researcher's response was to say, 'You may believe that, but you're wrong – in fact studies of children from your culture show exactly the same pattern as these other studies.' Once you begin to entertain this notion that culture can be wrong, pretty soon you can actually be quite comfortable with it.

The reason that we're in this room, the reason that anyone would ever define themselves as being a child advocate, or a social advocate, or someone who's sought social reform, is precisely because you think your own culture is in error. This is certainly what motivates American researchers and child advocates to say that the fact that our society will not ratify the UN Convention on the Rights of the Child is because our culture is pig-headed and stupid about a lot of things including these issues. That's not the problem for most people. For most enlightened people, the problem is to think that they might say that somebody else's culture is in error. This is something with which our nineteenth century forebearers had no problem. They were quite prepared to go throughout the world saying: 'Your culture is wrong.' In the late twentieth century and the beginning of the twenty-first century, we have perhaps retreated too far from that understanding that culture can be in error. In fact, in many cases there's a kind of slavish acceptance of cultural patterns which are quite demonstrably dangerous, damaging and probably wrong, because we're afraid of replicating the sins of our imperialist ancestors. It's worth thinking about.

From an ecological point of view, it's very difficult to think of what could be a universal right of children. If context is so important, if it always 'depends', is there anything which could be understood to be universal enough to be the kind of scientific foundation for a model of children's rights? I think there are at least two possibilities. The first one is the universality of rejection as a negative psychological influence in the lives of children. I would point to the work of Ronald Rohner, an anthropologist, who some years ago looked at the question of rejection (Rohner, 1975). Using the Human Area of Relations Files, he was able to study rejection in something like 118 cultures around the world. Rohner concluded from those anthropological data sources, that although cultures differ in how they define rejection, in every culture rejection produced negative outcomes in children. So much so that Rohner identifies rejection as being a psychological malignancy, a psychological cancer. Why? Because rejection undermines the development of self worth, because rejection undermines the sense of personal integrity, because rejection undermines positive identity. For a whole host of reasons, Rohner argued – and I think quite successfully – that rejection is a universal pathogen, if you will, a universal toxin in human development. If indeed that is true, then we'd have a position of strength to say that one of the fundamental rights of any child should be to acceptance. And that would spin from it a whole series of implications, a whole series of scientific foundations for social criticism underlying our concept of advancing the rights of children.

Let me give you an example of such an implication. A number of studies have pointed out that it is not poverty but income inequality that is really the most important economic influence on psychological and behavioural development. Poverty is an interesting concept, particularly if you try to apply it cross-nationally. In the United States we define poverty as families having less than about 14,000 dollars per year – US dollars – for a family of four. In India the standard for poverty is an individual who has less than 2,300 calories per day. Using the American standard in the United States, we find about 20 per cent of Americans are poor. Using the Indian standard in India, they find that about 20 per cent of the Indian population is poor. However, if we tried to transpose those standards and said using the American standard, what per cent of India is poor we'd probably get 95 per cent or something. If we used the Indian standard against the United States and say what per cent is poor we'd be virtually zero. There must be something wrong with that because every American knows there are poor people in America and every Indian knows there are affluent Indians.

The issue is not absolute resources, but the psychological significance of economic resources. Poverty is actually a measure of what you do not have in the context of what you could reasonably expect to have. That quickly moves us to the centrality of economic inequality rather than absolute levels of resources as the primary psychological issue. In other domains the absolute level of resources may be significant. Sufficient nourishment during pregnancy, if it has to do with health care in a market economy, and in this case actual dollar amounts may be significant, but I think if we're talking about the psychological impact of wealth, it is mainly a question of inequality. A number of studies point out the fact that when you compare nations and measure the level of inequality, that measure of inequality is correlated with violence within the society. The greater the inequality, the higher the level of violence. Why would that be? It's because in situations of relative inequality, to be at the bottom implies a negative identification of self.

Now there is a lot of research in one way or another skirting this issue, but I think I never heard it expressed more directly and clearly than from the lips of a boy I was interviewing in a court case once. After the formal interview the boy asked if he could ask me a question about my own upbringing and I said yes. He said, 'Dr G, when you were growing up, did you grow up poor or regular?' *Poor or regular*. I thought this captured what income inequality is really about. Is there a perception that by being poor, you are irregular? And this of course opens the door to Rohner's fundamental issue of acceptance and rejection – that in situations of income inequality, the psychological risk is that you will perceive rejection and a devaluing of self because of your inadequate relative economic position. It does no good to poor American children to point out that if they were in India they'd be rich. It is the reference group of the child that matters.

The Luxembourg Income Study (Rainwater & Smeeding, 1995) compares income inequality among eighteen Western European North Atlantic countries. The measure used is how many times higher the income of the top 10 per cent of the income distribution is versus the bottom 10 per cent after income taxes and income transfers. The range goes from about two to one (the top 10 per cent to the bottom 10 per cent) for Sweden to more than six to one for the United States. And among the eighteen countries, no country other than the United States gets above four to one. Canada's about four, the United States is over six.

This is the kind of thinking that gives us the possibility of going beyond very narrow thinking about children's rights to these broader ways of thinking. Rather than simply requiring us to talk with those we already agree with, it gives us some way to enter into a discussion and a dialogue across cultural lines. It gives us, in fact, a kind of scientific/ intellectual foundation for really approaching the issue of multiculturalism. Fundamentally, multiculturalism is the proposition that every culture has something to learn and to teach other cultures, because if each culture is an imperfect approximation based on a particular context, then chances are it has successful conclusions and inadequate conclusions. By sharing across cultural lines we can profit from the successes of one culture perhaps as a way to counteract the deficiencies and failures of our own.

I think this is a difficult proposition, given the history of colonialism which has not been particularly multicultural, but it is a way forward through the UN Convention to some point in the future. In many ways, the best way to understand the UN Convention is as a draft document of multiculturalism, of an effort to say: here's a kind of transcendent effort to take the best of the world's cultures and form it into a coherent statement about what it can and should mean to be a child. It is imperfect to be sure, incomplete as was made clear earlier, but nonetheless an important step. Acceptance is one of the fundamental universal foundations for thinking about children's rights. I think there may be another, and I save it for last because I don't think it has quite the same research foundation that acceptance and rejection has.

The second universality I would offer is the universality of children as being fundamentally spiritual beings, the understanding that to understand human beings as only animals with complicated brains is an incomplete and inadequate conceptualisation of the human being. And once we begin to recognise this understanding of human beings as spiritual beings, it opens up other vistas for understanding and approaching children's rights because it clearly implies the right of the child to have access to their spirituality. It clearly implies criteria for evaluating social environments in terms of their willingness and ability to foster and nurture the spiritual development of the child.

This certainly provides a basis for critiquing narrow, shallow and materialistic conceptions of human development. In the United States, for example, one could say that one of the major issues facing children and youth is the enormous cultural imagery which would define them as being only consumers and only shallow entertainment vehicles. You could say the ultimate cultural experience for an American teenager would be to go to the shopping mall with their pager, to eat at McDonalds, use their credit card, watch a violent, sexy movie and go home. And the fact that this is acceptable is one source of concern about the ability of human beings to be at least initially and superficially duped and misled. But it becomes clear, particularly when you look at youth who are deprived of this materialistic successful existence, that this is not enough because it becomes clear that those children and youth who are deprived of that materialistic experience and who are able to find some basis for a successful life are the ones who do so through their spiritual development.

There's an emerging research base on the role of spirituality in development, there is a research review conducted by Andrew Weaver and his colleagues at the University of Hawaii, accumulating research showing that children involved in *non-punitive*, spirituality oriented religion are buffered from major social pathologies of all kinds (Weaver, Flannelly, Flannelly, Koenig & Larson, 1998). I think that's a foundation that will grow in coming years and should be one of the frontiers for child development research in the next century – a more adequate and comprehensive understanding of the role of spirituality in development and its central importance in anchoring human behaviour, in organising human behaviour in a positive way and bringing worth and value to human experience.

Let me close with one final thought about all of this, and that is that the ecological perspective on the rights of children leads us ultimately to a focus on the most important mechanism or intervening variable, the extent to which we are able to treat children as subjectivities rather than instrumentalities, the extent to which we are able to strip away cultural impediments to seeing the fundamental subjectivity of children is one of the big issues we have to wrestle with.

To my way of thinking, what allows Sudanese parents, generation after generation, to subject their girls to tortuous violation of their bodies is that the girls' subjective experience of themselves is made secondary to some instrumentality and the instrumentalities involved are several. One is to say that your girl will not be marriageable if this procedure is not done because she will be deviant. A second is that the patriarchal structure of Sudanese society is organised around eliminating sexual gratification for women and therefore the physiological disruption of the organs of pleasure for girls is seen as necessary to complete and continue that patriarchal domination. Third, the actual incidence and the prevalence of this genital mutilation has increased among some traditional groups in Sudan as they perceive themselves as modernising, because they perceive this as being a sign of those groups in Sudan who are the most affluent and successful and who have the greatest access to resources; some traditional groups have instigated and initiated this procedure as a way of getting themselves more modernised.

All of these are really about the instrumentalising of children. The sign of hope here is that when these sorts of traditional culture patterns (whether they occur in economically modern societies or in economically primitive societies), and these kinds of instrumentalities are subjected to some higher order thinking, some higher order level of self awareness, they are often revealed for what they are. That is, Sudanese girls and women who come to a consciousness based on exposure to world culture or alternative cultures, often come to an appreciation of what has been done to them. There is a marvellous book about this in Sudan written by a Sudanese physician who was a leader in the campaign against genital mutilation. In part it's about translating her awareness of what had actually been done into a campaign to try to reduce the practice in the future. That same process of awareness can come to each of us, and one would hope sooner rather than later. In fiction, there has been one consistent metaphor that has been used to try to stimulate that. Those of you who watched New Zealand television earlier this week may have seen, on July 4th, the American film *Independence Day* – a film in which some terrible alien presence shows up with the intent of exterminating the human population so that they can have the planet for themselves. An earlier generation may remember the film called *The Day The Earth Stood Still* with a similar theme. Both of these films offer the idea that if the earth were faced with some alien threat, a threat which promised to exterminate human life, it would bring forth a kind of recognition of the universal subjective equality of all human beings and that it would lead to a transcending of cultural and political definitions and categories.

In both films, that is what is promised – that all human beings are able to see that there are not hundreds of races but one race, and that cultures are really secondary to fundamental humanity. This device used often in films and literature of some superordinate threat, we would hope will not be the only way to achieve this goal. What we've been offered is an alternative. William James offered what he called the need for a 'moral equivalent to war'and we have it before us in the UN Convention on the Rights of the Child which, if it is anything, is an attempt to aid us in transcending individual and collective limitations on behalf of some universal commitment to the subjective value of children, and that is something well worth achieving.

References

Bronfenbrenner, U., & Mahoney, M. (Eds). (1975). *Influences on human development.* Hinsdale Ill: Dryden Press.

Chomsky, N. (1957). *Syntactic structures.* The Hague: Mouton.

Mednick, S.A., & Kandel, E. (1998). Genetic and perinatal factors in violence. In S.A. Mednick., & T. Moffit (Eds), *Biological contributions to crime causation.* Dordrecht, The Netherlands: Martinus Nijhoff, pp. 121-34.

Rainwater, L., & Smeeding, T. (1995). U.S. Doing poorly compared to others. National Center for Children in Poverty. *News and Issues, 5*(3), 4ff.

Rohner, R. (1975). *They love me, they love me not.* New Haven. CT: Human Relations Area Files Press.

Tharp, R.G., & Gallimore, R. (1988). *Rousing minds to life. Teaching, learning and schooling in social context.* Cambridge: Cambridge University Press.

Weaver, A.J., Flannelly, L.T., Flannelly, K.J., Koenig, H.G., & Larsen, D.B. (1998). An analysis of research on religious and spiritual variables in three major mental health nursing journals, 1991-1995. *Issues in Mental Health Nursing, 19*(3), 263-76.

Werner, E.E. (1982*). Vulnerable but invincible: A longitudinal study of resilient children and youth*. New York: McGraw-Hill.

Whorf, B.L. (1956). Science and linguistics. In J.B. Carrroll (Ed)., *Language, thought and reality: Selected writings of Benjamin Lee Whorf.* Cambridge, MA: MIT Press.

Note

1 This chapter is a transcript of a keynote address. Gary Melton's paper follows in chapter 10 of this book.

Judicial and legislative conceptions of childhood and children's voices in family law

MARK HENAGHAN AND PAULINE TAPP

Introduction

Why does our system permit a child aged ten years to be tried before a judge and jury for murder (S 272(2) CYP&F Act, 1989) yet be very reluctant to accept as valid the wishes expressed by a child about family matters which affect them or to permit the child to be involved in Family Court proceedings? To what extent is the system's ambivalence about respecting a child's voice a concern that recognising a child's autonomy may erode the dependent status of children and result in harm to children as a class (Seymour, 1992)? Is the concern that recognising children's autonomy will erode the power of adults and alter the balance of authority and responsibility which currently exists between the family and the state and hence threaten the institution of the family (Melton, 1983; Harre, 1986; Roche, 1996)?

One of the functions of family law is to express contemporary values and beliefs about the family (Schneider, 1992). Family law tells us about the conceptions of childhood held by law makers and the law makers' perceptions of children's relationships with their families and with society. In turn society's views of children are influenced by the law. Freeman has commented that legislation becomes '... a potent symbol of legitimacy [which] has the ... ability to set new standards of what is right and wrong' (Freeman, 1998, p. 345).

This paper focuses on the autonomy rights granted to children by Articles 12 and 13 of the United Nations Convention on the Rights of the Child (UNCROC) and will seek to show that all too often the New Zealand family law system fails to regard children as individuals with rights who are entitled to be treated with dignity and respect and to be provided with an environment which will give them the best opportunity of developing into healthy, autonomous citizens able to participate fully in a democracy. This failure is the result of conceptions of childhood held by our law makers, and system constraints.

The ability of the family law system to 'hear' the perspective of a child is constrained by a number of factors. These include statutory language emphasising the child's welfare first and foremost as a member of a family, whanau or family group and the importance given to family autonomy by Part 11 of the Family Proceedings Act 1980[1]. A child's perspective has statutory limits of age, maturity and culture placed on it. This occurs, for example, in s23(2) of the Guardianship Act 1968 where the qualification affects the extent to which a judge make take account of a child's views. The qualification is unnecessary to protect the child because s23(1) directs the court to regard the welfare of the child as the first and paramount consideration.

The Family Court's jurisdiction concerning children is 'childwork' (Oldman, 1994), work done by adults in the organisation and control of children. Such work has the potential to restrict the system's ability to hear the child. A feature of childwork is the reduction of the child to a psychological object – one that is in the process of 'becoming' not 'being'.

The potential value of feedback from the child is illustrated by the decisions in *K v K (No. 1)* (1988) and *K v K (No. 2)* (1988). The decisions concerned a long, bitter custody dispute between the parents of an eleven-year-old boy. Warrant action had been used a number of times to attempt to enforce a shared custody order. The father regarded himself as a devout Roman Catholic and was seriously aggrieved by the mother's action in withdrawing from the marital bed and embittered by the Family Court's grant of a separation order. The boy had consistently expressed a wish, to all who would listen, that he be permitted to live with his father. He said he preferred the relaxed atmosphere in his father's home, the fact that his older siblings lived there, and that his friends, hobbies and sporting interests were in the area. The social worker and child psychologist who reported to the court did not ascertain the child's wishes because they considered he should not be asked to express a preference between his parents. In an interview with the child McGechan J found the child to be intelligent and well able to express a clear preference. His Honour accepted that the child's wish to live with his father was genuine but discounted it as being 'hedonistic and immature' (No. 1, p. 276), based on immediate considerations rather than a long term view of his needs. His Honour made the child a ward of the court and gave the day-to-day care to the mother, the father to have access after a two-week 'settling down' period. The orders were said to be justified because of His Honour's opinion that the child would not suffer severe damage because his express wish to live with his father was not granted and, most importantly, because:

> No child should be brought up to believe he not only can but must disobey the law if it appears to him to be against his religion. Further, while as with all authority, there is room for balanced criticism of the judicial system, there is no room for the upbringing of a child in absurd beliefs that the courts of this country indulge in lies, favouritism, racial and religious bigotry, and corruption. I have the greatest concern at the prospect of an impressionable child being brought up in an atmosphere in which attitudes of this kind are expressed and accusations of this nature made. To do so would be entirely contrary to his welfare in a major respect. (*K v K*, No. 1, 1988, p. 279).

Three months after the orders were made the director-general of the Department of Social Welfare, as the court's agent, asked for the orders to be reviewed because the boy was suffering in his mother's care. McGechan J ordered a psychiatric report in an attempt to seek advice about whether the child's wishes were obsessional and what harm he might come to if his wish to live with his father was thwarted. Holland J, in the second judgement, stated he had gained no assistance from the report. He decided that the boy should no longer be used as a shuttlecock by his parents and that it was not in the boy's interest to remain in the custody of his mother. The child was placed in his father's custody and the mother granted access. This situation illustrates that a court order founded on generalised conceptions about welfare (negative parental attitudes to authority will be accepted by a child, both parents are equally able to parent, children's emotions are shallow and can safely be set aside) designed to produce a certain type of adult, is unlikely to be effective when it goes against the consistently expressed, clear wishes of an eleven-year-old who has given explanations for his wishes that were valid from his perspective. If the Family Court system is not to exploit children, in the sense that childwork is directed to adult perceived interests, the system must become open to the idea of children as partners. It must accept that children have a valid perspective that should be factored into its objectives and processes. Children should not be seen solely as objects of concern, developing beings who are too inexperienced and immature to be partners in adult endeavours.

Which professional ascertains the child's views will affect the method used to communicate, the type of questions asked, what the adult hears and the interpretation and weight given to any view expressed by the child. There has been a noticeable change in how the views of children are ascertained. In the 1970s and 1980s the judiciary, especially the judges of the High Court, regarded it as their statutory duty to speak with the child. Counsel for the Child was often not appointed. (See, for example, *A v A*, 1978; *D v D*, 1978; *Jury*, 1984.)

The professionalisation of the Family Court, especially the increased use of an expert reporter to ascertain the views of the child, has increasingly collapsed the distinction between subsections (1) and (2) of section 23 of the Guardianship Act 1968 and put the child's views through the filter of the welfare principle. This is contrary to s23(2) which, like Article 12 of the UNCROC, clearly requires that the child be given an opportunity to have their view as such put before the court. The weight to be given to the view is to be determined by the court having regard to the judge's perception of the child's age and maturity and the paramountcy of the judicial view of the child's welfare. In this context it is significant to note the views of specialist report writers on whether it was the role of counsel for the child to have direct contact with the child. Only 60 per cent thought it was in CYP&F Act 1989 cases, and 70 per cent thought it was in cases under the Guardianship Act (Gray & Martin,

1998). This section will illustrate how the voice of a child is subject to the filter of the current conceptions of welfare. For example, where the current belief is that children generally benefit from continued contact with both parents after parental separation, the wishes of a child who resists contact with a parent may be discounted as those of an immature child whose focus is immediate and hedonistic.[2]

Section 23(2) requires that the child's wishes be weighed according to the judge's conception of the maturity of the child and the age at which a child is capable of rational decision making. Gold (1998) opines that the New Zealand Family Court generally gives careful consideration to the views of teenagers, may consider the views of children aged from eight to twelve years, but seems to have a presumption that parents of children that age know best, and gives priority to the views of parents of a child aged less than eight years. Seymour (1992) states that the courts have a tendency to assess a child's capacity for mature, independent thought by reference to what the court considers to be in the child's best interests. A child who expresses a view contrary to the court's perception of welfare may be held to lack capacity to express a view which should be given weight. There have not been many empirical studies on children's competence in participating in family decision making. Garrison (1991) studied the responses of 144 children aged nine to fourteen from intact families to two hypothetical custody dilemmas. Their responses were compared to those of twenty-four, eighteen-year-olds and evaluated by fourty-four domestic relations judges. The object of the exercise was for the children to state their considered preference and give a rational reason for the choice. The nine- and ten-year-olds were as competent as the fourteen- and eighteen-year-olds in terms of the reasonableness of preference, or the rationality of reasons given.

In many cases the system constraints and adult conceptions about childhood result in decisions about what is for the welfare of children as a class, and whether or not a child is of an age and maturity to give weight to their views, being made on the basis of grand overarching generalisations which result in our learning 'not about children's perspectives, but about adult concepts of childhood' (Oakley, 1994, pp. 22–23).

Conceptions of childhood

> Children are seen as having to 'mature' before they obtain freedom to act on behalf of themselves .... protection [of children] may be suggested even when it is not strictly necessary for the sake of children, but rather works to protect adults or adult social orders against disturbance from the presence of children. This is exactly the point at which protection threatens to slide into unwarranted dominance (Qvortrup, 1990, pp. 79–80).

Different adult conceptions of childhood will result in different opinions about the right of a child to express a view and the relevance of the child's voice. Those who see children as primarily immature, subject to pressure and requiring protection, will have a different view from those who place primary emphasis on family autonomy, and see the child's interests as subsumed within those of the child's family. Feminists may regard the child's interests as inseparable from those of the child's mother. A different view will be held by those who regard the child as a social actor and right holder who will benefit from having their autonomy recognised (Trinder, 1997). This section considers some of the conceptions of childhood which appear to be influential in our family law system.

The legal system is crucial in defining adult society's view of children. Our system too often holds the out-of-date view of children as 'not-yet-adults'. The common law has traditionally viewed children as unreliable witnesses being prone to fantasy and suggestible (ALRC & HREOC, 1997, para 14.5).

The conceptions of childhood used in the Family Court appear to have been influenced by the heavy reliance the court places on the perceptions of psychologists. The nineteenth-century biological and philosophical theories which are the bases of child development theory, when combined with the basic concept within child psychology of socialisation, have resulted in children being seen as developing people whom adults must train for membership in the adult world (Mayall, 1994). Melton (1983-84) opines that conceptions of children as dependent, vulnerable, in need of protection, are likely to be based more on normative notions as to the proper role of children in society than on research as to how children behave when their autonomy is recognised. There may also be a tendency to conflate children's legal powerlessness, dependence, lack of choice and inarticulateness (*N v D [Guardianship]*, 1993) with the actual capacities of children.

Children's socio-cultural contexts will affect how they construct their reality and will in turn be affected by their participation in society. Childhood is culturally defined. Different cultures permit children to have different powers and levels of participation at different ages. (This is recognised in s5(d) CYP&F Act 1989.) This tends to show that it is not biology but adult social power rules which determine the boundaries between childhood and adulthood. Children's competence is thus defined by the power and interests perceived by adults as relevant to adult constructions of the world (Qvortrup, 1994). It is thus unwise for us to use assumptions about children's interests and abilities that are based on data from other eras and other cultures. New Zealand has in recent years become a multicultural society. Our legal system has yet to deal fully with the tensions that can exist between Western concepts of legal authority, and of the importance of psychological attachment to a child's welfare, and concepts of authority in other cultures and the emphasis in other cultures on group identity. Treadwell (1999) discusses a case where the Family Court had removed a seven-year-old boy on the grounds that his long-term interests lay in living in a home where his heritage and cultural background would be better supported, but the decision was reversed on appeal.

The changes in socio-economic circumstances in New Zealand in this century have effected changes in the conceptions of motherhood, fatherhood, gender and state-group relations, all of which have affected conceptions of childhood. The legal system has been slow to reflect these changes and to accept the conception of childhood required by our ratification of the UNCROC.

Lansdown (1994) argues that there is a tendency to rely too heavily on a presumption of children's biological and psychological vulnerability in developing our law, policy and practice, and insufficient focus on the extent to which their lack of civil status creates that vulnerability. Perceiving the child primarily as a victim, as in need of protection, can effectively silence the child, as occurs with the presumption in s16B of the Guardianship Act 1968, noted earlier.

Other conceptions of childhood commonly held by actors in the legal system include the belief that children think short-term rather than long-term and only want to get their own way. Thomas and O'Kane (1998) discuss an exercise in which they asked several groups of children to rank in order of importance reasons for being involved in decision making. The children consistently put at the top of the list 'to be listened to', 'to let me have my say' or 'to be supported'; and at the bottom 'to get what I want'. When social workers were asked to rank the statements as they thought the children would, several groups put at the top of the list 'to get what I want'.

An often cited reason for not inviting children to express a view in family matters is the belief that disputes between parents are adult concerns, adults have the responsibility for resolving them, and children may be harmed by being placed in a conflict of loyalty if they are invited to express a view. This fails not only to recognise UNCROC but also fails to recognise that the whole family has an interest in the resolution of the matter. It overlooks that children will be aware that a problem exists, will know better than anyone else what has happened to them and what is important to them and may have a valid option for resolution of the matter. Also it is naive to believe that adults will be unaware if their child has a clear preference between the options being offered. It should be remembered that:

> ... there is a difference between asking a child to give evidence in relation to a dispute of fact ... and allowing a child the opportunity to express his or her wishes as to the outcome of a matter. Children should not be required or pressured to do so but it may be appropriate for mature children to give evidence of their wishes where they freely indicate a desire to do so. In those cases, the voluntary involvement of children in family decision making processes can be of real benefit to children, to the court and to the ultimate decision (ALRC & HREOC, 1997, para 8.16).

A solution which fails to take account of a child's perspective has a reduced chance of meeting the child's reality and of being accepted by the child and therefore being effective. When the legal system equates the welfare of the child with family autonomy it effectively silences the voice of children. The system's emphasis on family autonomy, the belief that the adults in the family should and will protect a child's interests, is the reason so few areas in family law, in practice, provide space for the voice of the child. Yet the dominant concept in family law – that children are vulnerable, unformed creatures in need of protection – is at odds with the legal system's use of the child as a witness (albeit with some protection) in criminal matters, its prosecution of children for murder and manslaughter, and the involvement of young people in proceedings in the Youth Court. The legal system's conceptions of childhood have more to do with the needs of the system and society as perceived by adults, than with children's rights or current research evidence on children's capabilities and interests.

Legislative policy – The privatisation of family responsibility and the voice of the child

The common law system developed around a concern for property rights. Not unnaturally, it traditionally regarded children as the property and responsibility of their parents (Freeman, 1983). The state's growing concern for a healthy, educated population after the First World War and the depression which followed, combined with a growing international interest in human rights, gradually led to an official willingness to depart from a strict policy of family autonomy.[3] In the 1980s and the 1990s the international community began to recognise the interdependence of the human family and accepted that the attainment of freedom, justice, peace and sustainable development in the world requires that the whole community accept responsibility for ensuring the rights and well-being of children (Report of the Solicitor General of the United Nations to the General Assembly, 1995). New Zealand's ratification of the United Nations Convention on the Rights of the Child on 13 March 1993 occurred after the ideology and fiscal policies of the New Right had firmly embedded a return to the policies of family responsibility epitomised in the February 1998 Public Discussion Document: Towards a Code of Social and Family Responsibility (Shipley & Peters, 1998; Kelsey, 1995). That New Zealand's acceptance of obligations under UNCROC did not deflect the government from this economic path, which resulted in disadvantage to children, and led to adverse comment from the Committee on the Rights of the Child in 1997 (Committee on the Rights of the Child, 1997, para 26).

The next section will consider legislation concerned with family matters to outline how policies of family autonomy and private ordering fail to accord children the dignity and respect to which they are entitled and silences their voices. It is argued that any short-term benefits to the public purse from such policies will be heavily outweighed by the longer term damage to society of adults who lack the self-esteem and skills to actively and fully participate in a healthy democracy, because as children they were treated as passive and dependent and denied the opportunities required to develop into autonomous citizens.

The protection of children – The Children, Young Persons and Their Families Act 1989 and the Domestic Violence Act 1995. Cultural and fiscal influences (Tapp, Geddis & Taylor, 1992; Smith, 1998) resulted in the CYP&F Act 1989 which subsumes the child's voice in that of the family, whanau, hapu, iwi and family group. The child and the young person are perceived as members of such groups rather than as unique individuals with rights who are entitled to respect. The Act has a family group perspective. In his Second Reading speech on the Bill, the Minister of Social Welfare, the Hon. Michael Cullen, said:

> The Bill recognises that the well-being of children and young persons is bound in with the well-being of their families. … Put briefly, the Bill places greater emphasis on the interests and authority of families. It reduces the power of the State and of professionals to make decisions for children and young people irrespective of their families. … The second central feature of the Bill I want to explain is the emphasis it places on the role of kin in making decisions for children and young persons. (Cullen, 1989, pp. 10246-10247)

This emphasis on the child as a member of a family and wider cultural group is made clear by the principle in s5(c), which provides that consideration must always be given to how a decision will affect the welfare of the child or young person and the stability of the child's or young person's family, whanau, hapu, iwi and family group. Section 5(d) provides for weight to be given to the wishes of a child or young person which is appropriate having regard to their age, maturity and culture. Research shows that in the family group conference process, which is the dominant decision-making mechanism in the legislation, the child's and young person's voice is all too often lost in the squabble of adult voices (Gilling, Patterson & Walker, 1995; McKenzie, 1996).

The Domestic Violence Act 1995 is adult focused. It makes provision for applications by a child, via a representative, for a protection order because the CYP&F Act 1989 was seen as being inadequate to protect children (Tapp, 1996), yet there is little, if any, mention of children in the Parliamentary debates on the legislation. The Act appears to be founded on the belief that the parent (generally the mother) who has a protection order is willing and able to protect their child. Sadly this is not always the case. Battered women who wish to return to their abuser may be unable to understand the harm a violent home inflicts on a child (see, for example *E v S*, 1996). Where the adult protected person consents to the presence of the abuser in their home, even children who have individual protection orders are powerless to protect themselves by excluding the abuser, as the Act does not give the child the right to apply for an occupation or tenancy order – *Arvidson v Croft* [1996]. Once again children are seen as the responsibility of their parents, and their rights as individuals are ignored.

Adult interests and the right of the child to identity. The Status of Children Amendment Act 1987 is a classic example of legislation which directly affects the child, but which was passed solely to meet adult interests. The legislator's conception of the child is as a creation and possession of adults. The legislation was enacted to clarify the legal status of children conceived by named reproductive techniques using donated material and to protect donors from any responsibility arising from paternity or maternity. The Act deems the child's mother to be the woman who gave birth and her partner (legal or de facto) who consented to the procedure to be the father. Where the woman who gave birth was not cohabiting in a heterosexual relationship, or her partner did not consent to the procedure no man has the legal rights and responsibilities of being a father. Despite the evidence from adoption research that many children wish to have information about their origins (which persuaded the government to pass the Adult Adoption Information Act 1985) the Status of Children Amendment Act 1987 does not require the keeping of records so that children conceived by assisted reproductive technologies can trace their genetic origins. In the debate on the Bill, the Minister of Justice, Rt Hon Geoffrey Palmer, commented in relation to the need for information of children already born and those yet to be conceived: 'We do not yet know whether the people concerned will want information or, if they do want it, what kind of information they will require' (Palmer, 1986, p. 3874).

New Zealand's obligations under UNCROC and the research evidence (Adair & Rumble, 1998) that children conceived by ART do wish to have access to information about their origins illustrates the vital importance of children's perceptions and voices informing legislative policy. The UNCROC requires that law makers recognise children as important partners in formulating policy which will meet the interests of all members of society.

Children's voices in access cases

This section considers a number of access cases to illustrate how system constraints and conceptions of childhood have affected the court's reception of children's voices. It raises a number of questions. Does the family law system regard the child as a social actor with agency who creates their own reality through interaction with others and whose perception of reality is entitled to respect? Does the Family Court provide the child with a role model which is consistent with the court's philosophy of self-determination? Do the court processes acknowledge and nurture a child's developing autonomy?

An application by a parent for access with a child will be determined by the Family Court under the provisions of the Guardianship Act 1968. Section 23(1) of that Act requires the court to regard the welfare of the child as the first and paramount consideration when determining the application. Section 23(2) directs the court to ascertain the wishes of the child and to take them into account, having regard to the child's age and maturity. The courts have a long history of considering the wishes of the child when determining their welfare (see *Re L (An Infant)*, 1914). How the court balances the two tasks in section 23 has a significant effect on its reception of the voice of a child.

The dominant conception in the last fifteen years has been the importance for a child's welfare of the child maintaining contact with both parents. A corollary to this has been the belief in the importance of a child having the opportunity for contact with siblings and extended family. This conception was so strongly held that it was initially referred to as a parental right. Wranghan J in *M v M (Child Access)* [1973], a decision often cited in New Zealand, introduced the more modern terminology of the right of the child and stated the conception effectively as a presumption which, as such, would have a significant effect on the reception of the child's voice.

> ... the companionship of a parent is in any ordinary circumstance of such immense value to the child that there is a basic right in him to such companionship. I for my part would prefer to call it a basic right in the child rather than a basic right in the parent. This only means this, that no court should deprive a child of access to either parent unless it is wholly satisfied that it is in the interests of the child that access should cease, and that is a conclusion at which a court should be extremely slow to arrive (p. 85).

Article 9 of the United Nations Convention on Rights of the Child says the child has a right to contact with the other parent unless it is not in the interests of the child. In 1982 the New Zealand Court of Appeal held that only in exceptional circumstances should a child be deprived of the benefit of a direct link with a parent – *M v M* (1981-82). Similarly, Jeffries J said in *R v C* (1985) 'As a starting point of principle, in family law a parent is entitled to access to a child unless there are grave and weighty reasons why access should be denied' (p. 12).

The courts' belief in the importance of access has been so strong that judges have been prepared to order contact under very artificial conditions. In *G v Adams & G* (1985) Barker J granted a father, who had kidnapped a four-year-old, access of one hour so the father could give the child a Christmas present before the father returned to Australia. The father was ordered to be searched before the meeting which was to occur in the presence of a plain-clothes member of the police. Counsel for the child, counsel for the father, the psychologist employed by the father, and the mother were given permission to be present. In *Sharman* (1988) Anderson J commented that access is important because 'there is a compelling and instinctive desire on the part of people to know their lineage; to know who their parents were; to place themselves in the pattern of time and history by reference to their immediate antecedents' (p. 94). His Honour warned the mother that if she continued to resist access he could ensure access by making the child a ward of the court and removing her to a boarding school. The eight-year-old child had been in the care of her mother for all but the first five months of her life when the parents had lived together. She regarded her mother's partner as her father. His Honour ordered a twelve month trial period of access of four hours per month with a counsellor available to supervise, and letters and phone communication consistent with the advice of the counsellor. Although the child was represented by counsel, the judgement makes no mention of any wishes of the child.

In *Shannon* (1988) Judge Boshier said, 'The Guardianship Act itself creates fundamental guardianship rights of both parents and to deny those rights without a proper cause would unquestionably not be in the best interests of children' (p. 316). His Honour accepted that there was possibly some truth in the mother's allegation that the children, aged six and four years, had been sexually abused by the father. The children displayed negativity towards the father. Because His Honour was of the view that it was important for the children that they grow up knowing their father and having the benefit of his strengths, he made orders that for three months the children and the parents receive separate counselling with the object of restoring contact between the children and the father. After counselling the children were to be reintroduced to their father by the psychologist. Then access was to occur for three hours per month for three months, after which time it could be increased.

The court's acceptance of the generalised conception that contact is for the welfare of children is so strong that some judges fail to consider the importance for a child's well-being of being shown respect and of having their views seriously considered. They simply conclude that the judge's view that the welfare of children requires access to both parents outweighs the wish of this child not to have contact with a parent. They overlook that Article 9, the right to contact, when read with Article 12 also encompasses the right not to have contact if that is the child's wish and is in accord with the child's best interests: *DGSW v R* (1997).

In *P v P* (1984) Barker J's conviction that the welfare of children requires contact with their mother and that it is not for their welfare to live with a father who is antagonistic to the mother, resulted in His Honour refusing to accept the wishes of two children to live with their father, consistently expressed since His Honour first granted custody to the mother in 1978, when the boys were aged eight and six years. When the matter returned to court in 1984 the children, now fourteen and twelve years of age, again expressed the wish to live with their father to the judge, counsel for the children, and the expert employed by the mother. They said that they preferred to live with their father because 'he spends time with us and really cares for us' (p. 12) and because the mother and her partner often argue (p. 14). His Honour said he would have been prepared to regard the wishes of a fourteen-year-old as determinative but, for some unstated reason, he was not prepared to accord the same weight to the wishes of the twelve-year-old. A decision on the father's application for custody was deferred for eight months, when His Honour indicated he might give more weight to the boy's wishes if they remained the same. However, His Honour made the significant comment: 'The father in particular must realise that he is on trial so far as access is concerned. If he does not change his attitude, his chances on a reconsideration of the custody position ... might not be good' (p. 226). This comment indicates that the judge's belief in the importance of the children having the opportunity for positive contact with their mother is so strong as to justify creating the appearance of placing the children in a situation where they could be seen as being the subject of emotional pressure on the father. This does not accord the children the respect they are entitled to and does not place an appropriate focus on the welfare of these children in this situation.

Similarly in *H v C* (1986), the generalised belief that contact between mother and child is vital for the child ('It is only in the most extraordinary circumstances that a court would ever deprive a mother of access to her child' (p. 35)) and in the importance of the authority of the court, led Holland J to over ride the wishes of an eleven-year-old girl not to have contact with her mother. His Honour said he was prepared to enforce access by issuing a warrant (p. 35). His Honour interviewed the child and warned her:

> ... that if a child of 11 is able to defy authority merely to do what she wants, it may show that her present environment was unsatisfactory. She immediately questioned whether I was proposing to remove her from her father. I pointed out to her that her insistence on doing what she wanted could hurt people and could hurt her mother, her father and her grandmother. She denied that it could hurt her father and her grandmother, but when I pointed out to her that she might possibly show that her father and grandmother were unsuited to care for her she then indicated that if that was so then she would see her mother (p. 34).

In *F v F* (1991) Judge Bremner accepted that a four-year-old, who did not wish to see her father, believed that he had sexually abused her, but ordered access because 'There are definite advantages to a child in having access to both parents in a separation situation' (p. 404).

These cases can be compared with *Simpson* (1986) in which Judge Gilbert held that access is desirable only where there is a chance of it being meaningful and beneficial. Such a chance does not exist where there is such antagonism between the parents that access would put the children in a battle zone. The three children aged thirteen, eleven and eight-and-a-half years, who were in their mother's care, were totally resistant to access with their father. His Honour commented: 'It is unthinkable, in my opinion, that I should make arrangements for access that will have to be enforced by a social worker or a police constable or both' (p. 642).

The belief in the importance of access has so outweighed consideration of the views and interests of the child that a number of judges have justified overriding the child's expressed wishes because of their belief that children are resilient and can cope, or the belief that children's feelings are so temporary that the child will suffer only short-term stress from having their wishes set aside. It was revealed in the High Court decision in *D v D* [1978] that in the lower court an order had been made, removing a seven-and-a-half-year-old child from the care of his mother to his father despite the boy's clear, consistently expressed wish to remain with his mother, because of the court's belief that it was not in the child's welfare to live with a woman who had admitted a sexual association since her separation from the child's father. The social worker who reported to the court and the lower court judge were both of the view that 'the boy would adjust if the choice of the court was not in accordance with his [view]' (p. 479). Jeffries J in the High Court did not agree and granted custody to the mother because she was said to be the child's psychological parent.

In *C v D* (1991) Judge Boshier said, 'Recognition that contact with both parents is by and large important for reasons of familial and psycho-social development is reflected in boundless cases' (p. 342). The case dealt with an application for access by a 'father' who was transsexual and living as a woman, to two children aged seven and fourteen years. The fourteen-year-old boy did not want contact with his father. Judge Boshier opined: 'To postpone access here might be to merely cause enduring injury. Whatever *short term* difficulty there is, is in my view, regrettable, but perhaps inevitable' (p. 344, emphasis added). Orders were made that physical access occur only after the children had received appropriate therapy, with access initially to be supervised by the therapist. In fact the boy never agreed to see his father and the father, to his credit, did not pursue the matter. Similarly in *T v T* (1998) his Honour commented

> '... it is generally the position that children ... living primarily with their mother, will benefit from having good quality time with [their father]. To not pursue that ideal is to forfeit a significant part of the children's overall development. It is never a factor to be forfeited lightly' (p. 137).

Although numerous judges appear to believe that social science research supports their conception that contact between a child and their non-resident parent generally advances the welfare of the child, research justifying this conception is at best ambivalent. Maclean and Eekelaar (1997) take from the research that any effects on the child of such contact appear to come from a multiplicity of influences and cannot simply be attributed to contact with the non-resident parent. This must raise queries about such an embedded judicial conception. Whose interests does the conception consciously or unconsciously promote? What practical consequences flow from the application of the conception? Arguably, presuming that contact promotes the child's welfare makes the judicial task easier in that it softens the 'winner-loser' dichotomy and provides some 'justice' for both parties. One practical consequence of the conception is to deflect the focus from *this* child, *their* wishes and rights, to the generalised child constructed by the judicial gaze, which is influenced by judicial understanding of psychology and the constraints of the legal system.

Examples of hearing and respecting the child

Although the ultimate order was contrary to the wishes of children aged twelve and nine years, there is some indication in *CL v CL* (1985) that Judge Inglis QC had heard the children and was prepared to take their views seriously so far as was consistent with His Honour's view of their welfare. The children wished to live with their mother and had 'voted with their feet' and returned to their mother after the court had granted custody to the father in 1981. Three different judges over the years of litigation between the parents had expressed concern at the malevolent influence on the children of the mother's lover. It appears that the lover was racist. The children and their father were visibly West Indian. Counsel for the children and counsel to assist had expressed the view that the children had been encouraged, or not discouraged, to run away from their father to live with their mother, who had persisted in trying to reverse the custody order. The twelve-year-old had also consistently expressed the wish that the parents reconcile. His Honour decided that the children's long-term welfare required that they live with their father but, in a possible recognition of the children's views, His Honour asked the father to show and demonstrate his real affection for the children. There was some indication that the children had said they found their mother's home to be warm and affectionate and their father's to have an 'austere atmosphere'. His Honour also directed that the children be given an explanation that the decision made by the court 'was not made at the request of the father, but was the result of an impartial inquiry into the children's long-term interests' (p. 464). This may have been a reference to the fact that the father had declined to be represented because he was sick of litigation or it may have been an attempt to explain the court's reasoning to the children and to assist them to understand that somehow the court could protect them from being pawns in the battle between their parents.

In *Pooley v Llewelyn* [1985] Judge Inglis QC accorded children aged thirteen and eleven years the dignity and respect of speaking with them about the options for giving effect to their father's desire to see them. The children were resistant to access with their father. Orders were made which gave effect to the type of contact the children had agreed to in their discussion with the judge. His Honour commented that '[the children] are to be approached, not as children, but as young people with minds and feelings of their own' (p. 634). Judge Boshier in *T v T* (1998) also adopted this more modern approach which recognises children as persons with rights whose co-operation is vital if the court's orders are to be effective. In his judgement His Honour said that because he was so concerned about the outcome of the case he had consulted with the children aged thirteen, nine, seven and five years about his views and the orders he proposed to make, and had elicited their responses. The two older children were firmly of the view that they did not want contact with their father. His Honour recognised this, and the expert report writer's opinion that the children should not be forced to have contact. To convey a clear message to the two older children, His Honour made an order for general access by the father. Such an order opened the way for the children to initiate access when, and if, they so desired. In *DGSW v R* (1997) Judge von Dadelszen accorded the young person the respect of speaking with her about the matter before the court.

Why does the system fail to always respect the voice of children and to understand their perspective? Too often judges appear to see a conflict between the child's welfare and the child's views, rather than understand that the child's views are an element of welfare and that all the elements of welfare must be considered and balanced in a way which both respects the child and her/his rights and is most likely to assist the child to develop into a healthy, autonomous adult. Is the system concerned that granting the child the respect and dignity to which they are entitled (by giving them the information and context they require to form and express their views, by considering their views seriously from the child's perspective and by giving the child an explanation for any decision) might require inconvenient or expensive changes in the system, or might undermine the role and authority of the court or the family? Perhaps it is bureaucratically and emotionally easier not to involve children and to tell ourselves that by not involving them we are protecting them from adult responsibility. The evidence that children are aware of problems between their parents, and often wish to be informed and to express a view, makes this wish to protect them at best illusory, and at worst simply an excuse.

> To be serious about what children do themselves may be seen as subversive to adults' definition of the rules of the game (Qvortrup, 1994, p. 2).

Conclusion

It is accepted that our courts have an obligation to found their decisions about contact between parents and children upon the judge's view of the welfare of the child and that this may require them to make an order contrary to the wishes of the child concerned. However, our obligations under the Convention on the Rights of the Child require that the child be given an opportunity to form and express a view, and that the decision of the court is based on an understanding of this child's perspective and rights and not on generalised beliefs about the importance of contact with both parents or of the transience of children's emotions and pain. It also requires that the child is given an explanation of the decision and the reasons for it in language, and in a context, which are appropriate for the child. It should not be assumed that a child's views will be the result of, or even open to, coercion to any greater degree than the views of an adult. Decision makers should be prepared to acknowledge the validity of a child's perspective for the child even if, from an adult perspective, giving effect to the child's views would not be for the welfare of the child. Any such conclusion should only be reached consciously and with the realisation of the harm that can occur to a child who feels unheard.

The dominant understanding of childhood given by the cases discussed in this paper is that the Family Court is involved in 'childwork' – children are the objects of concern, the subjects of legal applications. The court is constrained by legal categories and the concepts of legal relevance which follow from those categories, the options the parties propose and, above all, by available finances. All this is adult focused. Within such a system it is perhaps inevitable that generalised conceptions about the type of parenting required to produce the desired type of future citizen will appear to underlie most decisions. The focus will be on the parents, or the applicant and the respondent. Rarely will the focus be first and foremost on the child as a partner in the family system who may have a valid and vital perspective which he/she wishes to communicate. The Family Court is in a unique and uneasy situation in a common law system which accepts judges as law makers. The hearing of an application under the Guardianship Act 1968 has both adversary and inquisitorial features. The judge must decide a *lis* between the parties and at the same time must regard the welfare of the child as the first and paramount consideration. Family Court proceedings are held in private. Hence the public's only access to the law in action is through published judgements. Such 'system' matters may provide some explanation for what, from the judgements, appear to be inconsistent judicial attitudes towards children and their rights.

The same judge may speak with children and assist them to develop options which will meet their parent's request, will sometimes respect and give effect to the children's perspective, and will use innovative means to ensure a parent is able to understand their children's perspective; yet in other cases will fail to even mention children's perspectives and presume that children will adjust to whatever the judge determines to be in their welfare. System matters may explain how judges justify saying that giving a child the chance to voice a preference allows them to manipulate the situation, yet themselves attempt to obtain what they deem desirable by threatening the child with warrant action if the child does not abide by the court's order.

Extreme caution is required when using judgements to make assumptions about judicial beliefs. A judgement is the court's answer to the request by the parties to resolve a matter for them. Except to the extent that it addresses questions of law, the judgement will be addressed to the parties – the adults – and will contain the information the judge believes they require to enable them to understand, accept and implement the court's order. Judgements may also be influenced by unstated matters such as the judge's perceptions of the parties, their lifestyles and their perceived values.

The position and role of the Family Court in the New Zealand legal system make it vital that all professionals involved with the court are aware of their conceptions and values, especially their often subconscious and unexamined conceptions of childhood, mothering and fathering, so they can attempt to ensure that such conceptions do not replace a focus on the interests, rights and perspective of *this* child, their unique strengths and weaknesses. All must deconstruct their conceptions to understand whose interests they serve, what ideology they are pushing and what are the practical consequences for the child of applying the conception rather than focusing on the unique child. The child, who is not present in court and rarely seen by the judge, can easily be overlooked and not heard. Yet it is the child's well-being that is paramount, and at the very least the child deserves to be heard and treated with respect as an individual.

References

Adair, V., & Rumble, A. (1998). *Telling the story: Infertile parents with donor conceived children*. Manuscript submitted for publication.

Australian Law Reform Commission & Human Rights and Equal Opportunities Commission. (1997). *Seen and heard: Priority for children in the legal process*. ALRC & HREOC Report 84, Australia.

Committee on the Rights of the Child. (1997). *Concluding observations of the Committee on the Rights of the Child: New Zealand* CRC/C/15/ADD.

Cullen, M. (1989). 497 NZPD 10245, 24 April 1989.

Freeman, M. (1983). *The rights and wrongs of children*. London: Frances Pinter.

Freeman, M. (1998). The next Children's Act? *Family Law*, *28*, 341-8.

Garrison, E. (1991). Children's competence to participate in divorce custody decisionmaking. *Journal of Clinical Child Psychology*, *20* (1), 78-87.

Gilling, M., Patterson, L., & Walker, B. (1995). *Family members' experiences of the care and protection Family Group Conference process*. Wellington: Social Policy Agency.

Gold, M. (1998). The voice of children in the Family Court. In N.J. Taylor & A.B. Smith (Eds), *Enhancing children's potential: Minimising risk and maximising resiliency*. Dunedin: University of Otago, Children's Issues Centre, pp. 132-6.

Gray, A., & Martin, P. (1998). *The role of counsel for the child: A research report*. Wellington: Department for Courts.

Harre, R. (1986). The step to social constructionism. In M. Richards & P. Light (Eds), *Children of social worlds. Development in a social context*. Cambridge: Harvard University Press, pp. 287-96.

Kelsey, J. (1995). *The New Zealand experiment: A world model for structural adjustment?* Auckland: Auckland University Press.

Lansdown, G. (1994). Children's rights. In B. Mayall (Ed.), *Children's childhood's: Observed and experienced*. London: The Falmer Press, pp. 33-44.

Maclean, M., & Eekelaar, J. (1997). *The parental obligation*. Oxford: Hart Publishing.

Mayall, B. (Ed.). (1994). *Children's childhoods: Observed and experienced.* London: The Falmer Press.

McKenzie, M. (1996). Family decision-making as a preventive solution in child protection. In N.J. Taylor & A.B. Smith (Eds), *Investing in children: Primary prevention strategies.* Dunedin: University of Otago, Children's Issues Centre. pp. 243-53.

Melton, G. (1983). Decision making by children. In G. Melton, G. Koocher, & M. Saks (Eds), *Children's competence to consent.* New York: Plenum Press, pp. 21-40.

Melton, G. (1983–84). Developmental psychology and the law: The State of the Art. *Journal of Family Law, 22,* 445-82.

Oakley, A. (1994). Women and children first and last: Parallels and differences between children's and women's studies. In B. Mayall (Ed.), *Children's childhoods: Observed and experienced.* London: The Falmer Press, pp. 13-34.

Oldman, D. (1994). Childhood as a mode of production. In B. Mayall (Ed.), *Children's childhoods: Observed and experienced.* London: The Falmer Press, pp. 153-66.

Palmer, J. (1986). 473 NZPD 3868, 13 August 1986.

Qvortrup, J. (1990). A voice for children in statistical and social accounting: A plea for children's right to be heard. In A. James & A. Prout (Eds), *Constructing and reconstructing childhood: Contemporary issues in the sociology of childhood.* London: The Falmer Press, pp. 78-98.

Qvortrup, J. (1994). Childhood matters: An introduction. In J. Qvortrup, M. Bardy, G. Sgritta, & H. Wintersberger (Eds), *Childhood matters: Social theory, practice and policy.* Aldershot: Avebury Press, pp. 1-24.

Report of the Royal Commission of Inquiry. (1972). *Social security in New Zealand.* Wellington: Government Printer.

Report of the Solicitor General of the UN to the General Assembly. (1995). *Social development, including questions relating to the world social situation and to youth, ageing and disabled persons and the family.* A/50/370, NY; UN.

Roche, J. (1996). The politics of children's rights. In J. Brannen & M. O'Brien (Eds), *Children in families: Research and policy.* London: The Falmer Press, pp. 26-40.

Schneider, C.E. (1992). The channelling function in family law. *Hofstra Law Review, 20* (3), 495-532.

Seymour, J. (1992). An 'uncontrollable' child: A case study in children's and parents' rights. In P. Alston, S. Parker, & J. Seymour (Eds), *Children, rights and the law*. Oxford: Clarendon Press, pp. 98-118.

Shipley, J., & Peters, W. (1998). *Towards a code of social and family responsibility. Public discussion document*. Wellington: Department of Social Welfare.

Smith, C. (1998). Beyond the tip of the iceberg. *Social Work Now, 11*, 33-40.

Tapp, P. (1996). Family law. *New Zealand Law Review, part 11*, 187-96.

Tapp, P., Geddis, D., & Taylor, N. (1992). Protecting the family. In M. Henaghan & B. Atkin (Eds), *Family law policy in New Zealand.* Auckland: Oxford University Press, pp. 168-209.

Thomas, N., & O'Kane, C. (1998). When children's wishes and feelings clash with their 'best interests'. *International Journal of Children's Rights, 6*, 137-54.

Treadwell, P. (1999). Suffer little children: The disintegration of child protection. *Butterworths Family Law Journal, 3*(1), 3-5.

Trinder, L. (1997). Competing constructions of childhood: Children's rights and children's wishes in divorce. *Journal of Social Welfare and Family Law, 19* (3), 291-305.

Cases

A v A [1978] 1 NZLR 278.
Arvidson v Croft [1996] NZFLR 741.
C v D (1991) 8 FRNZ 338.
D v D [1978] 1 NZLR 476.
CL v CL (1985) 3 NZFLR 455.
D v D [1978] 1 NZLR 476.
DGSW v R (1997) 16 FRNZ 357.
E v S (1996) 15 FRNZ 550.
F v F (1991) 8 FRNZ 400.
G v Adams & G (1985) 2 FRNZ 14.
H v C (1986) 2 FRNZ 32.
Jury (1984) 3 NZFLR 33.
K v K (No 1) (1988) 5 NZFLR 257.
K v K (No 2) (1988) 5 NZFLR 283.
M v M (1981-1982) 1 NZFLR FLN 131.
M v M (Child Access) [1973] 2 All ER 81.
N v D [Guardianship] (1993) 11 FRNZ 303, 306.
P v P (1984) 1 FRNZ 221.
Pooley v Llewelyn [1985] 3 NZFLR 628.
R v C (1985) 2 FRNZ 8.
Re L (An Infant) (1914) XXXIII S Ct 849, 896.
Shannon (1988) 5 NZFLR 305.
Sharman (1988) 5 NZFLR 91.
Simpson (1986) 2 FRNZ 637.
T v T (1998) 17 FRNZ 133.

Notes

1 Section 23 of the Guardianship Act 1968 and sections 4, 5, 6 & 13 of the Children, Young Persons and Their Families Act 1989.
2 See *K v K (No. 1)* (1988) and *K v K (No. 2)* (1988).
3 The Domestic Purposes benefit was introduced in 1973 by an amendment inserting s27B into the Social Security Act 1964 (Report of the Royal Commission of Inquiry, 1972).

· 6 ·

Assessing the impact of the economic reforms on Maori tamariki and rangatahi

CINDY A. KIRO

Introduction

While little has been published about the effects of the economic reforms on children and young people, there has been a growing body of literature on the economic reforms themselves which occurred in New Zealand from 1984 (Kelsey, 1993, 1995; Easton, 1997a, 1997b; Cheyne, O'Brien & Belgrave, 1997; Hazeldine, 1998; Jesson, 1999; Boston, Dalziel & St. John, 1999; Te Puni Kokiri, 1998; Williams, Frater & Stephens, 1999). This literature reflects a consensus about the speed and scope of the reforms, and suggests significant long-term effects to these reforms. While the economic reforms were the primary goal of the Fourth Labour Government, they inevitably stretched to encompass and require social reforms, and it is this combination of reforms which will be examined in this paper. This preoccupation with all things economic remains today, and can also be seen mirrored in the approach of iwi authorities to Maori development.

The reason for the lack of material on children and young people is in part due to the absence of forethought and monitoring by successive governments on the effects of these reforms on children and young people in New Zealand. One possible explanation for this lack of monitoring could be the conviction which seemed to grab everyone involved in government administration in the period between the late 1980s and early 1990s – namely that major change was needed to lift the living standards of all New Zealanders.

Such conviction seems particularly misplaced in the cold light of day when considering the likely effects of significant economic and social policy reforms on our most vulnerable members of society – for whom it would take some time to adapt to the new order of things. In particular, it seems obvious in hindsight, that Maori tamariki (children) and rangatahi (young people) would be especially affected by the economic and social reforms given what we understand about the way in which ethnicity and socio-economic status act to multiply disadvantage for these populations. However, such an analysis has been largely absent from the literature of those who advocated for the reforms and amongst those who have critiqued these reforms. This paper aims to fills some of this void by providing some observations on the effects of these economic and social reforms on Maori tamariki and rangatahi. I will map out the economic and social changes that have swept New Zealand since 1984, when the neo-liberal revolution began. I will then describe how this relates to Maori children and young people with reference to outcomes for both their whanau (families) and themselves. Following this, I will propose an alternative way of conceptualising the changes that have occurred; and, lastly, suggest a future direction for Maori children and young people.

The problem of proof

Before moving on to the substance of this paper it is worth pointing out how difficult and fraught it is to link public policy reforms to discrete outcomes in the lives of children and young people. However, this doesn't mean we shouldn't try, and certainly considerable thinking and discussion has gone on amongst those concerned about children and young people in New Zealand, including discussions around the associations between the various elements of these reforms. It is this discourse that I draw on in this paper also.

Maori tamariki and rangatahi

Maori children and young people have distinctive and important needs arising from their status as indigenous children. As such, they share many experiences in common with other indigenous children, in particular their experience of colonisation and its devastating effects. The right of Maori children to ongoing contact with their whanau, hapu and iwi (family, subtribe and tribe) as a means of securing their cultural identity was reinforced through the 1986 report Puao-te-ata-tu, by the Ministerial Advisory Committee on a Maori Perspective for the Department of Social Welfare. This report would contribute in part to the groundbreaking Children, Young Persons and Their Families Act in 1989 by attempting to involve families in decision making around their youngsters through Family Group Conferences.

Maori enjoy a distinctive culture, language and values which have experienced a renaissance from the 1970s, but which remain under threat of erosion by the dominant English culture which colonised New Zealand last century. Maori tamariki and rangatahi are linked by whakapapa (or genealogy) to their tupuna (or forebears) and most commonly lived in extended village whanau, which built up to constitute a hapu (Cram & Pitama, 1998). These traditional family systems have eroded over time and now many children and young people live in vastly different family arrangements than they did a hundred years ago. While this pattern is also true for non-Maori, the experience of institutionalised racism and continual erosion of culture has meant even greater pressure on those elements of whanau, hapu and iwi which remain. Partly in response to this, new Maori structures have emerged to cope with the burden of change impacting Maori during the massive urbanisation of the 1950s, and dislocation created by the neo-liberal economic reforms of the 1980s and 1990s (see Waitangi Tribunal report, 1998).

Maori children made up a quarter (24.5 per cent) of the total proportion of children in the population in 1996 and this is projected to grow by 2051 to over a third (33.5 per cent) of all children in the population. Numbers of Pacific Island and Asian children have increased relative to the numbers of children of Pakeha (or European) descent, which have declined between 1986 and 1996 from 72.6 per cent to 62.4 per cent (Statistics New Zealand, 1999). This diversification of the population is a reflection of the changing patterns of fertility and immigration amongst New Zealand families (Statistics New Zealand, 1999; Shirley, Koopman-Boyden, Pool & St. John, 1997).

Maori have a younger population profile than non-Maori (see Figure 6.1) partly because they continue to have children at younger ages than non-Maori (Pool, cited Shirley et al., 1997).

> Young Pakeha have gone back to the patterns of childbearing which characterised their grandparents in the 1930s, and thus are following radically different parenting strategies from those seen in the baby boom, an era that stands out as aberrant. Consequently, from the mid-1970s there have been increases in age-specific fertility at all ages over 27 years, even at 40–49, and marked decreases in fertility at younger ages. In short, Pakeha fertility has achieved reprise of past patterns by repositioning to older ages (Shirley et al., 1997, p. 221).

In contrast Maori fertility, while dropping, is now seen as aberrant and, as Shirley et al. (1997) explain, this difference provides fuel for moral outrage over young parents:

> Over recent years teenage fertility has declined significantly for both Maori and Pakeha, a trend associated with an upward shift in ages of marriage and childbearing, to such an extent that age-specific fertility patterns are totally different from those in

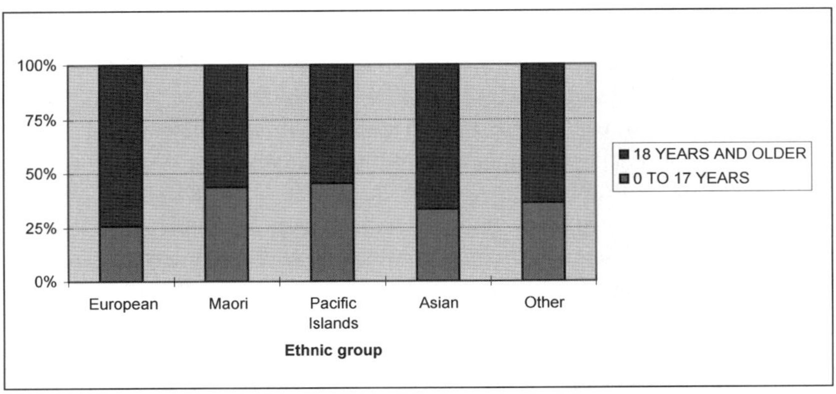

Figure 6.1: Percentage under age of eighteen years for ethnic groups 1996.[1]

the baby boom. It is thus somewhat curious that policy concerns about this phenomenon, verging on moral panic, have reached a crescendo in the 1990s when rates are much lower than in the baby boom, the peak period of adolescent childbearing (p. 221).

The implications of this for Maori families are twofold: firstly, having children earlier means delaying educational and income generating opportunities that have long lasting effects on future employment prospects. Secondly, the accompanying moral panic stigmatises Maori as irresponsible, despite falls in Maori fertility and recent similarities in non-Maori patterns of fertility. This is further exacerbated by the rise in sole parent families, most of them headed by women who continue to earn less than men with the same qualifications and work experience. Solo mums are also stigmatised as immoral and bludgers – a reflection of the dominance of New Right thinking which values economic independence from the state, above all else. Maori children are growing up in disproportionate numbers of these families (41.2 per cent or two out of five Maori children) compared to non-Maori (16.6 per cent for children of European descent, 29.0 per cent for Pacific Islands' children and 12.2 per cent for Asian children) (Statistics New Zealand, 1999). They therefore experience the deep racism that exists in New Zealand, the grinding poverty of those who rely on government assistance or low-paid insecure jobs, and the stigma of not living with two parents.

The problem therefore is in part that the pro-natal government policies which supported baby boomers have now been replaced by policies which punish families with dependent children and young people. This occurs at the very time when those families undergoing massive structural unemployment, such as Maori families, most need government support as a bridge to a new employment market.

Before moving to a more thorough analysis of the impact of the economic reforms, I want to provide a brief overview of the economic and social reforms so we can properly understand the impact of unemployment, income, housing, health, education and cultural development on Maori children and young people.

The neo-liberal reforms in New Zealand

In 1984 New Zealand caught the neo-liberal economics cold that had been sweeping other OECD countries. Our economic system was highly centralised and protected and government spending had come to rely heavily on overseas borrowing to fund the interventionist policies of the Muldoon administration. New Zealand adopted neo-liberalism with a vengeance with the election in 1984 of the Lange government. Over the next six years, this government would implement the most sweeping economic and social reforms of any government since the first Labour government, which introduced the notion of the comprehensive welfare state with the Social Security Act of 1938.

These reforms included the floating of the New Zealand dollar, removal of all tariffs and subsidies to New Zealand exporters and manufacturers, sale of government assets – most notably our telecommunications, forests, rail and a host of other government activities. They also introduced 'Tomorrow's Schools' which was designed to improve the self-management of schools. The election in 1990 of the Bolger government would signal a fresh round of reforms including punitive benefit cuts in 1991 and again in 1998 (under the Shipley government), tax cuts between 1991 and 1998, the overturning of all labour relations legislation with the Employment Contracts Act 1991. They would also introduce user pays to health, make moves to privatise health, eliminate the truancy service for schools, then re-establish a pilot project on improving school attendance which would be extended nationally. In short, everything and anything was up for grabs from 1984 to the time of writing.

Early efforts focused on creating the right economic environment within which business could flourish and international investors would want to invest their money. This behaviour was based on a belief that the market, or at least a particular version of the market, would deliver superior results to those New Zealand had experienced in the period prior to 1984 (Hazeldine, 1998). Underlying these reforms have been a platform of ideas associated with neo-liberalism, which is worth explaining briefly. Neo-liberalism contains a set of normative ideas about how government and society should function. It draws on a critique of the welfare state and argues that it creates distortions which make it inherently inefficient, ensures mediocre economic performance, restricts individual choice and prevents maximisation of individual utilities (Tensenbel & Gauld, in press). Since neo-liberalism is not the focus of this paper I will summarise by saying that the underlying tenets of neo-liberalism concern the limitation of government and government expenditure, promotion of the individual and promotion of responsible economic policy through the unfettered operation of the marketplace where individual utility can be maximised. When distilled, these components seem almost unbelievable to most people. However, these ideas have dominated New Zealand's public policy agenda for the past fifteen years. They reveal a preoccupation with all things economic, as if economics were somehow disconnected from the very fabric of society within which this activity takes place. Of significance to Maori is the way in which so much of what constitutes neo-liberalism, undermines the collectivist values of traditional Maori society. And herein lies a great irony.

The social policies pursued by government under the domination of neo-liberalism have included devolution of services to communities of interest. For Maori this has meant devolving services in health, education (although this is centralising again), welfare, and employment. While Maori have been wary of the reforms agenda because of a concern with the limited resources to support such a shift in responsibility, they have also been quick to take up the opportunities offered by providing services to Maori themselves. This has allowed the expression of tino rangatiratanga (self-determination) sought by Maori for so long. However, little analysis has accompanied this shift in responsibility. In particular the devolution of services has been packaged as allowing 'local responses to local problems' but in effect has allowed the transfer of risk to those very communities of interest who are most vulnerable, and have been most affected by the withdrawal of the state during a period of considerable change. Maori should be especially wary of such a transfer of risk and responsibility because we carry the largest burden of illness, social despair and poverty within New Zealand society. If Maori were prepared and able to act in a united way together, overcoming iwi rivalries, iwi and Maori urban organisation warfare, then we would become a considerable political force for change within this society. However, as was recently pointed out at the Conference on Children and Family Violence, iwi leadership appears to prioritise economic development over the pain and suffering experienced currently by Maori. Long-term development and addressing the needs of those in pain currently is part of responsible government, expressed at both an iwi and national government level.

Before leaving this area, I should point out that there is evidence to suggest that the reforms in New Zealand have not delivered the economic benefits promised.[2] Jesson (1999) even went so far as to suggest that the reforms were really about freeing up the productive capacity of New Zealand for exploitation by the financial sector, in part by shifting public monies into private hands. He further argued that these reforms, while occurring around the world, were not inevitable as was painted by politicians and advocates, but were a choice.

Let us now consider the evidence of the effects of the economic and social reforms in New Zealand of the past fifteen years on Maori tamariki, rangatahi and their whanau.

How have the reforms affected Maori tamariki, rangatahi and their whanau?

Many of the indicators of social and economic well-being suggest Maori children are faring worse in comparison with non-Maori (Te Puni Kokiri, 1998). This is true across a range of economic and social indicators such as employment, income, housing tenure, educational achievement and health status. However, it does not account for cultural participation which may well be rising as more people identify themselves as Maori on the census and iwi invest their Treaty of Waitangi settlements monies.

These indicators also reflect the absence of a sufficiently holistic framework for understanding Maori well-being. A 1998 report by the Ministry of Health (1998a) on children's health identified alternative or additional measures for Maori tamariki and rangatahi. These include cultural affirmation, participation in recreation, safety (including spiritual, cultural, emotional and physical safety), social functioning and educational attainment (Ministry of Health, 1998b). Unfortunately these new measures are yet to be developed, let alone tested and analysed. The most significant effects have been in the deterioration of living standards of Maori families, who have been disproportionately affected by unemployment, rising rentals in metropolitan centres and increasing costs for items such as pharmaceuticals, school fees and food. In particular, it was from 1988 to 1992 that Maori families experienced the greatest job losses as a direct result of state restructuring. Partly as a response to these job losses, Maori women have increased their participation in the workforce (Te Puni Kokiri, 1998), but are mainly located in casual or part-time work which is poorly paid, insecure, and where little support exists for parental responsibilities such as child care.

Maori children and young people are over-represented in lone parent families headed by women (Te Puni Kokiri, 1998; Davey, 1998; Statistics New Zealand, 1998b). These families also tend to be amongst the poorest families and have fewer social supports than other families. This creates pressure for Maori children and young people in two respects. Firstly, their immediate material needs are less likely to be met with inadequate income and support to raise them. Secondly, the lack of support through whanau networks provides a point of tension, wherein cultural values appear to be undermined by the daily realities of these children's lives adding to a crisis of identity.

Specific economic reforms and their effects

The most important reforms occurred in relation to the labour market, with massive redundancies during the late 1980s. These redundancies resulted from the sale of public services such as New Zealand Rail, New Zealand Forests, New Zealand Post (including telecommunications) and ironically led to significant increases in benefit dependency amongst Maori (Kiro, 1998). Maori unemployment has remained consistently high during the period of the reforms, peaking in 1990–92 at around 20.5 per cent compared to the non-Maori rate of 7 per cent. By 1996 this rate remained at 19 per cent for Maori, compared to 6.3 per cent for non-Maori (Durie, 1998, based on Statistics New Zealand Household Labour Force Survey, September 1996). Despite this, Maori women's participation in the workforce increased from 15 per cent in 1991 to 25 per cent in 1996, but these were located mainly in part-time positions for those on the Domestic Purposes Benefit (Department of Social Welfare, 1996). Even where Maori do work, there is evidence to suggest that they do not earn the same money as non-Maori for doing the same work and having the same qualifications. These families continue to provide the basis for economic well-being for Maori tamariki and rangatahi. While traditional values reflect the view that children are taonga (a treasure) and historical accounts suggest extraordinary leniency in respect of Maori children by their whanau and hapu, today's realities ensure that life is less care-free and more of a daily struggle for survival.

The combination of structural unemployment and benefit cuts has increased the income inequality between Maori and non-Maori households even further. The gap between Maori and non-Maori household income grew from $5,500 in 1987 to $10,000 by 1997 (Williams, Frater & Stephens, 1999). A number of structural features associated with the Maori population contribute to this, including higher mortality and morbidity rates, higher fertility rates at younger ages, higher sole-parent rates and larger household sizes with more children per household. These households often exist on less income and in less secure housing tenure (Maori home ownership is lower than for non-Maori).

The introduction of market rentals to state houses in 1991 has significantly affected those low income families who relied on cheap housing to offset the effects of their low incomes. Stephens, Waldegrave and Frater (1995) found that the incidence of Maori poverty was 27.3 per cent and three times that of Pakeha. Pacific Islanders were four times higher than Pakeha. A later study by Stephens and Waldegrave found that the cost of housing rentals was a large component of household expenditure amongst low income families, sometimes taking as much as 60 per cent of the household income in metropolitan centres (Stephens & Waldegrave, 1996).

Such circumstances tend to establish a pattern of high mobility for Maori children that makes it more difficult to establish learning patterns and friendships within schools. Limited resources and lack of knowledge of the school culture also make it more likely that Maori children will participate less in school-based activities, again increasing the likelihood that children will not identify positively with their school environment. Maori absences from schools remain high (Lange & Kerslake, 1998).

Participation rates at secondary schools and tertiary institutions have grown for Maori during the 1990s; however, Maori rates remain lower than non-Maori, and again, appear to be concentrated in areas that are more susceptible to market changes. Furthermore, the number of Maori school leavers with no qualification remains unacceptably high and appears to have been climbing since 1994. A 1997 Ministry of Education report (cited by the National Advisory Committee on Health and Disability, 1998) found that over 60 per cent of Maori, Pacific people and members of other minority ethnic groups are functioning below the level of literacy required to effectively meet the demands of everyday life.

While Kohanga Reo and Kura Kaupapa Maori, which provide Maori immersion education, have been growing in number and percentage of Maori children involved, there has also been a dearth of research, and other changes in the education sector have negatively impacted.

> Mainstreaming has been a major feature of the changes in educational administration brought about by the Picot Report and the subsequent Education Act (1989) and Education Amendment Act (1990). Mainstreaming substantially affected the delivery of services previously provided to meet the particular needs of groups such as Maori.

> Maori Trade Training was abolished and brought down to a level pegging with other schools – except in some instances such as school transport provision. Mainstream, as the word implies, meant providing a relatively level playing field for all, despite the differences in need or ability (Jefferies, 1997, p. 17).

Government has put in place a number of initiatives intended to provide some relief to families, with schemes such as Family Start, Family Tax Credit, Community Services Card and so forth. However, a singular feature of these is their level of complexity and the way in which such highly targeted assistance has failed to reach many of those in extreme need.

Nor is the picture improved when considering the health evidence. This would require a paper in itself. Suffice to say that significant causes of child mortality (0–14 years) remain stubbornly resistant to the economic 'miracle' in New Zealand. Notably SIDS (Sudden Infant Death Syndrome), where the Maori rate is 4.5 times that of non-Maori, respiratory diseases, congenital disorders and injuries all contribute greatly to child mortality. Importantly, New Zealand's position relative to other countries continues to decline – a far cry from our 1970s position in the world. There are also worrying signs of increases in youth suicide rates amongst Maori and other 'new' illness such as eating disorders.

Universalism vs targeted assistance

The economic reforms have led to a targeted social assistance regime, providing a complicated and ever-changing landscape of government assistance to low income families. Furthermore, this targeting has led to more ethnically specific applications which, on the face of it, are more consistent with tino rangatiratanga than historical benefits through the state. A more careful examination, however, reveals a worrying trend. Direct government assistance has diminished by the cutting of benefits in 1991 and 1998. In addition, reduced government expenditure and policy changes in social services have affected those most in need by withdrawing such essential supports as state-subsidised housing and more extensive health services for children over six years.[3] They have also resulted in minimal dental services and an educational management structure reliant on voluntary labour. Many of these changes have had a marked impact on the living standards of children from low income families such as Maori. To explain more fully:

> The shift from centralised provision to decentralised service delivery and group-targeted services, especially since 1991, has focused on Maori 'problems', rather than on the non-culturally specific improvements in Maori social conditions resulting from universally provided benefits and mainstreaming (Cheyne, O'Brien & Belgrave, 1997, pp. 154–155).

Universal entitlement to the family benefit for those with dependent children, increased family incomes during the period of the welfare state. It did so without overtly drawing attention to specific Maori entitlement, since it was provided to all citizens, yet Maori were net beneficiaries of this scheme. Compare this to now, where:

> Group targeting – the result of mainstreaming health and education services along with services once provided by the Department of Maori Affairs – makes welfare provision much more culturally specific. This allows services to be tuned to tangata whenua needs in a way that could be seen to be more responsive to the Crown's Treaty obligations, but it also makes any attempts to transfer resources to Maori subject to Pakeha cries of separatism. Article II rights to redress economic impoverishment are more subject to a cultural veto by Pakeha, than Article III rights, which stress common citizenship (Cheyne, O'Brien & Belgrave, 1997, p. 155).

Such changes must pose questions about how the public of New Zealand will respond to increasing Maori need created by economic and social dislocation during the reforms of the late 1980s and 1990s in the face of lower public tolerance to such need, and the pervasiveness of these attitudes on Maori children and young people.

Well-being of tamariki, rangatahi and whanau

Maori tamariki and rangatahi needs are best served through the well-being of their whanau, hapu and iwi, as well as through positive reinforcement within mainstream Pakeha society. Positive role models, acknowledgement and common usage of tikanga and te reo assist in creating a more culturally diverse and engaging climate for Maori tamariki and rangatahi. While Maori society is not now, nor has it ever been, egalitarian or homogenous, it does have a humanitarian and collectivist past which could contribute to a more vibrant and rich culture for all New Zealanders. The huge burden of poverty, illness and disadvantage cannot be overcome by Maori efforts alone. They require the efforts of all New Zealanders and our international indigenous and non-indigenous colleagues.

Conclusion

The economic reforms began in New Zealand in 1984 and continue to the present (1999). They have had a profound affect on the lives of Maori children and young people by reshaping the wider socio-political context within which these children grow up. Their educational opportunities and access to welfare services including health and also in the direct impact on the incomes, employment, and life opportunities of their families contribute to this.

Much of the evidence of these effects is associative because of the paucity of data about long-term trends such as in education. Dramatic changes to those institutions which affect the daily lives of children such as schools, families and local communities, have not been monitored for their effects on children and young people. Evidence suggests that little thought was given to how such reforms would affect children and young people in New Zealand. This must cause grave concern for those worried about the future of our society. We know that youth suicide rates have grown exponentially during the period of economic reforms (Hassall, 1997), the result perhaps of a growing youth anomie. Official explanations continue to shy away from linking these reforms with this exponential growth in suicide.

There is also substantial evidence that most families have experienced a decline in income as a result of taxation benefits for the highest income families, and cuts in benefits for those families reliant on government assistance (Easton, 1997b). What is clear is that the trend is towards growing inequality in incomes (Podder & Chatterjee, 1998; Statistics New Zealand, 1998b), which is part of a worldwide trend of growing inequality amongst those countries who have pursued neo-liberal economics in public policy.

The picture of growing inequality is most worrying for Maori tamariki and rangatahi, along with Pacific Island families, as it is they who have experienced the greatest decline in incomes and overall well-being during the period of the reforms. Positive developments such as with Kohanga Reo, Maori health providers, increased rates of secondary and tertiary participation and so forth, have almost invariably been the result of Maori efforts to bridge the gap created by the withdrawal of the state, or the provision of inappropriate state services.

Overall the picture for Maori tamariki and rangatahi as we enter the new millennium is a bleak one. Maori well-being is more likely in a social and cultural milieu that is more tolerant and where universal benefits are the norm. Furthermore, we require some truly visionary Maori leadership who reject the belief that only economic development will lead us to the promised land. Humanitarianism, not economic prosperity alone, is a pre-requisite for a healthy society.

References

Boston, J., Dalziel, P., & St. John, S. (1999). *Redesigning the welfare state in New Zealand: Problems, policies, prospects*. Auckland: Oxford University Press.

Cheyne, C., O'Brien M., & Belgrave M. (1997). *Social policy in Aotearoa New Zealand: A critical introduction*. Auckland: Oxford University Press.

Children, Young Persons and Their Families Act, 1989. New Zealand Parliament, Government Printers, No. 24.

Cram, F., & Pitama S. (1998). Ko toku whanau, ko toku mana. In V. Adair & R. Dixon (Eds), *The family in Aotearoa New Zealand*. Auckland: Longman, pp. 130-57.

Davey, J.A. (1998). *Tracking social change in New Zealand: From birth to death IV*. Wellington: Institute of Policy Studies.

Department of Social Welfare. (1996). Briefing papers to the Minister of Social Welfare.

Durie, M.H. (1998). *Te mana, te kawanatanga: The politics of Maori self-determination*. Auckland: Oxford University Press.

Easton, B. (1997a). *The commercialisation of New Zealand*. Auckland: Auckland University Press.

Easton, B. (1997b). *In stormy seas: The post-war New Zealand economy*. Dunedin: University of Otago Press.

Hassall, I. (1997). Why are so many young people killing themselves? *Butterworths Family Law Journal*, *2*(7), 153-58.

Hazeldine, T. (1998). *Taking New Zealand seriously*. Auckland: Auckland University Press.

Jefferies, R. (1997). *Maori participation in tertiary education: Barriers and strategies to overcome them*. Report prepared for Te Puni Kokiri. Wellington: Ministry of Maori Development.

Jesson, B. (1999). *Only their purpose is mad: The money-men take over New Zealand*. Auckland: Dunmore Press.

Kelsey, J. (1993). *Rolling back the state*. Wellington: Bridget Williams Books.

Kelsey, J. (1995). *The New Zealand experiment*. Auckland: Auckland University Press/ Bridget Williams Books.

Kiro, C.A. (1998). Maori, the welfare state and market economy. In Te Pumanawa Hauora (Ed.), *Proceedings of Te Oru Rangahau Maori Research and Development Conference*. Palmerston North, NZ: Massey University, Te Putahi-a-Toi School of Maori Studies, pp. 294-302.

Lange, D., & Kerslake, J. (1998). *School absences, truancy and suspensions*. Wellington: Ministry of Education.

Ministerial Advisory Committee on a Maori perspective for the Department of Social Welfare. (1986). *Puao-te-ata-tu* (Daybreak). Wellington: Department of Social Welfare.

Ministry of Health. (1998a). *Child health strategy*. Wellington: Ministry of Health.

Ministry of Health. (1998b). *Our children's health*. Wellington: Ministry of Health.

National Advisory Committee on Health and Disability. (1998). *The social, cultural and economic determinants of health in New Zealand: Action to improve health*. Wellington: National Advisory Committee on Health and Disability.

Podder, N. & Chatterjee, S. (1998, September). *Sharing the national cake in post reform New Zealand: Income inequality trends in terms of income sources*. Paper presented at the Annual Conference of the New Zealand Association of Economists, Wellington, New Zealand.

Shirley, I., Koopman-Boyden, P., Pool, I., & St. John, S. (1997). Family change and family policies: New Zealand. In S.B. Kamerman & A.J. Kahn (Eds), *Family change and family policies in Great Britain, Canada, New Zealand and the United States*. Oxford: Clarendon Press, pp. 207-303.

Statistics New Zealand. (1998a). *1996 census of population and dwellings: Population structure and internal migration*. Wellington: Statistics New Zealand.

Statistics New Zealand. (1998b). *Incomes*. Wellington: Statistics New Zealand.

Statistics New Zealand. (1999). *Children*. Wellington: Statistics New Zealand.

Stephens, R., & Waldegrave, C. (1996). Measuring poverty in New Zealand. In P. Crampton & P. Howden-Chapman (Eds), *Socioeconomic inequalities and health: Proceedings of the Socioeconomic Inequalities and Health Conference, Wellington, 9-10 December1996*. Wellington: Victoria University, pp. 105-20.

Stephens, R., Waldegrave, C., & Frater, P. (1995). Measuring poverty in New Zealand. *Social Policy Journal of New Zealand, 5*, 88-112.

Tensenbel T., & Gauld R. (in press). What models and theories are there to help us analyse policy? In P. Davis & T. Ashton (Eds), *Health and public policy*. Auckland: Oxford University Press.

Te Puni Kokiri (Ministry of Maori Development). (1998). *Progress towards closing social and economic gaps between Maori and non-Maori*: A report to the Minister of Maori Affairs. Wellington: Te Puni Kokiri.

Waitangi Tribunal. (1998). *Te Whanau o Waipareira report*. Wellington: GP Publications.

Williams, J., Frater, P., & Stephens, R. (1999). *Income and Maori Quantitative Project*. Report prepared by BERL for Te Puni Kokiri (Ministry of Maori Development). Unpublished manuscript.

Notes

1 Source: Statistics New Zealand (1998a). Note: Respondents could identify up to three ethnic groups. Figure shows total responses. There were 1,124,604 responses from 990,615 respondents.

2 See Dalziel and Lattimore's analysis from 1996 on the New Zealand macroeconomy, in Hazeldine (1998), p. 34.

3 Currently New Zealand policy allows children under six years of age to be subsidised up to $32 per visit – if a general practitioner charges more than this rate, then the patient pays the remainder as a co-payment charge. Nationally approximately 75 per cent of all general practitioners make no additional charge for children under six years.

• 7 •

The rights of the Samoan child

AIONO DR FANAAFI LE TAGALOA

Suffer the children to come unto Me, and forbid them not for of such is the kingdom of God. (Mark 10:14)

O au o matua, fanau. (Upu tuu a Samoa)

Samoan identity and heritage

I believe that where a person sits, as it were, within the ideal social organisation of culture, language and society, is germane to the theme of this conference. In Samoa, the ideal social organisation is the *Faamatai*, where people are arrayed upon a three-fold base, of the *Faasinomaga* or 'points of reference' pertaining to identity. The first base of the *Faasinomaga* of the Samoan's identity is the *matai* title to which he/she is heir. Every Samoan is heir to a matai title, whether he/she lives in Samoa, is born overseas, or is an issue of a mixed-marital union. As long as the parents are, or one of the parents is, Samoan, the person is automatically heir to the matai title of his/her *Faasinomaga.* A Samoan can be heir to more than one matai title. If there is a Samoan who says that he/she is not heir to a matai title, the denial is a choice and personal preference.

The second base of the *Faasinomaga* of the Samoan is the land owned by the matai title. The land tenure of the *Faamatai* states clearly that the *matai* title owns the land. It holds the 'title deed', while the title-holder or the heir chosen by all heirs is the trustee and protector of the *aiga* (extended family) land, and verbal tradition. Since a Samoan is connected as heir to more than one matai title, he/she has access to more than one land or property.

The third base of the *Faasinomaga* is the *Gagana* or Samoan language. There is only one language from the eastern-most Manua to Savaii in the west. The use of this language for social communication, for worship, in the deliberations of the *fono* and in the everyday life of the *aiga* or family has never been disrupted, interrupted, or had to be relearned. In the linguistic philosophy of the Gagana, the Samoan is instructed to use it as the proper food and nourishment, particularly for the young and youthful heir.

One basic right

I have introduced the ideal social organisation of the *Faamatai*, because I wish to consider the Samoan child not as a mere child, but as an heir to the matai title, heir to the land owned by the matai title, and heir to the Samoan language. Considering that the Samoan child is an heir to all that, justifies the view that the Samoan child has only *one right* – the others are consequential to this one right: *The one RIGHT is the right to life regardless of how conceived.*

In Old Samoa, the *nunuavaga* or marital unions were formally recognised and ritualistically celebrated, the grand affair as well as the small, blessed by the matai of the family. There were also births outside the formal unions or the children of the night (*tama o le po*); but however conceived, the child is an heir of the matai titles of the maternal/paternal sides: *As an heir, the opportunity to live and enjoy life is not a privilege, but a human right.*

The United Nations Convention on the Rights of Children (UNCROC) refers to the right of the child to a name, the right of children to parents, a right to an identity and so on. But the Samoan child is an heir to all these through the Faasinomaga and automatically has these rights as long as he/she lives and is allowed to survive.

The missionary record refers to the practice of infanticide by women who did not want to spoil their beauty by breast feeding their babies. There is also reference to cases of illegitimate pregnancies that were too shameful to be allowed to reach full-term. But these must have represented a very small percentage, and could have been recorded as peculiarities of the people viewed through the spectacles of the Victorians.

In modern times life is all-important, and the survival of the heir is of the essence. The Samoan parent is mindful of the welfare of the child, newly born as well as yet to be born, this generation and future ones, because he/she is an heir and as such has the right to live, no matter how conceived.

The preciousness of life and its preservation – the viewing of life as a right of the Samoan child (heir) is the unstated feeling and emotional support of the legislation against abortion. It is also the rationale for the unstated, almost unconscious, attitude of protective trust, that the Samoans have, that seems to say: 'We believe and trust that you will not harm or endanger the child.'

Of course what has been said does not mean that there has never been the wish to abort, or actual termination of unwanted pregnancies. There are abortions, often as a consequence of other problems, such as fear of physical abuse, shame because of real or imagined social status, ignorance and low level of educational background, physical illness, lack of self-discipline, alcoholism, unemployment, the ugliness of incest and so on.

The police and hospital officials I interviewed about the rights of children said that the Samoan of modern times still regards life as the most essential right of the child. Of the few babies that were literally thrown away but survived, or left as foundlings, all have been formally/officially adopted, mainly by people connected with the Health Department. One of the police officials said that a number of girls who became pregnant and did not want to keep their babies were being advised to consult a newly established centre for adoption. This centre is called 'Adopt-us Centre', is registered as an NGO., gives counselling services to young pregnant mothers, and acts as an adoption agency. The founder and coordinator of the Adopt-us Centre has no medical background, but the Centre enjoys the services and advice of two qualified medical doctors and a New Zealand trained Samoan lawyer.

The co-ordinator counsels young pregnant girls to have a regard for the lives they are bearing. About 90 per cent of the girls come with the expressed wish to abort the pregnancy. But when they were asked for the reasons why, they almost all gave fear of parental disapproval and loss of face as the main reason. One or two said that they were unable financially to care for the babies and one or two did not want to be reminded of an error of judgement.

The Adopt-us Centre follows the open adoption system. This is explained to the girls, especially the emphasis on availability of all information. The identity of the natural father, of the girls' parents and family is known, and the agreement of the girls to be medically examined is gained (many were well on with their pregnancies and had never seen a doctor) as well as their permission to allow the Centre to contact and inform their parents, especially their mothers, about the situation of their daughters.

The case of the Adopt-us Centre is an example of the general feelings of concern and caring that Samoans have towards children. The parents, like most parents, may be greatly disappointed and angry to begin with, but they usually rally around and take back their daughter and especially the young grandchild. As they usually say, 'How can I harm those eyes, those innocent eyes, that did not ask to be born?'

There is no government service for adoption; the counselling available comes as part of the hospital-based service – a planned parenthood and maternal welfare centre – mainly for regular pregnancies. The police also offer counselling, usually when there is an incident of an attempted abortion or some other violation of the law. The numbers are not overwhelming and I believe this is because of the importance of the right of an heir to life.

As an heir to the *matai* title the child, even before he or she is born, has a name and an aiga (an extended family) to which he/she belongs. When the child is born, the placenta or the *fanua* is named his/her brother or sister, which is called the *Uso*. The matai of the family usually selects some suitable spot of the aiga land, or the second base of the *Faasinomaga* (or Identity) where the *Uso* is planted. In other words the heir lives, survives, while the Uso is planted in the land where he/she belongs and has access to. The other word in the Samoan language for land is *Fanua* but as has been mentioned, *fanua* is also the placenta.

The *Uso* is planted in the *fanua*, not buried, suggesting that the newly born child lives and grows and so will the Uso. The symbolism is powerful and evocative, underscoring the closeness of the right of the heir to life and land in the Samoan cosmogony. Consequently, there is no need to write a law giving the child the right to land and property; as long as he/she lives as an heir, he/she will have access to land.

Physical discipline and culture

The right of the Samoan child to life is in jeopardy sometimes because of ignorance, and poor levels of parental education. I refer to the physical abuse that some parents give to their children. Both in Samoa and overseas, a false notion has come about and is used as an explanation for the use of physical abuse, beatings, and cruel measures. *The false notion is that beating is in accordance with Samoan culture, practice and philosophy*. The quote of sparing the rod and spoiling the child is also used as a biblical justification of the thrashing. Recently, I gave a talk to a Samoan congregation in San Francisco on the importance of teaching Samoan language and culture to the Samoan children and young people, particularly those born in San Francisco. I referred to the Samoan language as a part of the *Faasinomaga* and the identity as well as the linguistic principle that has been handed down from time immemorial: *Fafaga Tama a manu i fuga o laau ma ia, ae fafaga tama a tagata i upu ma tala*; which means: 'Feed the young of animals with fruit of trees and fish, but feed the young of Man with words and speech.' I stressed the importance of speaking with the children, teaching good and appropriate vocabulary and encouraging self-discipline and assuming that there are no generation gaps.

Afterwards, one of the female members of the congregation asked for advice about disciplining children: 'The law in this land is very severe – if we use physical means like whipping when we discipline, and you know Aiono, we Samoans always discipline our children by the *sasa* just as the Bible says.' I was pleased to have the opportunity to speak on this false disciplinary measure. I pointed to her one method of child-rearing as contained in the Samoan words of wisdom 'feed the animals with bacon and eggs, bread and butter, but feed the child with words' and that, as a teacher and mother, I discipline with words, not the whip. Use of the whip is not a Samoan way of disciplining. Rather, words and the use of appropriate speech as instructed by our *Tofamanino* and philosophy.

Often, we feel the need to use physical measures – the whip, the fists – because we lack the proper words. We become abusive because of loss of face or being put on the spot for negligence. That is when we 'hit out' when really we should kick ourselves for neglecting to speak, to share, and feed our children the diet our culture and philosophy has prescribed. Disciplining with words through speech is hard on the parent and (from the reaction of my son at nine years old) on the child also. I remember speaking to my son on one occasion and he said 'Please, Mum, it would be easier for me if you use the *salu tuaniu* – that would not be as sharp as your words.'

Physical abuse is also used as an unthinking response for other reasons. The pressures of modern life, the inability to hold a job, the distress that can come to a Samoan parent with the realisation that his child is better educated; the infidelity of husband or wife; or the violation of the *va-tapuia* or incest.

The Samoan child has a right to his culture and philosophy. Therefore part of the heritage he/she is heir to must be recognised, provided and safeguarded. It is assumed that Samoan children have a common cultural and philosophic experience but that is not true of the Samoan child's situation. For example, the culture, the language, the philosophy of formal schooling, of the church, of government is alien and non- Samoan.

Therefore the culture and language, and especially the unconscious philosophical underpinnings of an international convention like UNCROC can be quite strange to the Samoan whose rights and concerns the Convention is supposed to promote. That is the reason why I insist that the Samoan child has a right to his/her culture. There is a lack of consideration of the specific way people have of viewing, of thinking, of feeling about world-wide issues. To me, personally, even the way the rights are stated in the Convention can be offputting. For example, the rights are addressed to the child defined as anyone who is under the age of eighteen years, which in some cultural and social considerations make the child not a child at all; and the direct address of 'you have a right to' can have different effects on the parents and the so-called child.

A Samoan child living in San Francisco, for example, learns very quickly to be like other seventeen-year-olds in his/her school and neighbourhood, tending to be outspoken and individualistic all the time, when in public and when in the closeness of the aiga. The language that comes easily to him/her is the English language. His/her knowledge of English often outstrips that of the parents, and can lead to disrespect or condescension towards the less educated parent.

Often the parent in this situation has difficulty because of not having the required knowledge and level of understanding of the English language to enable an analysis of the situation and to speak knowledgeably of the foreign ways. The parent also lacks the language to express his or her own way of thinking, of feeling, of establishing a dialogue. If communication between child and parent breaks down, how can one hope to get through to the other?

A very tragic incident recently occurred concerning the death of an eight-year-old girl on the island of Savaii which was reported on the local news. It was on a Sunday morning; the husband was making the stone oven and was about to put the white-hot stones on the food to be baked when the wife called out to him to 'Hit that naughty girl!' The wife must have been punishing the little girl and the latter got away and ran to the father for refuge. Tragically, the husband heard the wife and turned just as the girl reached him, and he hit her with the tongs that he had been using to put the white-hot stones on the food. They reported that the little girl died four or five hours later. This incident has already been cited by some as an example of the negative influence of Samoan culture. Such a statement is erroneous and unjust. The case is complex, and involves in the first place the personalities and psyche of husband, wife and child; the relationships between them and the community; it involves the many and specific pressures from within and from without on the couple, all of which should be explored before blaming the Samoan culture.

The reported incident is in fact very un-Samoan and anti-community. To begin with, Sunday is a special day in Samoa, particularly in the village. All preparations for the day are to be done quietly and with due respect to the holiness of God and consideration of others. Even the smoke of the stone oven is considered undesirable in the breathing of the people – therefore the stone ovens are distanced from the living quarters and cooking is done in the early hours of the morning to avoid the pollution over the awakening village. Sunday is the day when all unpeaceful incidents are avoided because it is a day holy to God and also for the consideration of others in the community. Therefore a wife who beats her eight-year-old child in the circumstances of a Sunday morning in a Samoan village needs to be examined very carefully for the reason and justification for violating the Sunday morning quietness. In the setting of the Samoan culture, it is very hard for the neighbours not to intervene, in matters like this. I have heard of parents who, when another person tries to intervene, become quite abusive and say: 'Don't interfere – it's my child, I can beat him to death!' Such an attitude is very un-Samoan and does not prevent intervention, because the words stem from anger, deep emotional upset and even temporary insanity. Samoans always intervene or interfere in situations like this because life, whether of a child or an adult, must be protected. The Samoan philosophy expresses this in the expression: *E leai se aoga o se tamaalii pe a le ola ai seisi*, which means: 'You are inhumane (and therefore not an aristocrat) if you cannot save the life of anybody.' I believe in the appropriateness of this aspect of Samoan life to any Samoan in our times, whether in Samoa or in foreign climes. The Samoan culture and philosophy are important and relevant and the Samoan must not lose respect for them.

Language

I wholeheartedly believe in the importance of culture, philosophy, language and the consequent rights of Samoan children to that culture, philosophy and language. Speaking of the right to language refers back to the brief description of the three bases of the identity of the Samoan. I was privileged to meet the late Princess Te Puea; the late Lady Salamasina Malietoa kindly took me to Ngaruawahia. Princess Te Puea spoke of the importance of the Maori language – not just the speech but the rhetoric of the language. She mentioned one New

Zealand leader who had to learn the Maori language because when he visited the marae of his mother's tribe he was politely but firmly told that if he did not know the language of the marae then he'd better sit down and be silent.

The relationship of the Samoan to his or her language is similar. You are not Samoan if you do not know how to speak the language. There are Samoans who will deny this, maybe using themselves as an example. But it is important to know the language of the *malae* – the rhetoric and metaphor, there are situations where you cannot cross the barriers unless you know the 'password'.

If a Samoan child has a right to language, then he/she or she should not be made to speak only the English language of formal school. There are several expressions that bear out Samoans' right to speech – for example, *O le mea a le Tamalii le fetalai; E le paoa e le tasi le isi; E saolele le finagalo o le tuamafa filimalae*. Every Samoan has the right to speak, but there is a responsibility for this to be appropriate and of good quality.

I am reminded of a lesson on what democracy is. My teacher said, 'Supposing you walk down Queen Street in Auckland at five o'clock in the afternoon swinging your arms around; you have the democratic right to do that if that is your wish. But the moment you hit someone with your arms swinging then your democratic right to walk, act, as you please, ends.' So the Samoan child has the right to speak but the responsibility of knowing the right and the proper words to use, as well as knowing the appropriate moment and situations to apply this right. *It is essential when we speak of rights to keep clearly in our mind's eye responsibility; for in pushing our right irresponsibly, we can violate the right of the other person.*

Samoan culture and philosophy holds that to speak is a human right, not a privilege. It also stresses the importance of timing; of knowing the correct and proper words of the particular moment and situation and the wisdom to know when to be silent. When a responsibility is thus given equal emphasis to a right, the Samoan child and adult can speak his mind freely and with temerity. As a Samoan, I know I have the right to speak and if I require an audience with the Head of State, I have the confidence to seek the opportunity to speak to His Highness, knowing that the Head of State as a matai would recognise my right to speak, as well as his own right to speak or remain silent. Behaviour that is responsible must go with every right that we seek. We seek the right to speak, therefore we should be conscious and aware of the enormity of the responsibility; especially in a society where the spoken word has mana, because of the philosophical concept of the *Sau* – the breath of life, that creates, that blesses, that curses. It is by word of mouth that the blessings are passed on; that the total milieu of the social life – the culture, the language, the philosophy, that make the Samoan a separate and peculiar human being – is conveyed. In the world where much of a muchness is becoming standard, and the media addresses the masses. I still believe in the necessity of speaking the essence of one's own particular language and vocabulary. It calms the mind and promotes disciplined behaviour, beginning with the child.

Work

The United Nations Convention makes much of the right of children to proper employment. This is very important and the Samoan child must also have the right to be considered and protected from sweated labour and abuse associated with child labour. The Samoan child is taught very early in life to serve others, beginning with the aiga, and gradually the community elders. When there is food to be shared the Samoan child is often sent with a basket of food to the neighbours or to the *matua tausi* or the elderly. A lesson in how to perform this act is usually done at home before the child sets out, for example, 'Come Tele, take this vaisalo for the old lady Mele. Don't go to the front but enter from the back of the house. Sit down before you speak; say, 'This is the vaisalo for the old lady Mele sent by my parents."

In modern times there is legislation – the Infants Ordinance of 1967 – which defines the child as anyone under sixteen years of age and defines the categories of child labour in Samoa. There are three such categories:

1.The formal employment sector under contract as paid workers. At present, no one under fifteen years of age is known to be employed in the formal sector. The minimum legal age for employment is sixteen years and for apprenticeship seventeen years.

2. Semi-formal employment sector. Here the child is engaged as a non-paid worker in family-run, commercial or semi-commercial operations as part of the normal household chores. This is the most problematic sector mainly because the coverage by legislation is unclear. It is difficult to differentiate between engagement as workers and as family members doing normal family chores. Presently, many children are known to be engaged in this work sector.

3.The non-formal employment sector. Where the child is a non-paid family worker in non-commercial, subsistence activities. Again there are problems in this area but according to the Commissioner of Labour they are not too serious. There are problems where children are employed in domestic work not suitable to their physical capacity or likely to be injurious to their health, or engaged in domestic work instead of attending school.

But anyone with eyes can observe some of the young people hawking a variety of goods in the town of Apia near the supermarket stores, restaurants, hotels, banks, and car parks. In the beginning the goods offered for sale were garlands of fresh flowers or ulas, offered to tourists or sailors off the cruise ships. This was something that earned the sellers and the makers of the ulas some hard cash and was usually done in the later afternoon and evening. Gradually the items sold became varied and some of the sellers seemed to be fully employed. In the last two years or so, I have noticed children selling 'shop goods' – items like batteries for radios and cameras, and deodorants, mothballs, toilet soaps, hair bands, as well as homemade banana, taro, and breadfruit chips, woven fans and coconut stringers or *tauaga*. On Saturdays and on school holidays, sellers hawk fresh vegetables like cucumbers, tomatoes, beans, pumpkins, cabbage, yam cooked in coconut cream, umu-baked *faapapa*, as well as octopus, and sea eels.

There is much public criticism of these activities. In preparing this paper, I undertook a mini-survey, buying some of these goods and asking the sellers many questions. I must have interviewed something like thirty children, usually in the afternoons or on Saturdays, which are the times and days of their operations. All the children I interviewed were polite and seemed not to mind my questions. Most wore clothes commonly worn by Samoan children and seemed to be in good health. There were four boys, probably aged fourteen or fifteen and one older, who were hawking matches. I bought a packet and I asked where they got their matches from. The answer surprised me because I thought they were probably 'circulating' some of the wares from their family stalls at the flea market. But they said they got their matches from a recently established wholesale business in town. I asked whether they were employed by the company and they answered, 'After school we go there to get the items we sell and, like selling the newspaper, we get paid on how much we sell.' 'Are you related to the owner of the company?' I asked, and they said, 'No.' When I asked them whether they attended school, they laughed and said, 'Yes, except this guy (pointing to the older one) who has a wife.' They were probably having me on but I looked at the older youth and said to the four boys, 'He should not be hawking boxes of matches, don't you think?'

I met the four sellers of matches later on that same afternoon, for they brought to me a young man who was selling taro chips. I asked the taro chips seller where he got his chips from. He answered that his mother makes them at home and after school and on Saturdays he sells them. The chips were going at a dollar a bag. I asked the seller the name of his school and he mentioned a government intermediate school in town. As several buyers were waiting in line, I stopped questioning to allow the seller to serve his customers. But one of the sellers of matches took upon himself to select five bags of taro chips that I wanted and handed them to me and saying that he was from the same school as the seller of taro chips.

One Saturday, a young child approached my car and asked if I wanted a plaited fan or Ili. The fans were three *Tala* each and quite well woven. I bought a fan and asked whether she made them herself, she shook her head, saying that her mother wove them. Their village is about half an hour from Apia on the west bus route. She comes to Apia to sell the fans on some Saturdays and she attends the village school and is in year six. Then, I was waylaid by a very little boy, perhaps six years old. He looked rather delicate and could hardly manage the sales talk, especially when his nose was running very badly. No mother could resist the sad eyes. He was selling two iced coconuts which means their stall with a 'cooler' must have been close by. I bought the two coconuts (one *tala* each) even though I am allergic to coconut.

One seller of tauaga, or coconut strainer, introduced an interesting element into what appeared to be a simple selling of home-produced, homemade goods by children during their free time. This seller did not hawk his strainers in town but in suburban areas like Alafua, Lotopa and Pesega. He carries his tauaga in a large bag, an empty container of sugar. He did not attend school and said that his parents allow him to stay away from school. The source of his tauaga is the produce market at Fugalei. He actually buys from the village farmers and then divides each tauaga to make three or four and sells the 'repackaged' *tauaga* for a *tala* each. Tauaga can be fluffed out to look quite big. The particular seller said that he makes twenty *tala* a day which compares well with the take-home earnings of an unskilled labourer at one *tala* and thirty-nine *sene* an hour.

I also came across young children who sold nothing but hung around restaurants and banks begging. In Apia, a handful of individuals actually beg because they say they are handicapped, some because they are mute, others because they are 'crazy' from drinking, smoking and sniffing poisonous drugs and chemicals. In Apia, a town with a population of 35,000 to 37,000, I counted seven adults who sometimes stopped some member of the public and begged. The majority do not bother you but simply roam around town, some picking up the litter and dumping it in the trashcans provided. In fact, it seems that even in this breakdown in our social system and people's behaviour, something of the pride of the Samoan and his preference to ask help only from family or friends is retained.

How long this feeling of personal pride will act as personal buffer and restraint, I cannot predict. All I know and firmly believe in is the ability of the *Faasinomaga* or the identity of the Samoan to protect and provide for members of the *aiga* when in need, in straitened circumstances, or in breakdown in their inner beings, their *mauli* and psyche.

In recent months, more petty thieving and entering into private houses to steal has been reported and police investigations and finger printing have suggested that some young people's fingers have been involved. This 'Oliver Twist Variation' is new, because house-breaking and thieving has been done by adults who are former jail inmates known to the police. The inmates of our two prisons (one on Upolu and one on Savaii) usually spend their free weekends in their *aiga* and village and if a robbery occurs in the weekend, the police are quick to pick them up as suspects. But the suspected involvement of young fingers is new and a cause of anxiety.

In the area of child labour, I feel that there is no need to claim a right for the Samoan child, for the legislation as well as the sense of responsibility of the

Samoan parent for his child are sufficient. Samoan parents love and care for their children especially the young, who are often spoilt. The government is reviewing the labour laws to include the semi-formal sectors, specifically banning the employment of the child during normal school hours and at night and stressing the need for a policy of compulsory education. A review of existing legislation should also be undertaken to consider some of the areas highlighted by the Convention on the Rights of the Child and to introduce penalties which are more effective deterrents.

Education

Formal schooling in Samoa is not compulsory. In 1969 a statistical survey was undertaken by the Department of Education, which revealed that 4 per cent of the total school population reached the levels where the two external examinations, the New Zealand School Certificate and University Entrance, are taken and 82 per cent of the school age population were at school. In the Department of Education's Annual Report tabled in Parliament in April 1997, the statistics showed that 4 per cent of the school population reached School Certificate and University Entrance examinations level but 60 per cent of the school-age population were in school. In other words, the number reaching examination levels was constant over this roughly twenty-year period, but the school age population had dropped by about 20 per cent. But schooling is not compulsory. A positive factor from the point of view of the school administrator and classroom teachers is that the children are in school because they want to be, or their parents have persuaded them that going to school is good and proper. The government elementary school system has a place for every Samoan child. Education used to be from primary one to standard four, but now formal schooling begins at kindergarten, and includes primary school, post-primary school, 'polytechnic' and university.

In the area of education, some very important issues need to be examined sensitively and with care. The proposed right of the Samoan child (and heir) to his or her culture, *Tofamanino*, and language stems from this reported situation. If only 4 per cent of school children reached form five and six and are allowed to sit the external examinations, what happened to the 96 per cent?

In August 1997, the SCALA (NGO) launched two projects: one, the *Puagagana* or monolingual dictionary of the Samoan language, and the second, the Le Amosa – the School for Further Schooling. Le Amosa addresses the unstated, unanswered question of what happened to the 96 per cent of school pupils who were eliminated from sitting the School Certificate and/or University Entrance (or the SPPEC now administered from Suva by the South Pacific Education Board).

As already mentioned or inferred, being able to speak English and pass examinations in a foreign language is very important to the political leaders of

Samoa, as well as to the majority of parents. So every effort is given to the promotion of English and that is the reason for the 4 per cent. Only 4 per cent are capable of handling the examinations in English. The 96 per cent do a tour of the private secondary schools, ever hoping to achieve the desirable School Certificate and SPPEC, for without the certificates they can not enter the tertiary level or be employed in 'white collar jobs'.

On 18 August 1997 Le Amosa launched its first class, and offered an alternative to anyone over eighteen years of age who was still interested in continuing schooling. Le Amosa teaches the usual school subjects but they are taught and explained in the Samoan language. The entry requirements for Le Amosa are to be over eighteen years, to be keen to continue schooling, not to have passed School Certificate or SPPEC, and to understand, read and write Samoan. The first year has encouraged us that this can be an alternative to help Samoans to become thinking, thoughtful, and effective members of society. We try to realise the many natural talents of the students and at the same time lift their self-confidence and morale, particularly those who have been labelled as 'dropouts', 'dumb ones' and 'idiots'. We also try and correct poor study habits inculcated through rote-learning and memorisation of material in an alien language and culture.

Although education is not compulsory I feel that the need to claim the right to schooling for the Samoan child (in Samoa) is not pressing. The Samoan child overseas, however, receives benefits under the excellent educational legislation, policies, opportunities and provisions in other countries. The roles played by the parents or the pastors in the overseas Samoan community are critical to the successful use of the many opportunities for schooling. Unlike in the homeland, the opportunities (for example, in New Zealand) are many, and both Samoan child and parent can take these for granted and many may not be challenged to make good use of them. Sometimes there are problems for the Samoan student in New Zealand, Australia and the United States of America because of language. Even for Samoans born overseas, the foreign language can be a linguistic barrier to self-expression, spoken (accent) and written language, and in the racist prejudices of *papalagi* students and teachers.

Conclusion

Highlighting these issues at this conference, and in the preparation of this paper, has been most beneficial and positive personally. I therefore express the hope that it has given you 'pause', however brief, in the consideration of our common task of making our Divinely created and beautiful world safe and prosperous and peaceful, by accepting the responsibility of putting the young of our societies as the first consideration. The realisation and acceptance that children have rights are important, stressing the one right that I am claiming for the Samoan Child: *The right to life and survival no matter how conceived.*

Victims of tokenism and hypocrisy: New Zealand's failure to implement the United Nations Convention on the Rights of the Child

Robert Ludbrook

Mankind owes to the child the best it has to give. (Preamble to the Declaration of the Rights of the Child, 1959)

Politicians, eager to be seen as child friendly, have often paid lip service to the well-being of children. But at the end of the day children have usually been let down. *In the power game other interests have been stronger. Children have always been, and still are, the victims of hypocrisy.* (Thomas Hammarberg, Member of the United Nations Committee on the Rights of the Child)

Abstract

This paper looks at the New Zealand government's response to the United Nations Convention on the Rights of the Child (UNCROC). It examines steps taken before and after ratification and concludes that New Zealand's approach to the Convention demonstrates a fundamental error. While the New Zealand government has paid lip service to UNCROC and its principles, it has failed in its basic obligations under the Convention. In reporting to international agencies, New Zealand has attempted to disguise its failure by resorting to untruths, half-truths, evasions and diplomatic obfuscation. Its approach to UNCROC has been one of tokenism and hypocrisy. Children are the victims.

The World Summit for Children (1990)

On 30 September 1990 the then New Zealand Minister of Social Welfare joined the President of the United States and many of the world's political leaders at the United Nations in New York for a World Summit for Children. The assembled world leaders signed their names to a *World Declaration on the Survival, Protection and Development of Children in the 1990s* (the *World Declaration*). The signatories acknowledged that the well-being of children required political action at the highest level and expressed their determination to take such action (United Nations, 1990, para. 18). Each country made a solemn commitment 'to give high priority to the rights of children: to their survival, their protection, and their development' (para. 19).

The World Summit adopted the principle of 'First Call for Children' agreeing that, when resources are limited, children should have first claim on available resources. This principle is a restatement of the principle from the United Nations Declaration on the Rights of the Child 1959, quoted above.

United Nations Convention on the Rights of the Child (1989)

After ten years of meetings and discussions, the General Assembly of the United Nations adopted the Convention on the Rights of the Child (UNCROC) in November 1989. New Zealand had been represented at meetings in Geneva where the wording of the Convention was debated and refined, and the government was fully informed of progress with UNCROC.

Before the General Assembly adopted UNCROC, New Zealand's Ministry of External Relations and Trade (MERT) had circulated copies of the final draft to lead government agencies inviting comment on the text (MERT, 1989). In February 1990 MERT sent a copy of the final text of UNCROC to these government agencies asking them to look at those provisions relevant to their work and assess whether any legislative changes would be necessary to ensure compliance (MERT, 1990). It was MERT's proclaimed policy to ratify international human rights instruments only if satisfied that New Zealand complied at the time of ratification. Most government agencies approached were slow to respond, and those that did reply provided little information about steps taken to assess whether laws in their area of responsibility complied with UNCROC. The Department of Social Welfare took three years to respond and then merely sent a ten-line fax saying that it saw no difficulties in ratification (Social Policy Agency, 1993). The Labour Department took eighteen months to send a detailed response opposing ratification on the grounds that, as a result of recent policy decisions, New Zealand employment legislation did not comply (Secretary of Labour, 1991). The Justice Department identified non-compliance in respect of adoption law and the mixing of adults and children in prisons. The Human Rights Commission provided a detailed response within three months pointing to a number of areas in which New Zealand law did not comply, including corporal punishment in home and schools, school expulsion procedures, lack of religious freedom for children in prisons and the minimum age for joining the armed forces. Inexplicably the Commissioner for Children was not consulted in relation to ratification, an omission pointed out to MERT by the Department of Health in 1993 (Department of Health, 1993).

New Zealand's ratification of the convention

New Zealand ratified UNCROC on 13 March 1993 binding the government to:

- *Respect and ensure the rights set forth in the Convention to each child within their jurisdiction without discrimination of any kind* (Article 2). Commentaries on UNCROC stress that 'to respect' means 'to refrain from any actions which would violate any of the rights' and 'ensure' implies an affirmative obligation to take whatever measures are necessary to enable individual children to enjoy and exercise their Convention rights (Alston, 1991).

- *Undertake all appropriate legislative, administrative and other measures for the implementation of the rights recognised in the convention* (Article 4). The Committee on the Rights of the Child has emphasised the particular importance that all domestic legislation be compatible with the Convention and that there is coordination of policy within and between all levels of government (UN Committee on the Rights of the Child, 1989, para. 12).
- *Submit regular reports to the Committee on the Rights of the Child on measures adopted to give effect to the rights set out in UNCROC and on progress made in the enjoyment by children of those rights* (Article 44.1). Such reports must indicate any factors affecting fulfilment of Convention obligations and must contain sufficient information to enable the Committee to have a comprehensive understanding of the reporting country's implementation of the Convention (UN Committee on the Rights of the Child, 1989, para. 6) .

UNCROC is more than a mission statement or statement of ideals. It moves on from the United Nations Declaration on the Rights of the Child (1959) which was a bare statement of rights with no monitoring mechanism and no means by which countries could make a formal commitment to give practical effect to its rights and principles.

The intention is that parties to UNCROC should progressively bring their laws, policies and practices into line with the Convention. Ratification is not intended to give countries an international badge of approval. It involves a commitment by governments to implement the principles of UNCROC and to ensure to each child within their boundaries the rights set forth in the Convention. The performance of state parties is monitored by the United Nations Committee on the Rights of the Child (UNCRC) which, after considering reports submitted by a state party, can make observations as to that country's compliance and recommendations regarding areas of non-compliance. When a country files a periodic report it is required to detail what action has been taken in respect of any areas of concern identified and suggestions made by UNCRC when it considered that country's previous report.

It needs to be emphasised that ratification of UNCROC was never intended as a statement from the ratifying country that its laws, policies and practices were fully compliant; it was a commitment to take all necessary steps to achieve this goal. This is known as the policy of 'progressive implementation' (Hodgkin & Newell, 1998, p. 5).

UNCROC obliges each country to file an initial report two years after ratification and subsequent reports at five yearly intervals. It was expected that, before filing their first reports, ratifying countries would review their laws, policies and practices to identify any areas of non-conformity or doubtful conformity and, on the basis of this review, develop a plan of action indicating what measures were necessary to ensure full compliance and setting goals and a time frame for progress towards meeting these goals (UN Committee on the Rights of the Child, 1989, para. 5).

The unwarranted assumption of full conformity

The New Zealand government started from the premise that New Zealand laws, policies and practices were in full conformity with the principles of UNCROC except in the three areas where reservations were entered.[1] This presumption was demonstrably incorrect, yet it has been constantly repeated over the years (e.g. Ministry of Foreign Affairs, 1997) to the puzzlement of many New Zealanders who could point to hundreds of areas of non-compliance (see NGO Report, 1996).

Before ratification the Ministry of Foreign Affairs approached the Departments of Justice, Social Welfare, Education, Labour, Health and Te Puni Kokiri and also the Human Rights Commission, sending them a draft of the Convention, indicating that ratification was being considered and asking them whether they were aware of any legislation inconsistent with the principles of the Convention. The views of the Commissioner for Children, Youth Affairs, Women's Affairs or the many other government agencies whose activities and policies impact on children were not sought at this time. Only the Labour Department, Justice Department and the Human Rights Commission made a considered response. Only the Labour Department indicated that it had reviewed employment legislation and looked at whether legislative changes would be necessary to ensure compliance. The other government departments approached made no response to the request that they identify any areas of non-compliance. It is significant that pre-ratification inquiries by MERT referred only to *legislation* and made no reference to government policies or administrative practices. UNCROC places an obligation on governments not only to bring their *law* into conformity with the Convention but also to take all necessary administrative and other measures to achieve full conformity. MERT later claimed in a memo to the Social and Family Committee of Cabinet that it had 'conducted an extensive review with interested Departments of New Zealand law and policy to determine its compatibility with all the provisions of the Convention' and that this review had shown 'there are few areas of divergence' (MERT, 1992, para. 4). In fact, only the Labour Department had indicated to MERT that it had reviewed relevant laws. It had advised that New Zealand law was incompatible with the principles of the Convention.

The myth of full compliance at the time of ratification became, through repetition, part of the government's received wisdom and engendered a sense of self-satisfaction which has subsequently dogged New Zealand's approach to its obligations under UNCROC. If New Zealand was fully compliant on ratification, the argument goes, no government action was needed.

An allied myth is that, because in terms of social and economic development New Zealand is so far ahead of the majority of countries that had ratified UNCROC, it can rest on its laurels. This attitude smacks of cultural arrogance and misconceives the nature and purpose of UNCROC which is to encourage parties to set goals and make progress towards full implementation.[2]

New Zealand's steps towards meeting its obligations under UNCROC

The New Zealand government decided prior to ratification not to appoint a central agency to oversee the review of laws, policies and practices to identify areas of non-compliance and to develop a draft Plan of Action with goals and a time frame for progress towards compliance. New Zealand was not alone in this respect: neither the United Kingdom nor Australia appointed central agencies. But in the United Kingdom a non-governmental organisation, the Children's Rights Development Group, undertook in 1992–93 a comprehensive audit of the state of the country's children and the laws, policies and practices which affect them, and the National Children's and Youth Law Centre in Australia developed a 1996 Charter of Children's Rights based on the Convention.

The New Zealand government accepted an offer from the Ministry of Youth Affairs (MYA) to be the 'lead agency' with responsibility for drafting New Zealand's first report (Ministry of Youth Affairs, 1992). MYA is a small, stand-alone Ministry charged with giving policy advice to government in relation to young people and young adults within the age range of twelve to twenty-five years (Ministry of Youth Affairs, 1996). Children under twelve (two-thirds of those encompassed by UNCROC) were outside MYA's statutory responsibilities. But MYA had a youth focus, was a policy agency and was independent of the major government agencies providing services for children and was willing to undertake the task. The Minister of Youth Affairs has not always been a member of Cabinet and this has limited the Ministry's political influence.

The role of MYA in the implementation of UNCROC appears never to have been clearly defined. Certainly MYA was given the task of drafting New Zealand's first report. It is less clear that they were given or that they accepted the more important role of overseeing compliance with the principles of UNCROC. The Cabinet Committee, MYA and MERT all appear to have some role but none was given overall responsibility. The result has been a paper trail between the three agencies and virtual stagnation of the process of implementation.

New Zealand's failure to complete a national plan of action

Assisted by the Commissioner for Children, MYA made hesitant progress towards developing a National Plan of Action for Children as required by the undertaking given by New Zealand at the World Summit in 1990. A background report *Children in New Zealand in the 1990s: A Response to the World Summit for Children* was published in August 1995. The report contains background and statistical information about New Zealand's children, including detailed information on child health issues, education and New Zealand's foreign aid (Ministry of Youth Affairs, 1995).

The focus of the report is on the areas in which New Zealand has performed well and it lacks self-criticism. On the issue of infant mortality, the report records with apparent pride that New Zealand has one of the lowest rates of infant death in the world (eleventh in 1991) but fails to record that its standing had fallen from sixth in the OECD in 1960 or that it was falling seriously behind other OECD countries in reducing the rate of infant mortality (it had fallen to seventeenth by 1996) (Kirton, 1997). There is little analysis of the poor health record of Maori and Pacific Island children or their social disadvantages in terms of housing, income and unemployment. There is no reference to the fact that some 40 per cent of the annual health budget was spent in meeting the needs of people over sixty. The education section is silent about the large and growing number of children not receiving education as a result of suspension, expulsion or truancy. There is no reference to the serious problem of bullying in schools.

Children in New Zealand in the 1990s was intended as the first part of New Zealand's response to the World Summit and provides a useful snapshot of the state of New Zealand's children, commenting that they enjoy a favoured status compared with children in many other countries but admitting that New Zealand is not a paradise for children and acknowledging that there is much to be done to improve the lives of some children, particularly those in low income families. However, it does not identify specific areas on non-compliance with UNCROC and contains no proposals or time frame for action. It contains no survey of legislation affecting children nor any recommendations with regard to legislative changes needed to achieve compliance with UNCROC.

The Office of the Commissioner for Children (OCC) and Social Policy Agency (SPA) pointed out to MYA that the report did no more than provide background material and was not a Plan of Action (Office of the Commissioner for Children, 1996). In late 1995 and early 1996 there were discussions between the government agencies and the Commissioner for Children as to whether the National Plan of Action would be a stand alone document or would be grafted onto the background report. The task of drafting a Plan of Action was never allocated. The OCC and SPA reiterated the need for a National Plan of

Action but were told that the government's position was to proceed 'softly, softly' on the Plan (Meeting Notes, 1996). The two-stage plan lapsed after stage one.

Comprehensive national strategy for children

In addition to the National Plan of Action, New Zealand was obliged by reason of ratification of UNCROC to develop a comprehensive national strategy for children or national plan for children's rights with specific goals (UN Committee on the Rights of the Child, 1989, para. 17). As far as can be ascertained no effort has been made to develop any comprehensive national strategy. This failure to meet a fundamental requirement of UNCROC attracted critical comment from the Committee on the Rights of the Child (UNCRC, 1997) but even this polite reprimand failed to move the government to action.

The government has failed and continues to fail to prepare a National Plan of Action as required by the World Summit of 1990 or a comprehensive national strategy for children as required by UNCROC (which it ratified in 1993).

First report to the UN Committee on the Rights of the Child (October 1995)

New Zealand's first report was due in March 1995 and was filed in October 1995. In terms of timeliness New Zealand was well ahead of Australia whose report was filed more than two years late.

In preparing its first report, the government had the advantage of detailed guidelines developed by CRC. It has also had the opportunity to consider the Committee's observations on the first reports of other developed countries – in particular Canada and the United Kingdom. A common theme in these observations is the importance of an examination of laws, policies and practices to ensure that these are fully compatible with UNCROC and the need for an overarching policy for children and a plan of action. New Zealand's first report is nearly a hundred pages in length and clearly involved a lot of work gathering and recording information about the state of New Zealand's children. It is seriously deficient as:

- the report makes the false claim that New Zealand ratified the Convention after completing a comprehensive review of existing legislation and policy and that New Zealand law and practice were found to be in full compliance. As discussed earlier, the pre-ratification review was superficial and selective. It covered only laws, not policies or practices. Only a few government departments were approached and only one indicated that they had made any effort to review legislation to assess compliance with UNCROC.
- the report deftly avoids any reference to the failure to develop a global strategy for children or National Plan of Action. The official *Guidelines*

for Reports asks for details of 'any steps taken or envisaged to adopt a comprehensive national strategy for children in the framework of the Convention' (UN Committee on the Rights of the Child, *General Guidelines*, 1989, para 17).

- the report merely records that government departments have been advised of their Convention obligations. This minimalist stance might better be described as a Plan of Inaction.
- in its introductory statement to CRC, the government delegation gave emphasis to the fact that the Human Rights Commission was reviewing all laws, government policies and practices to assess whether they were consistent with the Human Rights Act. This was proffered to CRC as an imminent, if belated, review of laws, policies and practices as required by UNCROC. It missed the point that the HRC Consistency 2000 review required by the Human Rights Act [s5 (l) (I) e (j)] related only to human rights obligations under the Human Rights Act and not to obligations under international human rights instruments such as UNCROC. The CRC was quick to pick this up, urging that the HRC review be extended to cover a review of compliance with UNCROC. Less than six months later the government, against the advice of the HRC, abandoned the Consistency 2000 Review.[3]
- the report strains to give a self-congratulatory rather than a self-critical review of the state of New Zealand's children. There are many excellent policies and programmes in New Zealand which justify a degree of pride. But UNCROC has a remedial purpose intended to bring international pressure to bear on countries to look at their laws and policies and to change any which are harming children.
- the report engages in selective reporting, highlighting worthy policies and achievements but remaining silent about failures to comply with UNCROC.
- the report smacks of hypocrisy in that it boasts that 'New Zealand is fully committed to upholding the Convention and takes very seriously the obligations assumed on ratification' (p. 6, para. 7) yet conceals that the government has not even started on the processes essential to compliance.

There is space for only three examples:

- the report is expansive about the positive features of the Children, Young Persons and their Families Act but fails to draw attention to the exclusion of seventeen-year-olds from the special rights and protections which it gives to younger children. The child protection and youth justice provisions in the CYPF Act apply only to children under the age of seventeen. The UNCROC definition of a child includes seventeen-year-olds. The jurisdiction of the Commissioner for Children is similarly restricted to under-seventeens. The report also fails to mention that when children are sent to the District Court or the High Court for sentence, these courts are not bound by the principles of the CYPF Act.

- the report fails to acknowledge the widespread breaches of Article 12 in New Zealand's education system. One such breach was pointed out by the Human Rights Commission prior to ratification. A post-ratification amendment to the Education Act allowed adult members of school boards of trustees to decide not to have a student representative on the Board and more than 40 per cent of boards of trustees have no student representative.
- the report refers to the Human Rights Act which makes it unlawful to discriminate on the grounds of a person's age but significantly fails to disclose that the age discrimination provisions do not apply to under-sixteens. The Act discriminates against the majority of children by denying them the protection afforded to adults.

UN Committee's observations on New Zealand's report (January 1997)

The Committee is unfailingly polite and diplomatic in its observations and recommendations on reports submitted by ratifying countries. It has to take great care to avoid any suggestion that it is interfering in the domestic affairs of a sovereign state. Obviously many countries are hard-pressed to find the resources to provide for the health, safety and well-being of children but that does not authorise more affluent countries to engage in self-congratulation rather than self-examination. The Committee raised a number of concerns:

- the broad nature of New Zealand's reservations to UNCROC. In endorsing the Vienna Declaration, the New Zealand government undertook to review these reservations but has failed to do so;
- the lack of any Plan of Action or global policy in respect of children incorporating the principles of UNCROC;
- the failure to bring New Zealand's domestic law in line with UNCROC, particularly in relation to youth justice and employment law;
- the need for a comprehensive review of all government policy, administrative practice and legislation having an impact on children to assess compliance with UNCROC;
- the need for the office of the Commissioner for Children to be strengthened and to be given greater independence and for the commissioner to be made an officer of Parliament;
- the danger that, in delegating to non-governmental organisation delivery of support services to children and families, there may be a falling off of standards unless government continues to monitor and evaluate such services;
- the lack of effective co-ordination between government departments in developing policies and delivering services for children;
- the lack of disaggregated statistical data, especially specific information

about vulnerable groups and about complaints made by children;
- a concern at the lack of information as to the extent to which New Zealand's economic reforms have affected the support services available for children and families;
- a concern at the disadvantages suffered by the growing number of children being brought up in single parent families;
- a serious concern about the high rate of youth suicide in New Zealand;
- a concern at the disadvantaged situation of Maori children reflecting the need for special measures aimed at protecting and promoting their rights;
- the lack of adequate support services for refugees and asylum seekers;
- the lack of a comprehensive policy to deal with youth employment and minimum ages for entering certain types of employment;
- a concern that s59 of the Crimes Act allows parents and carers to use corporal punishment as a means of parental discipline.

The CRC makes a series of practical recommendations for government action to address the areas of non-compliance identified in the report.

Government's response to the Committee's recommendations (1997-99)

The Committee's observations and recommendations attracted much publicity. The Minister of Youth Affairs commented that 'the process of having experts critique New Zealand's performance is a helpful mechanism in the on-going process of refining policies and programmes for children' and accepted that 'the Committee had identified some important areas that require attention' (MYA, 1997). Richard Prebble, leader of the ACT party, mounted a churlish and ill-informed attack against the Committee saying that they knew nothing about New Zealand's children and claiming its members were overpaid diplomats, many of them from dictatorships (Government Response, 1997).

One might have anticipated that the government would have seen the CRC report as a polite rebuke for its lack of progress in meeting its Convention obligations and would have galvanised it into giving priority to the task of addressing the failures identified by CRC. That was not to be. The matter was brought before the Cabinet committee on Health and Social Policy in May 1997 by the Minister of Foreign Affairs and the Minister of Youth Affairs (Government Response, 1997). The joint paper made no proposals for meeting CRC's criticisms but saw a need to assess areas of non-compliance. It proposed that MYA carry out the necessary assessment and report progress to the Cabinet Committee by 30 June 1998. One can be forgiven for asking why it was necessary for MYA to embark on a year-long assessment of areas of non-compliance when these had been clearly pointed out to the New Zealand government by CRC. Surely the need was for recommendations to Cabinet and to the relevant Ministers on what changes in law, policy and practice were needed to meet the CRC's criticisms. In June 1997, MYA arranged meetings in Wellington and Auckland and, when pressed in relation to the National Plan of Action, replied that there might not be a need for a National Plan because government departments would anyway be taking the necessary actions identified in any National Plan. The message that the government should be trusted to do whatever was necessary to meet its Convention obligations was not well received at these meetings.

By the June 1998 deadline, MYA made a 'progress report'. For reasons that are unexplained the report was not to the Cabinet Committee but to the Ministers of Foreign Affairs, Social Welfare and Maori Affairs. Somehow Cabinet seems to have dropped out of the loop. Any evidence of progress is conspicuously lacking. The report's key message was that preliminary work had begun on considering the fit between the concerns of the UN Committee and current policy initiatives. No detail is given about the 'preliminary work' nor any explanation why, a year on from the first report, MYA had done only 'preliminary work'. MYA agreed to make a further progress report by 30 June 1999 to the three ministers. In this second report, MYA has noticeably (and unexplainedly) shifted its focus from assessing areas of non-compliance towards planning for New Zealand's second report due in 2000. The impression is that any attempt to develop a National Plan or comprehensive strategic plan for children had been abandoned, as had any effort to address the other areas of concern raised by CRC. The second progress report avoids any reference to a National Plan of Action. It is silent about the CRC's strong recommendation that New Zealand review its reservations to the Convention. It proposes that MYA, in consultation with other government agencies, will continue analysing the recommendations of CRC and will file a third report to the Ministers (not Cabinet) by 30 June 2000 – a classic case of 'paralysis by analysis'?

The June 1999 report from MYA shows that (after two-and-a-half years) it is still analysing the recommendations of CRC. The only explanation for the lack of progress is that, because of an oversight, the work projects were not picked up in their work programme.

The recommendations of CRC are quite specific and implementation requires political will, not a seemingly interminable process of assessment and analysis. The New Zealand government's attitude to the CRC's observations can be characterised as one of deliberate inaction. There is no evidence that the criticisms and recommendations have been taken seriously or that government at Cabinet level or individual Ministers have ever considered what is needed to meet the obligations undertaken on ratification of UNCROC. This failure compounds the earlier failure to develop a National Plan of Action as agreed at the World Summit.

One can only speculate as to the government's reasons for taking its obligations so lightly. Its inaction is clearly deliberate and can probably be ascribed to a belief that it is improper for international human rights bodies to seek to influence policies of democratically elected governments. The New Zealand government is obviously aware that it is likely to face criticism domestically and from the international community if it continues to defy the urgings of the United Nations committee appointed to monitor compliance with UNCROC. To deflect domestic criticism, the June 1998 progress report proposes a Communication Strategy to promote the government's approach to implementation and to help ensure consistent messages to NGOs. Is this another example of the view that when you are in trouble you bring in the spin doctors and public relations consultants?

Judging from the reports referred to above, the government is more intent on providing excuses for non-compliance with UNCROC than in ensuring changes which are plainly necessary for compliance. These excuses include the lame comment that the performance of other industrialised countries has also been criticised by CRC, the repeated assurance that the government takes seriously its commitment to the rights and well-being of children, and the circular argument that preparation of the second report due in 2000 is a form of self-review of New Zealand's compliance.

Government actions inconsistent with UNCROC (1997–99)

Some government actions or initiatives since 1997 show a continuing disregard of the Convention in government policy-making and legislative initiatives. Some examples:

- The government aborted the Human Rights Commissions Consistency 2000 review which had earned praise from the CRC and would have ensured partial compliance with its obligation to review laws, policies and practices to assess their compatibility with UNCROC.
- The government consistently opposed moves to give the Commissioner for Children independence from the Department of Social Welfare, despite recommendations of the Mason Committee Review of the CYPF Act (Report of the Ministerial Review Team, Department of Social Welfare, 1992) and a recommendation of CRC (UN Committee on the Rights of the Child, 1997, para. 24) to this effect. It voted against private member's Bills in 1998 and 1999 intended to give the Commissioner greater independence.
- The government, when considering amendments to education legislation in 1998, refused to accept a series of amendments proposed by the Commissioner for Children which would have assured to school students rights established by UNCROC. The government for years neglected to take action to reduce the number of students denied their right to education as a result of exclusion from state schools.

- The government introduced in 1997 new Residential Care Regulations with draconian new search and seizure powers in respect of children in residential care (including children deemed to be in need of care and protection). These were in July 1997 criticised by the Parliamentary Regulations Review Committee which urged that if they were to be retained, they be introduced urgently in the form of a Bill so that they could be debated in Parliament and considered by a select committee. The government agreed but no Bill was introduced.
- The government in 1999 set up a working party to consider whether the age of criminal responsibility should be lowered (Inter-departmental Working Group to review Youth Court jurisdiction and sentencing 199899) thus bringing younger children into the criminal justice system.
- The government has failed to stem the decline in rates of immunisation of New Zealand children which have been reducing alarmingly.[4]

The New Zealand government appeared to be content to leave it to government departments to make any changes necessary to attain compliance with UNCROC. This is not enough. Government through Cabinet must monitor actions taken by government agencies. Two basic principles 'First call for children' and 'Progressive implementation of the Convention' provide signposts to the way ahead. The journey towards full implementation will not be easy but UNCROC requires New Zealand to take the first steps on the journey without further delay.

New Zealand's first report under Vienna Declaration (1998)

Obligations assumed by New Zealand under the Vienna Declaration and Programme of Action in June 1993 include a commitment to the effective implementation of the principles of UNCROC by all necessary legislative, administrative and other measures and the allocation of the maximum extent of available resources. Under the Vienna Declaration countries are required to report every five years. In its first report in 1998 New Zealand had to identify major obstacles to full implementation. The report states:

> ... New Zealand has made its initial report, to the Committee on the Rights of the Child, on implementation of the 1989 Convention. *This process was valuable in initiating a dialogue on matters of implementation and on conditions affecting children in New Zealand* on which the Committee issued some valuable observations which will further be addressed in New Zealand's next report. (New Zealand Report, 1998, p. 8). [Italics added.]

There is no reference in the report to the lack of any National Plan or comprehensive strategy for children (as required by the World Summit and UNCROC), to the criticisms and recommendations of the CRC or on the progress or lack of progress towards meeting these. On any interpretation, these must be seen as major obstacles to full implementation of UNCROC. The small section of the report headed 'Rights of Children' deals mainly with New Zealand's work in respect of international measures against child prostitution and child pornography. Reference to New Zealand's failure to meet fundamental obligations under UNCROC cannot have been overlooked through inadvertence. The Commissioner for Children referred explicitly to these when consulted by the Ministry of Foreign Affairs in January 1998 (Commissioner for Children, 1998).

Perhaps the most surprising aspect of the italicised passage above is that it trivialises the role of the CRC, reducing it almost to the level of a friendly chat over a cup of tea. In fact, New Zealand's delegation was asked to answer a series of probing questions which exposed many of the deficiencies in New Zealand's report and in this country's performance.

Summary

New Zealand is a comparatively affluent society blessed with a fine natural environment and pleasant climate. This country has pioneered many child-friendly and innovative social policies. There is a widespread perception that over the last ten years or so government economic and social policies have had a particularly harmful impact on many aspects of the lives of children. The United Nations Committee picked up these concerns and urged the New Zealand government to measure the impact of the economic reform process on this country's children. The Committee also urged that we gather much more sophisticated statistics so we can judge the impact of social policies on vulnerable and disadvantaged groups of children and can build up a profile of the sorts of issues that children complain about when given access to grievance procedures.

UNCROC has always been seen as the starting point for a programme of action which will refocus government policy by giving priority to the rights and needs of children and which will encourage governments to work towards progressive implementation of the Convention. In April 1999 a member of the New Zealand delegation at the Commission of Human Rights in Geneva in speaking of the near-universal acceptance of UNCROC commented that the real measure of success, however, is whether the Convention has brought about improvement in the everyday lives of children – in their homes, at school, in the workplace, the playground and the larger community – and she stressed the importance of a strong focus on the full implementation of the Convention (Geels, 1999). She failed to inform the Assembly of New Zealand's failure to review its existing laws, policies and practices or to develop a Plan of Action or global policy for improving the position of New Zealand children. Nor was there any mention of the lack of any government action to redress the failings identified by CRC.

Since it ratified UNCROC in March 1993, the New Zealand government has failed in its baseline obligations and has consequently not started on the process of self-review and forward planning which is basic to the commitment made on ratification. Despite the polite but firm reminder given by CRC in 1997 the government fails to address the fundamental requirements of UNCROC. It may be that it is official government policy to go 'softly, softly' on implementation of the UNCROC or it may be that the process of moving towards compliance has become bogged down in a miasma of bureaucratic inertia and a lack of any centralised responsibility. Six years after ratification, the New Zealand government has not taken the first steps towards compliance with UNCROC.

In the light of the inertia, evasiveness and diplomatic obfuscation on the part of the government it is time for non-government organisations to remind the government of its obligations and to ensure that the true facts are placed before the international community. There will be opportunities for the non-government sector to submit parallel reports to the United Nations both under the International Covenant on Civil and Political Rights (due this year) and UNCROC (due in March 2000).

The government must take heed of the likely damage to its international standing if it continues its minimalist approach to its Convention obligations. It must act and it must act now. It should seek the support of the Commissioner for Children and a range of non-government organisations to develop a draft National Plan of Action or global policy for children. A programme for consultation on the draft involving children and non-government organisations should be established. Only by taking this action can the government ensure that by the time it files its second report under UNCROC it has taken seriously its obligations in international law.

Until these baseline actions are completed there will be no progress. The Convention on the Rights of the Child will remain 'rights on paper', an empty mission statement, a dead letter, a false promise to the nation's children.

Conclusion

It would be hard for the government to point to any change since ratification of UNCROC which can be demonstrated to have enhanced the rights and interests of children in this country as well as giving practical effect to the principles of UNCROC. On the other hand, there are many examples of the rights of children being ignored, overridden or diminished as a result of government action or inaction. New Zealand's children are victims of tokenism and hypocrisy.

References

Alston, P. (1991). The legal framework of the Convention on the Rights of the Child. In *Bulletin of Human Rights* 91/2.

Commissioner for Children. (1998). *Submissions on Education Legislation Amendment Bill 1997* 5/2/98.

Department of Health. (1993). Letter to MERT, dated 3/2/93.

Department of Social Welfare. (1992). *Review of the Children, Young Persons and their Families Act 1989.* Dated February 1992.

Geels, D. (1999). Statement by Deborah Geels, Observer Delegation of New Zealand 55th Session of Commission on Human Rights, dated 14/4/99.

Government Response. (1997). Response to Report on U.N. Committee on the Rights of the Child's *Concluding Observations in Respect of New Zealand:* dated June 1997.

Hodgkin, R., & Newell, P. (1998). *Implementation handbook for the convention on the rights of the child.* New York: UNICEF.

Human Rights Commission. (1998). *Consistency 2000.* Wellington: Human Rights Commission.

Kirton, N. (1997). Opening address at National Child Health Summit. The Future for Child Health 14/7/97, Wellington.

Meeting Notes. (1996). Meeting on 29 /5/96 between senior officers of MYA, SPA and OCC.

MERT. (1989). Memo 701/7/6 dated 13/2/89.

MERT. (1990). Memo 701/7/6 dated 28/2/90.

MERT. (1992). Memo SOC (92) 55 dated 30/11/92 to Cabinet Social and Family Committee.

Ministry of Foreign Affairs. (1997). *Introductory statement by CEO of Ministry of Foreign Affairs,* Catherine Gibson to the Committee on the Rights of the Child dated 20/1/97.

Ministry of Youth Affairs. (1992). Handwritten Fax to MERT dated 3/2/92.

Ministry of Youth Affairs. (1995). *Children in New Zealand in the 1990s: A response to the World Summit for Children.* Wellington: Ministry of Youth Affairs.

Ministry of Youth Affairs. (1996). *Briefing to the incoming government.* Wellington: Ministry of Youth Affairs.

Ministry of Youth Affairs. (1997). Press Release 25/1/97.

New Zealand Report. (1998). *New Zealand report for the 1998 five-year implementation review of the Vienna declaration and plan of action.*

NZ jeopardises world child health goal. (1999, June 7). *The New Zealand Herald.*

NGO Initial Report under UNCROC. (1996). *Action for Children Aotearoa.*

Office of Commissioner for Children. (1996). Letter to MYA, dated 22/5/96.

Polio an ever-present threat and Whooping Cough revival predicted. (1999, July 19). *The New Zealand Herald.*

Secretary of Labour. (1991). Letter to MERT 9/9/91.

Social Policy Agency. (1993). Fax to MERT 3/2/93.

United Nations. (1959). *Declaration of the Rights of the Child.*

United Nations. (1990). *World Declaration on the Survival, Protection and Development of Children.* United Nations, New York, dated 30/9/90.

United Nations Committee on the Rights of the Child. (1989). *Guidelines for initial reports* CRC/C/5 paras 9-11; *General guidelines regarding the form and contents of periodic reports to be submitted by states parties under Article 44.1(b) of the Convention* CRC/C/58 11/10/96.

United Nations Committee on the Rights of the Child. (1997). *Concluding observations of the Committee on the Rights of the Child re the initial report of New Zealand,* CRC/C/15/ADD.71., 24 January 1997.

Notes

1 Preserving the right of the government to treat people differently according to their immigration status; reserving the right not to pass further laws nor take additional measures to protect children from harm, injury or exploitation in employment; reserving the right not to separate children deprived of their liberty from adults where there is a shortage of suitable facilities or it is considered to be for the benefit of the child.

2 Article 4 of UNCROC recognises that in the case of economic, social and cultural rights some countries may be limited in their ability to achieve full compliance by their lack of resources but no such limitation is recognised in relation to civil and political rights. There is nothing in UNCROC which suggests that economically developed countries have lesser responsibilities in meeting their obligations under the Convention.

3 Cabinet made a decision to abandon Consistency 2000 on 16 June 1997 and introduced legislation for this purpose on 19 August 1998 but was unable to get Parliamentary Support to pass the legislation. The Human Rights Commission published a partial report *Consistency 2000* 31/12/98 on work completed prior to abandonment but this contains no review of laws, policies or practices which breach UNCROC (Human Rights Commission, 1998).

4 New Zealand has slipped in its rate of immunisation for whooping cough, measles, mumps, rubella, hepatitis B, polio, diptheria, tetanus and Hib-type influenza (*Polio*, 1999).

The sociology of childhood: Children's autonomy and participation rights

BERRY MAYALL

Abstract

This paper first discusses why it is appropriate to reconsider models of children and of childhood, and how to do it. In particular the contributions of a sociology of childhood to shifting ideas about children and childhood are considered. Using frameworks for theoretical development devised by feminists, the paper considers how we may move on theoretically. It then draws on recent research with children conducted by the author to show how children themselves understand the social condition of childhood in the context of child-adult relationships. Children's understandings of interdependence (rather than autonomy) as a key value in life, and their emphasis on their provision, protection and participation rights are discussed.

The problem – why and how to rethink childhood

Why rethink childhood?

Just to set the scene, I will make my main point first. A summary: children's welfare has been inextricably woven into women's welfare and women's social condition. And women-and-children – hyphened, a composite noun – have become in the twentieth century the object of scrutiny, surveillance and intervention by ever-increasing numbers and types of professionals. There are a lot of us here today. But no children. It is hard to peer through the tangle of adults surrounding children and pronouncing on their needs, and to look clearly at children themselves. It is still more difficult to listen to children seriously, and yet more difficult to include children into society rather than excluding them. But this is what we must now do: extricate children, conceptually, from parents, the family and professionals. Study the social condition of childhood and write children into the script of the social order. Why must we do this? Because children, like other minority groups, lack a voice and have a right to be heard and their views taken into account. And because proper understanding of the social order requires consideration of all its members.

Let us start at the beginning of this problematic century, with one event in Europe. In 1900 the Swedish reformer Ellen Key wrote a powerfully polemical and eugenicist book, *The Century of the Child*, in which she argued that responsibility for children's health and welfare lay in the hands of women. Women must realise that:

> … the transformation of society begins with the unborn child, with the conditions for its coming into existence, its physical and psychical training. It must be the general conviction that the new instincts, the new feelings, the new thoughts, the new ideas, which mothers and fathers pass on into the flesh and blood of their children, will transform existence (Key, 1909, p. 100).

Women's central function was motherhood. They should be freed from patriarchal marriage arrangements, should promote their own health and should be free to choose a man fit enough to father healthy children. Healthy, happy adult relationships rather than marriage per se should be the basis for child-bearing and child-rearing. A mother should be paid by the state to stay at home with her children as their first educator, until they were ten. Children's daily lives in spacious natural surroundings should include Rousseau-esque explorations as well as social training. Ellen Key thus managed to offend the patriarchs, to infuriate the women's movement and to challenge the scholarisation of childhood. In the furore that followed the book's publication, Ellen Key fled Sweden. (She came back, though, and became not a mother but a matriarchal figure – holding court to radicals and artists in her beautiful house by a lake.)

Some of the reforms – or changes – she argued for have come about, in some countries. Some women are freer to choose partners than before; and some mothers (and a few fathers) are paid to stay at home – but only with very young children. In some countries, mothers' care of their children – as ever the key to children's welfare – has been backed by policies to decrease poverty and by the development of universalist child health services. Whilst many countries lack the resources to improve child health, there is general recognition of the crucial contributions made by mothers. But in critical respects Ellen Key's vision has not been fulfilled:

> Instead of the century of the child we got the century of child professionals (Stafseng, 1993, p. 77).

Indeed we might like to discuss what the century of the child might have looked like. But instead children and childhood have become the object of massive interventions. Whole armies of educators, health experts, psychologists and social workers work to modify childhood. The concept of children's needs – derived from professionals' concepts, assumptions, priorities and goals – justifies programmes of education, including the education of mothers, health promotion and social work practice (Woodhead, 1997). The perceived 'need' to monitor children's development has led to unprecedented surveillance of children – both at school and at home; in some Western societies children are virtually excluded as independent actors from public spaces. In most northern European countries, the scholarisation of childhood is well advanced; children attend nurseries, then school, then college. Childhood gets longer and longer; at one point in Mrs Thatcher's Britain, people up to age twenty-five were defined as dependants of their parents (in order to release the state from the obligation to support them). The concept of adolescence (itself an adult construction, and not a term used by young people themselves) extends beyond childhood the idea that young people are becomings, rather than people (Erikson, 1965). The insulting suggestion that a large social group of people are not people, but merely in process, has led to a pointed riposte:

> If young people are called adolescents, then the rest of us should be called mortescents (R. Frankenberg, personal communication).

In Britain, where health and psychological professionals have long aimed to modify mothers' behaviour (but not fathers' – why not? we should ask), we now have another increasingly influential set of professionals telling mothers what to do: education experts. Nowadays, mothers are meant to attend 'parenting classes'; to work with their children on literacy and numeracy; to supervise homework; and to promise to co-operate with the school to maximise their children's performance in nationally devised tests. Children not only attend school all day, but are increasingly encouraged to study in after-school centres; at younger and younger ages they are required to do homework.

Why is any of this problematic? Or to put it another way, why have I been asked to come and talk about the sociology of childhood? Why do I wish to argue that psychological knowledge is relevant but not sufficient? Why should we come at children and childhood from a new set of perspectives? I think there are two major points to be made here. And, as is the way with major points, they are interlinked.

In the first place, we have to be clear that childhood is a political issue. Theories about what children need, about how they develop and what input from adults is therefore appropriate, are indeed theories or stories (rather than facts) and practices that derive exclusively from adult perspectives. They derive from adults' study of children, contextualised and structured by adults' social and economic goals in specific societies. Yet in the name of 'scientific' formulas about child development and children's needs we separate childhood off from politics; we propose, conceptually, that children and childhood operate in an apolitical space.

In the second place – an interlinked point – in defining children as inferior, as objects essentially of adult socialisation, we depersonalise children. In proposing that we know best the best interests of the child, we deny children's rights. We deny children the right to participate in the structuring of their childhoods. Though we may work to protect children and provide for them, we find it much harder to take children seriously as contributors to social thinking and social policies.

You will note I say 'we' because it is critical to draw attention to us as an adult social group in contradistinction to children as a social group. Ask children how they understand and experience childhood (as I have) and you will find that they divide the social order into two separate (and somewhat opposing) social groups: children and adults. Children are those whom adults have defined as non-adults.

Why is it difficult to rethink childhood?

Rethinking children and rethinking childhood is difficult. Firstly, because there is a large and powerful body of knowledge on child development and socialisation. We must here pay tribute to the massive accumulation of knowledge assembled over the last century by Western psychologists and doctors. Piaget and Talcott Parsons are key figures (Jenks, 1996). In public and private spheres, probably we (we adults) are more accurately informed than ever before about children's development. The experiential knowledge of nineteenth century novelists gave us some first accounts; for instance, in England, the insights of Charles Dickens and George Eliot about the sensitivities and perceptions of children have later been substantiated and given theoretical underpinning through psychologists' work. The characters of David Copperfield and Maggie Tulliver reflect Dickens' and Eliot's own experiences of childhood, vividly recalled and still speaking to us today.

You could say that the child development industry has cornered the market in knowledge about children. Lawyers, doctors, social workers, educationalists and academics depend on child development theory as a basis for their work on, for and with children. They do so because it has high status, and by so doing they raise its status further. Cornering the market carries dangers of monopolisation. Don't we, at the least, need some complementary ideas about children to balance the insights psychology has provided? Not so much competition, rather complement.

One example here shows the problematics of developmentalism applied globally: how this one discipline dominates the world stage (see Boyden, 1990) and how its assumptions derive from Western ideas about what it is to be a person. As many people have noted (e.g. Stephens, 1995), the UN Convention on the Rights of the Child is itself contextualised in the concepts of dominant Western cultures. The Convention refers to a universal, free-standing, individual child, a child who is on a particular developmental trajectory. It implies that biologically-based relations between parents and children are more fundamental and natural than other sorts of family or community relations. In aiming to limit and regulate child labour, it questions the values of social worlds where children's lives are intricately involved with adult working lives, and where children's contributions to household economies are essential to life, as well as enabling children to participate in schooling (Woodhead, 1998).

The very solidity of knowledge structures itself makes it difficult to move forward. A professor of education (he was trained as a psychologist) at my place of work once asked me, 'Why do we need a sociology of childhood? Psychology already gives us a perfectly adequate set of approaches to children and childhood.' Well, as I shall try to show, we do need a sociology of childhood in order to draw attention to certain neglected features of childhood, to right children's wrongs and to provide a better account of how the social order works.

Secondly and more specifically, barriers to rethinking childhood also lie in the pleasing and reassuring vision of childhood that Western psychology proposes. The spaces and times of childhood are proposed as, ideally, protected from politics. Children are to be protected, in an apolitical arena of thought and practice. Just as women have been assigned to the private and the domestic, so we are taught to think of children as growing up there too, in a happy domain which enables them to develop, unmolested by the stresses of public life. Children therefore are presented to us as pre-people, outside the polity. And the kindergarten – where children grow and where they are grown – is emblematic of that attractive vision. Gardens, after all, offer both a natural environment where plants and people flourish, and a context for cultivation.

And thirdly, perhaps the greatest barrier to rethinking childhood is the set of labels we are taught to associate with the idea of childhood. To take a few terms applied to them – children are termed incompetent, unstable, credulous, unreliable, emotional. Whereas, as we know, adults are uniformly competent, stable, well informed, reliable and rational. All the more reason, then, for us reasoning adults to protect children in the kindergarten, until they reach the age of reason. And all the less reason to listen to their views. Durkheim (1922/1972) put the case succinctly:

> Education is the influence exercised by adult generations on those that are not yet ready for social life (p. 204).

Durkheim – though a sociologist – carries a good deal of responsibility for ensuring that the education industry has relied on psychological rather than on sociological knowledge as a basis for its work on children. To this day, mainstream sociologists assume as unproblematic the notion that children are to be understood merely as objects of socialisation at home and school, which will fit them to join society as adults (e.g. Giddens, 1997). Recent theoretical work on the fashionable sociology of the body, refers to children only as precursors to their adult status (Shilling, 1993; Turner, 1992).

Taking a basic step forward

However, through the recent pioneering work of a few scholars (Qvortrup, 1987, 1991; Qvortrup, Bardy, Sgritta & Wintersberger, 1994; James & Prout, 1990, 1997; Alanen, 1992), it has become clear that we need a fuller understanding of childhood than has been available till now. Essentially what has emerged is that study of children and childhood is a political enterprise, not a neutral scientific enterprise. To define children as incompetent, inadequate versions of adults, to individualise childhood and to propose childhood as politically neutral will not do. Further, to do so risks damaging children and childhood. Once you begin to look at the history of knowledge about children, you find yourself faced with political goals and interests. An example is linkages between intelligence testing and social goals. It was to suit the demands of the economy that children were to be sorted by intelligence levels and trained accordingly.

In my view, the basic step forward is to rescue children and childhood from a conceptual space which has commonly been regarded as apolitical (see Elshtain, 1981, especially Chapter 6, for discussion). It is to recognise interrelationships between knowledge and policy; it is to study children as a social group and childhood as a social phenomenon. The proper study of the social order has to include the social condition of childhood, and the contributions of children to it.

The sociological project is to work initially on the task of extracting children theoretically from the family in order to study their social positioning as a social group. A next step is to replace children in reciprocal relations with adults, and childhood with adulthood. Thus the sociological enterprise aims to locate the study of childhood in the study of societies. Cindy Kiro made these points in her keynote address with great force in discussing the social condition of Maori children and their families.

This enterprise requires reconsidering the division of labour between social groups. Traditional sociology, devised by nineteenth-century men, set up and reified two contrasting (and interlinked) dimensions of society: the public versus the private, and economy versus culture. Of course, in this scenario men occupied the public, economically productive spheres; women, naturally, occupied the private sphere and introduced their children to socially accepted norms and behaviours (that is, they socialised them into the local culture). But as women have pointed out, what women do at home is economically productive: it produces children – new people; and it provides the conditions through which family members are fit to go out to work. The private is not private – it intersects with the public. What happens to women and children at home is structured by public theories and policies, and what happens in the private domain affects the public domain. Indeed, the conceptual division of the social order into public and private, the economic and the cultural, begins to fall apart once you consider the work of women – and even more so now when you begin to consider the work of children.

What happens to children and childhood if we sociologise childhood?

How the sociology of childhood shifts adult understanding of children and childhood

The sociology of childhood has begun to shift adult understandings of what it is to be a child, and how this varies across time and across societies. On the one hand, the work is leading to greater respect for children and childhood; on the other hand, it is leading to fuller understanding of the wrongs suffered by children.

Taking children seriously as people leads to a shift in thinking. Firstly, children move from being objects of adult work, to being competent, contributing social actors. Secondly, at a broader level, when facing the age-old debates about agency and structure, we can consider the extent to which children may be regarded as agents intersecting with the structures surrounding their lives. This can mean considering how far children are effective in altering the conditions of their own childhoods. Thirdly, the idea that adult views are sufficient for defining children's needs has to give way to the understanding that children's own wishes and expressed needs are relevant to the construction and implementation of social policies and practices. So in all these respects, children gain in stature.

But the new knowledge arising from these new approaches to children and childhood also reveals the wrongs suffered by children, and the unacceptably poor condition of childhood itself. For when one studies children as a social group, in any society (that I know about) one is forced to recognise the subordination of that group in the social order. Childhood as social status is defined within the generational order as inferior to adulthood. How children live their childhoods looks heavily structured by what adults want of childhood. A case in point is schooling, where children's days are largely controlled by adult agendas. Furthermore, adults justify their control over children through a naturalisation of the condition of childhood: it is for the good of children that their school-days are as they are; if children do well at school, the argument goes, jobs, security and happiness lie ahead. (Currently in the UK, the increasingly instrumental policies pushed through by successive governments are leading to a backlash – in the name of more Rousseau-esque models of how childhood should be lived.)

Given this duality in our understandings of childhood, where children emerge as competent actors who are heavily controlled and subordinated, the rights of children become not only of crucial importance to the quality of childhood, but also problematic. For in order to honour children's participation rights we must establish the conditions in which they can be honoured. That is, as already stressed, we adults have to carry out the work of protecting children and providing for them so that they have a securely based arena within which they may participate in working through issues that affect them (Wintersberger, 1996).

The problematics lie in the control elements inherent in protection and provision – for if children are based in a controlled situation, then their ability to participate may be limited.

At the root of the dilemmas faced by adults and children when adults try to honour the three Ps (protection, provision, participation) are valuations of autonomy or of interdependence. Western philosophers from John Locke onwards through to John Stuart Mill have proposed the autonomous rational man as the ideal. Indeed the notion of competence has been regarded in liberal contract theory as a quality of the autonomous man, who is capable of deciding whether to opt into the social order, or social contract. He is a man who makes decisions for himself, in his own interests. These are points criticised by feminists, who note that the man in the ivory tower depends on other people to feed him and keep him clean, and even to keep him company (Grimshaw, 1986). As I shall describe later, children themselves respect the principle of interdependence in human relationships. John O'Neill has put it very well, in his proposal for a 'covenant society' (1994). In such a society, people respect the principle of reciprocity. This means recognition of civic obligation to each other; that recognition in turn affords us our ideas of our own moral worth. He identifies three kinds of obligation. The norm of reciprocity requires that we repay people on grounds of what they have done for us in the past. The 'no strangers' norm tells us that no-one must be excluded from obligation; the old, the young, female and male, are all part of a reciprocal society. And the norm of reciprocity between generations requires enactment of responsibility by children to parents as well as by parents to children. If we accept children's accounts and John O'Neill's formula, we can agree that his covenant society helps to do away with the notion of contracts and conflicts between autonomous individuals. This vision does away with competence as a precondition for participation. Then maybe children's rights to provision, protection and participation can be honoured within social relationships which recognise interdependence.

> In a covenant theory of the state and community it is recognised that gender, age, infirmity, health, intelligence and strength are the very element of moral and political life and require of us a judicious weighting of the moral contributions of both justice and care in dealing with one another (O'Neill, 1994, pp. 41-42).

How can we move on theoretically

I have given so far a brief sketch of where we are at in trying to rethink childhood as a social phenomenon. In the rest of this paper, I should like to do two things. The first is to suggest ways in which we can move on theoretically; and the second is to tell you briefly how children in a recent study see their social situation.

In my view, we can take lessons from the work of another subordinated group to help us understand the condition of childhood and how to amend it. Women over two centuries and with considerable force in the last thirty years have counterbalanced how men describe their social position with their own understandings (e.g. Smith, 1988). This work provides a model for thinking about childhood. Women have analysed their work as comprising four stages, and we can use these to think about childhood: (1) critique; (2) deconstruction; (3) the development of a defining concept; and (4) the development of a child standpoint.

The first step is a critique. We may consider where childhood is situated in dominant understandings. A key term here is family; children are familialised. Children's success is deemed to depend on what the family provides. They are the object of parental – mainly maternal – care. Children are also individualised. The child's development is seen as the product of individual relationships. Individualisation also implies problematisation. Given a normal loving mother and father children will develop normally. But in the absence of this, children are likely to develop abnormally. Maladjustment, pathological development, and so forth are common outcomes.

The second stage of study is deconstruction. Here we can provide an analysis of what underlies the social assignment of children to family, individualisation, and problematisation. A key consideration here is how a given society conceptualises the division of responsibility between the state and parents for child welfare and rearing. Thus in some socialist societies, the state takes a major share of responsibility for child welfare, for equalling out children's opportunities. Free schooling and health care are examples. In some societies, much more responsibility is assigned to parents. A linked issue is how far direct money transfers are made to children. Family poverty as fecklessness is one vision, government responsibility to finance children is another. A third kind of analysis might be of ideologies of manhood or citizenship. Thus an emphasis on the individual competitive man may account for policies on the family and education. If we had time here and if we could imagine it, we might think how a society which valued interdependence would structure schools (if indeed such a society had schools at all). Presumably somewhat differently from the institutions we are familiar with. What would area planning and housing look like if we favoured community responsibility for children and intergenerational reciprocal relationships? Then, it can be argued that childhood is commonly problematised: in a competitive, industrialised society, what are we to do with children? We can hide them away, work to make them conform, but these measures may lead to further problematising ideas – that children are either victims or threats.

The third stage in women's studies aims to arrive at a key defining concept. Just as gender helped people to understand women's relations to men, so generation can help us understand children's relationships with adults. Using the concept of generation we can both look at how things are now, and consider how they might be. Currently, the concept of generation shows us how adults regard themselves as different from and superior to children. Generation crossed with gender tells us how mother-child relations are structured. Mothers' own subordination in both private and public spheres is the basis for the mother as object of the psy complex in her childcare work (Donzelot, 1980), and as servant of the education system in the requirement that she work with and on her children to maximise their school success. In trying to improve children's lot, the concept of generation allows us to think how relationships between the generations might be improved.

The fourth stage in rethinking childhood, as in women's studies, is to develop a standpoint. Here we have to work on means of developing a child standpoint. Again, this means both recognising how things are and using children's understandings to help improve the condition of childhood. Paying attention to what children say in research contexts has become popular in some countries. Initial fears among researchers that children – being incompetent – would not be able to provide good data are being superseded with concerns that interpretation of what they say gives too much power to adults. In the last few years, adults have begun to recognise that children and young people can carry out their own research. Perhaps in years to come, it will be common for children to design their own research, and disseminate it, perhaps in partnership with adults, and as participants in intergenerational research.

In the last part of this paper, I should like to tell you how some London children understood and experienced their childhoods. Their views provide a commentary on many of the points made so far.

Lessons from empirical research

In my current study with nine-year-olds in London[1] I have been doing two things: discussing with them how they understand the social status of childhood, motherhood and fatherhood; and asking them to reflect on their daily lives. The fifty-seven children were situated in two school classes, one from each of two schools. The girls and boys make up a multi-ethnic, mixed social class sample. I note here briefly some of the key findings arising from what the children said. You may like to consider how far these children's accounts resonate with those of children you know.

Social positions

- Children regard parents as having ultimate responsibilities, mothers for childcare and fathers for resourcing the family.
- Children accept their low status vis-à-vis adults. They regard themselves as rightly subordinate to adults, one of whose responsibilities is to teach them moral standards.

Responsibility

Children enjoy their freedom from adult responsibility. But their accounts show they take or are delegated responsibility for housework, childcare and school work.

Free time

Children think they have a right to free time for play, for pursuing their own interests. But adult domination of time means they often have to argue for free time.

Negotiation

Children have to negotiate for free time, for goods and services, for adult time, for time with friends, for money, for transport. As subordinates, they are dependent on adult say-so. The principal person with whom they negotiate is their mother, who runs the household.

Apprenticeship

Children describe childhood as apprenticeship (among other things!). They identify the central tasks of childhood as comprising three components:

- becoming a good enough member of one's family and culture;
- working on the project of one's own life (including getting an education, building friendships, considering the future);
- negotiating with adults in order to carve out time for oneself and to resist adult demands.

Moral status

Children find that their moral status is dubious in the eyes of adults. Children are often not believed, often wrongly blamed. And they are not always accorded respect for their moral competence.

Moral agency

- Children understand themselves as people not as imperfect beings. Their accounts show that they operate as moral agents in constructing and reconstructing relationships with relatives and friends.
- Children's accounts indicate that they contribute to the division of labour in building and maintaining the social order of the home, in their work at school, in developing social lives in the neighbourhood.
- Children recognise the central importance of child-family relationships and the slightly lesser importance of child-child relations. They emphasise interdependence and reciprocity, rather than lonely autonomy, as central values.

The three Ps

Children think they have rights to protection and to provision (and on the whole their parents meet these rights). They also emphasise their participation rights, but find that these are not always respected. Parents only sometimes, and school staff hardly ever, respect their participation rights.

Conclusions

Over the last ten years, I have listened to children's accounts of childhood, child-adult relationships, and the rights and wrongs of children (Mayall, 1994a, 1994b, 1996; Mayall, Bendelow, Barker, Storey & Veltman, 1996; Kelley, Mayall & Hood, 1997). I think some major general points emerge from children's accounts.

Firstly, children think sociologically. They divide the social order into two groups of people: adults and those whom adults define as non-adults – that is, children. Children regard childhood as relational. That is, they see clearly that the character and quality of their childhoods is structured through their relationships with adults, and most importantly with parents and teachers.

Secondly, children subscribe to a paradox: they agree with adults that childhood is a period of life – an apprenticeship – when people are rightly subordinated to those with more experience and knowledge. Being protected by adults from absolute responsibilities is one kind of right children identify (Hughes, 1988). On the other hand, being an apprentice is only half the story of childhood. Children forcibly indicate that they are moral agents who carry out important activities, both in the structuring and progressing of their own lives, and in making and remaking relationships within the family and with friends.

Thirdly, and this is very disturbing, children are clear that their moral status, and in particular their participation rights, are constantly in question. Adult conceptualisations of children as incomplete people, and adult assumptions that their own agendas matter more than children's, lead to them downgrading children as moral agents. In turn, children's own subordination to adults leads them to adopt whatever tactics they can in order to assert their rights; these tactics, which include wheedling, lying, demanding, refusing, themselves reinforce adult prejudices. The fact that – in the UK – children are regarded as adult responsibilities in public places further serves to solidify adult views that children are moral incompetents.

Fourthly, children have important lessons for moral philosophers on issues of autonomy and interdependence. Whilst Western liberal thinkers (all of them men) have regarded the autonomous, independent moral agent as the highest form of life, children, like women, regard relationships as the cornerstone of their lives. It is of crucial importance to them to work with and through family relationships, to care about those who live elsewhere as well as those they live with. Children's accounts centre on such matters – on the health, well-being and problems of those they love. And of course the best thing about school is friends; for whilst the formal school agenda is dictated by national curricula, authority figures and timetables, relationships with friends provide the forum that allows them to make sense of school, to put up with it and even enjoy it.

So children provide us with a unique, specific set of 'takes' on the social order, which both help us to understand how it works, and provide pointers towards ways of improving childhoods.

Thus, I would argue, the sociology of childhood helps us to consider important issues in children's rights. In this talk I have tried to give an account of the positioning of children in the social order, and very briefly I have listed how children themselves understand their childhoods. From my point of view, these macro and micro perspectives, linked together, suggest relevant ways of thinking about rights. Children, like women, see that they are positioned in social relationships, not just as individuals but as group members. Children are required to operate through intergenerational relations – with parents, with teachers. It is through these child–adult relations that they learn. And the character of their daily lives is structured through the goals, control, permission and affection (and sometimes anger) of adults. An important part of what they learn is that other people's happiness depends on their input. Thus it comes as no surprise that the children who talked with me stressed interdependence and reciprocity, rather than lonely autonomy. Children therefore are adding to the arguments raised by feminist philosophers (such as Grimshaw, 1986; Griffiths & Whitford, 1988) which challenge the long, over-long, Western European tradition whereby rational man, in lonely autonomy, is the measure of virtue.

Sociology also throws light on issues to do with respecting children's participation rights. For if we understand children not just as individuals but as members of a social group, then we are forced to reflect on that group's rights to participate in constructing the social order, social polices and practices. But sociology also reveals, in stark form, the subordination of children as a group to adults as a group – a subordination that children themselves accept. This leads to difficulties. As a subordinate and marginalised group, children find they have dubious moral status. Adult vision of children comprises developmentalism, adult socialisation duties, and responsibility for protection and provision. All these combine to foster adult suspicion of children – to disbelieve them, to blame them, to suspect their moral competence, to assign moral responsibility to adults rather than to children. Under these circumstances, it is hard for children to take the initiative and participate in social affairs, and it is hard for adults to permit them to, and very hard for children and adults to work together on anything like equal terms.

Should I end on an up-note? I think so, for there are reasons to rejoice. I think the last few years have shown a huge increase in knowledge about children and childhood; this includes information on the social condition of childhood, and theoretical and policy-oriented study in sociology, anthropology and psychology. Sociological study of children and childhood is showing that they are fit for sociology! And work has begun on making sociology fit for children! This is not an ivory tower comment. We need the theoretical work to help understand how to move forward in policy terms. I think, too, that the UN Convention is providing at least a basis for arguing for children's welfare across the world, though it's a long road. Even in the UK, notable in the Western

European world for its neglect of child-oriented policies, people are beginning to think about consulting children, about child-impact statements, about how childhood can be improved. The Internet is providing children with the means of talking with each other about issues that concern them. Children hold conferences, run newspapers, participate in community meetings, and carry out their own research. They discuss rights with local authority rights officers. Perhaps, a hundred years on, helped along by the UN Convention, the century of the child will dawn!

References

Alanen, L. (1992). *Modern childhood? Exploring the 'child question' in sociology*. Research Report 50. Finland: University of Jyvaskyla.

Boyden, J. (1990). Childhood and the policy makers: A comparative perspective on the globalization of childhood. In A. James & A. Prout (Eds), *Constructing and reconstructing childhood: Contemporary issues in the sociological study of childhood.* London: The Falmer Press, pp. 184-215.

Donzelot, J. (1980). *The policing of families: Welfare versus the state*. London: Hutchinson.

Durkheim, E. (1972). Education and society. In A. Giddens (Ed.), *Emile Durkheim: Selected readings.* Cambridge: Cambridge University Press, pp. 203-18. (Original work published 1922).

Elshtain, J.B. (1981). *Public man, private woman: Women in social and political thought.* Princeton, NJ: Princeton University Press.

Erikson, E. (1965). *Childhood and society.* Harmondsworth: Penguin in association with the Hogarth Press.

Giddens, A. (1997). *Sociology* (3rd edn). Oxford: Polity Press in association with Blackwell Publishers.

Griffiths, M.G., & Whitford, M.W. (Eds). (1988). *Feminist perspectives in philosophy.* London: Macmillan Press.

Grimshaw, J. (1986). *Feminist philosophers: Women's perspectives on philosophical traditions.* London: Harvester Wheatsheaf.

Hughes, J. (1988). The philosopher's child. In M.G. Griffiths & M.W. Whitford (Eds), *Feminist perspectives in philosophy.* London: Macmillan Press, pp. 72-89.

James, A., & Prout, A. (Eds). (1990/1997). *Constructing and reconstructing childhood: Contemporary issues in the sociological study of childhood.* London: The Falmer Press.

Jenks, C. (1996). *Childhood.* London: Routledge.

Kelley, P., Mayall, B., & Hood, S. (1997). Children's accounts of risk. *Childhood, 4*(3), 305-324.

Key, E. (1909/1900). *The century of the child.* London: G.P. Putnam's and Sons.

Mayall, B. (1994a). *Negotiating health: Children at home and primary school.* London: Cassell.

Mayall, B. (1994b). Children in action at home and school. In B. Mayall (Ed.), *Children's childhood's: Observed and experienced.* London: The Falmer Press. pp. 114-27.

Mayall, B. (1996). *Children, health and the social order*. Buckingham: Open University Press.

Mayall, B., Bendelow, G., Barker, S., Storey, P., & Veltman, M. (1996). *Children's health in primary schools*. London: The Falmer Press.

O'Neill, J. (1994). *The missing child in liberal theory.* Toronto: University of Toronto Press.

Qvortrup, J. (1987). Introduction. *International Journal of Sociology, 17*(3), 3-37.

Qvortrup, J. (1991). *Childhood as a social phenomenon – an introduction to a series of national reports* (2nd edn). Eurosocial Report 36/0. Vienna: European Centre.

Qvortrup, J., Bardy, M., Sgritta, G., & Wintersberger, H. (Eds). (1994). *Childhood matters: Social theory, practice and politics.* Aldershot: Avebury Press.

Shilling, C. (1993). *The body and social theory.* London: Sage.

Smith, D.E. (1988). *The everyday world as problematic: Towards a feminist sociology.* Buckingham: Open University Press.

Stafseng, O. (1993). A sociology of childhood and youth – the need of both? In J. Qvortrup (Ed.), *Childhood as a social phenomenon: Lessons from an international project.* Eurosocial report 47.1993. Vienna: European Centre, pp. 71-90.

Stephens, S. (Ed.). (1995). *Children and the politics of culture.* Princeton, NJ: Princeton University Press.

Turner, B. (1992). *Regulating bodies: Essays in medical sociology.* London: Routledge.

Wintersberger, H. (Ed.). (1996). *Children on the way from marginality towards citizenship. Childhood policies: Conceptual and practical issues.* Eurosocial Report 61/1996. Vienna: European Centre.

Woodhead, M. (1997). Psychology and the cultural construction of children's needs. In A. James & A. Prout (Eds), *Constructing and reconstructing childhood: Contemporary issues in the sociological study of childhood.* London: The Falmer Press, pp. 63-84.

Woodhead, M. (1998). *Children's perspectives on their working lives.* Stockholm: Radda Barnen.

Note

1 This study 'Negotiating Childhoods' is funded 1997-99 on the ESRC Children 5–16 Programme.

Parents *and* children: Legal reform to facilitate children's participation[1]

Gary B. Melton

Abstract

The mandate in the law and ethics of human rights to take children seriously as people usually should not be framed as deference to parents or children. Rather, careful efforts to promote the participation of children – to help them to feel that they are heard – will usually bring parents (and other adults) and children together in shared decision making. Such a recognition reframes the core problem of children's law to be the creation of structures to facilitate such inter-generational involvement, not the choice of the age at which children's decisions should be recognised as authoritative.

Few discussions are as apt to raise the participants' blood pressure as much as a seminar on children's (or parents' or teachers') rights, and few are as apt to result in policy that is inconsistent, unreasoned, and just plain incoherent. Besides that, such discussions by their nature touch on the most fundamental relationships in society (even the survival of the society), they also are inherently complex. Six facts contribute to such complexity and difficulty in generating workable children's law.

First, decisions pertaining to children almost always directly affect the interests of others. Accordingly, the recognition of autonomy for children and youth cannot rest simply on their competence (the issue that historically has dominated children's law), because the question remains whether they should be permitted, in effect, to make decisions on behalf of other family members, especially their parents. Attention needs to be given, therefore, to ways of routinely considering the interests of all of the affected parties in the family.

Second, notwithstanding the special place of parents in their children's lives, parents are by no means the only adults who have responsibility for children's care and education and who may be involved in decision making about the children, often on a daily basis. Teachers, recreation leaders, health professionals, juvenile probation officers, child welfare workers, foster parents, clergy, Scout leaders, extended family, and, in some cultures, community elders, among others, may share responsibility for protecting children and enhancing their development. Moreover, many of these individuals act directly or indirectly on behalf of the state in doing so, with or without parental concurrence. Children's law must take these interests into account.

Third, establishment of a policy, without more, that children may make a particular decision independently typically leaves a host of important issues unresolved. For example, children might be given the power to decide whether to choose the courses that they will take in school, but that recognition of autonomy does not answer (a) whether they may reject particular assignments or conditions of attendance, (b) whether they may exercise control over personal information elicited in their classes, and (c) if a fee is charged for a course, who will bear the financial responsibility. Of course, the converse is also true; children may be given authority to decide one of the corollary questions but not the threshold question in regard to enrolment in particular courses. Further, on any or all of these issues, children might be permitted to *participate* in the decision making but not to make the final decision.

Hence, children's law cannot be meaningfully reduced to a single question of 'Who will decide?' The historic focus on that question inevitably leads to a disconnection from the practical problems of everyday life.

Fourth, if the complex interests at stake are to be accommodated, a *process* is likely to be required, not a single *event*. This principle often applies to any particular party. For example, Katz (1984) and other students of informed consent have argued that the reduction of the process of development of a partnership between health professional and patient to the act of signing a consent form – an often incomprehensible form at that – has robbed the concept of informed consent of any ethical meaning. When multiple parties are involved, as is almost inherently the case when children's interests are at stake, the need for a process to promote discussion among the affected parties is even clearer. An ethically coherent children's policy would routinely encourage or demand such conversations.

Fifth, a corollary to the fourth point is that vindication of the interests at stake – in particular, giving concerned parties a say – may require development of *structures* to facilitate such participation. For example, if students are to believe that they are free to tell teachers that particular assignments are too intrusive and embarrassing for them as individuals, they probably will need already to have experienced or observed situations that will build their trust that their concerns will be heard and taken seriously. Similarly, solicitation of parents' concerns will be more natural if forums already exist for exchange of experiences and ideas with their children's teachers. In either instance, the situation will be substantially less troublesome if agreements have already been reached about the kinds of circumstances in which personal privacy will be respected and those in which a discussion among multiple parties is necessary.

Sixth, although the children's law casebooks are filled with dramatic examples of the interplay of interests in matters involving children, such issues pervade everyday life in the institutions of which children are a part (families, schools, pediatric clinics, religious congregations, etc.). A coherent children's policy would go beyond the dramatic questions of life and death and of custody and freedom to the norms by which community settings operate in their ordinary interactions with children.

In that regard, the critical question is not so much whether children will be granted absolute autonomy and privacy but instead whether they will be treated with respect. As Zimring (1982) has sagely framed the problem, *the central issue is not whether we should treat children like adults but instead whether we should treat them like people* – and, I would add, whether we should do so routinely in everyday life.

Principles for policy

In that context, as Zimring (1982) has further argued, the norm that should prevail is a *rebuttable presumption of liberty*. To be clear, Zimring was not arguing, as I am not, that government ought to enforce a rebuttable presumption of liberty for children within the family. He was saying, however, that a norm of deference to liberty is desirable, as a matter of ethics, absent a good reason to the contrary. Further, I would add, given the state's interest in democratic socialisation, it is sound public policy for government to facilitate the experience of choice for children in settings outside the family (perhaps most of all in everyday matters in schools and other community institutions).

There are two complementary qualifiers to the rebuttable presumption of liberty. First, as already noted, the fact that the interests of multiple parties are almost always at stake in matters involving children must be taken into account. Such a principle ordinarily implies the need for structures to promote *shared* decision making.

Second, taken together, the dual values of autonomy and beneficence imply that children should have opportunities for increasing independence in contexts in which risk is minimised. As a general matter, *self-determination* is less important than *participation* in decision making. Nothing is more fundamental to the experience of being taken seriously than simply having a say, being heard politely, and having one's perspective considered – in effect, being part of a conversation about matters of personal significance (see generally Lind & Tyler, 1988; Tyler & Degoey, 1995). In the same vein, children's interests are most likely to be promoted when they are given opportunities for *graduated* decision making – in effect, 'learner's permits' (see Zimring, 1982) that enable gradual assumption of independence so that full autonomy is not exercised until there is some experience with the decision or task.

In short, the human-rights mandate to take children seriously as people usually should not be framed as deference to parents *or* children. Rather, careful efforts to promote the participation of children (as well as parents and other interested adults) – to help them to feel that they are heard – will usually bring parents *and* children together in shared decision making.

The principal purposes of this paper are to explicate the rationale for such an approach, to explain its foundation in international human rights law, and to describe ways that it can be applied. Before undertaking such an analysis, however, it is useful to contrast the framework that is currently in place in most Western countries.

The state of the law

Perhaps the most fundamental question facing legal policy makers concerned with children's issues is *how best to create a society in which, consistent with fundamental legal values, there is respect for children as persons*. Policy makers have implicitly framed this question as a problem of discerning the point at which children are sufficiently mature that their interests trump those of their parents. Consequently, a grand purpose typically has been reduced in legislation and litigation to a question about who will decide the fate of a child of a particular age or competence in a particular context: *'How old should children be before they have the right to …?'*

When this question is presented to a group of adults, almost any word placed in the blank is likely to stimulate a spirited discussion – a result that is unsurprising when one considers the range of interests and ideologies typically at stake in children's issues. Indeed, the only conclusion that may draw a consensus is that policy on the point typically has not been very thoughtful. For example, in the United States during the Vietnam War, the slogan that anyone who is old enough to fight is old enough to vote generalised simplistically to old enough to fight, old enough to sign contracts, drink alcoholic beverages, consent to medical care, and so on. The rush to a conclusion without careful consideration of the relevant factors was followed predictably by the surfacing of issues about particular decisions that might be initiated justifiably earlier or later than age 18. Notably, Congress ultimately made federal highway funds contingent on states' raising the drinking age to 21 (National Minimum Drinking Age, 1984).

Meanwhile, states have often broadened the authority of minors under 18 to make other kinds of decisions, particularly in regard to access to some forms of health care. In some cases, states have lowered the minimum age for consent to various types of health care (Alabama, 1998). In others, age-grading has been replaced, at least implicitly, by a mature minor rule, in which the threshold for autonomy appears to have been individualized (Virginia, 1998).

The lack of apparent thoughtfulness about the specific age at which minors may exercise particular choices independently is perhaps less important as a practical matter, however, than the lack of attention to some more subtle questions. For example, the focus on who will decide often misses critical corollary questions. As already noted, the decision that minors can contract for a particular service independently does not by itself answer the questions of whether they may do so confidentially or whether they will be permitted to do so without fee. Focusing on the identity of the decision maker, statutes typically are silent about the corollary questions. The result is that service providers have little idea how to implement the standard for decision making and little incentive to increase minors' autonomy and privacy when legislators intended such an outcome (see, for example, Melton, 1981, describing the results of Virginia's removal of any age threshold for minors' independent consent to psychotherapy).

Even when the corollary questions are addressed in part, they rarely are considered systematically. For example, Nebraska (1998) has a statute permitting minors independently to seek diagnosis and treatment for sexually transmitted diseases. That statute expressly permits minors to seek such services confidentially and makes their parents liable for the cost. In an era in American health care of prior approvals, co-payments, and deductibles, one can only imagine a notice coming to parents about payment for an unspecified health service provided to an unspecified patient for an unspecified reason!

The clashing of symbols

Moreover, the emphasis on who will decide – children of any given age *or* their parents – often results in overlooking the fundamental question at issue. One of the most important US Supreme Court cases on children's rights, *Parham v J.R.* (1979), is illustrative (see Melton, Lyons, & Spaulding, 1998). By the time that *Parham* reached the Supreme Court, it focused on a question of procedural due process: Does the Constitution permit psychiatric hospitalisation of minors by their parents without a hearing? By contrast, when the case had first entered the federal courts, it was primarily a case of substantive due process: When a state permits psychiatric hospitalisation of minors in its facilities, does the Constitution require it to generate less restrictive alternatives?

The procedural question invited – and elicited – voluminous verbiage by the justices about the nature of childhood and family life. The ultimate focus was on the symbolic question of the dominance of parents *or* children, while the ubiquitous theme of children's law cases (Melton, 1987) missed the central point that parents *and* children have strong interests in avoiding unnecessary disruptions of family relationships (see Melton, 1996). The development of alternatives to hospitalisation minimises threats to the integrity of the family, protects the option of family preservation for the parents, and avoids undue restrictions on the child's liberty and intrusions on his or her privacy. It also better satisfies the state's interest in cost-effective amelioration of threats to the child's healthy socialisation. When families are in crisis, the question of who will decide is simply not as critical – even for protection of children's liberty – as that of what can be done.

The Misdirected Focus on Competence

Much of the debate about the relative dominance of parents and children has rested ultimately on assumptions about children's competence (see generally Melton, Koocher, & Saks, 1983). Like many courts in other jurisdictions (Wadlington, 1973), the US Supreme Court has been inconsistent and often unclear in its concept of competence or maturity (see, e.g., *Hodgson v Minnesota,* 1990, p. 474 [Marshall J, dissenting]). Scholars have debated whether the court's assumptions have been based on a view of competence as equivalent to understanding of and reasoning about risks and benefits of various choices (see, e.g., the analyses in Melton et al., 1983) or, more broadly, as synonymous with 'judgement' (see, for example, Scott, 1992; Scott, Reppucci, & Woolard, 1995).

Regardless, however, of the definition underlying the court's reasoning, questions of competence have been given undue emphasis in deciding cases, enacting legislation, and promulgating regulations about the limits of minors' autonomy and privacy. There are six key points here.

First, as cognitive psychologists (e.g., Kahneman & Tversky, 1984; Nisbett & Ross, 1980; Tversky & Kahneman, 1974, 1981) have shown vividly, adult reasoning is far from ideal. (Remember the approach that you took the last time that you bought a car!) It is unfair to hold children to a higher standard.

Second, virtually all commentators believe that the court has exaggerated the cognitive differences between adults and adolescents. In perhaps the most skeptical article on prevailing scholarship on children's competence, Gardner and his colleagues (Gardner, Scherer, & Tester, 1989) have criticised commentators who have concluded that developmental research indicates that adolescents aged fourteen and older are indistinguishable from adults in their competence to make decisions, where competence is defined in the terms identified by Lidz et al. (1984). Gardner et al. (1989) acknowledged, however, that a number of studies showed that older children and adolescents are reasonably skilled in identifying risks and benefits of various health procedures.

Two of the authors of the Gardner et al. article (Scherer & Gardner, 1990) subsequently praised an American Psychological Association brief (on which Gardner consulted) in *Hodgson v. Minnesota* (1990) as 'a narrowly drawn statement of the current research' (p. 1174). That brief's conclusions in regard to adolescents' competence in abortion decision making were substantially the same as earlier briefs that Gardner et al. criticised:

> *Psychological research and theory about cognitive, social and moral development strongly supports the conclusion that most adolescents are competent to make informed decisions about important life decisions.*
>
> … Research consistently supports the conclusion that there is a predictable development during late childhood and early adolescence of the capacity to think rationally about increasingly complex problems and decisions. Although there are several competing theories of cognitive development, these theories each recognize that a revolution in rationality occurs during early adolescence.

> … In fact, by middle adolescence (age 14–15) young people develop abilities similar to adults in reasoning about moral dilemmas, understanding social rules and laws, reasoning about interpersonal relationships and interpersonal problems, and reasoning about custody preference during parental divorce. … Thus, by age 14 most adolescents have developed adult-like intellectual and social capacities including specific abilities outlined in the law as necessary for understanding treatment alternatives, considering risks and benefits, and giving legally competent consent (Schneider, Bersoff, & Podolsky, 1989, pp. 18–20, footnotes and citations omitted).

Third, even when cognitive immaturity can be demonstrated, the risk of harm may be minimal – at least insofar as the fear is that marginally competent children will make decisions contrary to adults' perceptions of the children's interests. For example, even though they usually are unable to give adult-like rationalisations for decisions, elementary-school children typically follow adult models when they are permitted to make many routine personal decisions (e.g., whether to go to the school nurse; see, e.g., Lewis, 1983), whether in hypothetical or real-life situations.

Indeed, the ironic caution that emerges from research on children's competence as decision makers is that, absent affirmative effort to show children and youth that they really do have a choice, they often will simply adopt the stance that they believe adult authorities wish them to take (cf. Scherer, 1991; Scherer & Reppucci, 1988). For example, adolescent participants in Belter and Grisso's (1984) research did not show their prowess in identifying risks of psychotherapy until such behaviour was modelled. Similarly, Abramovitch, Freedman, Thoden, & Nikolich (1991) found that, although even five- and six-year-old children comprehended the information that they could withdraw from participation in research, most believed that they could exercise that option only temporarily. Children from disadvantaged populations may be especially likely to believe, perhaps realistically, that they do not have meaningful choices (see, e.g., Ginsburg et al., 1995; Lewis, 1983; Melton, 1980).

Fourth, children often may benefit from the experience of decision making even if their skill in generating and expressing reasons for their decisions is underdeveloped. There is a huge body of research showing that, for children as well as adults, perceived and actual control are highly correlated and that perceived control is related to mental health, educational achievement, and treatment compliance (see generally Melton, 1983, and citations therein). Perhaps the most direct effect of participation is in the development of democratic values and behaviour; participation begets further civic involvement across the lifespan. In that regard, it is important to note that political socialisation apparently occurs primarily in middle childhood (Melton & Limber, 1992), not adolescence, as many educators and psychologists believe.

Fifth, at other times, minors may not be especially skilled in reasoning, and they may not benefit from decision making per se, but society wants them to have easy independent access to services for other reasons. Evaluation and treatment for sexually transmitted diseases, matters of both personal and public health, are illustrative. The common provision in state law for independent consent to substance abuse counselling – but often not to treatment for other physical and mental health problems – may also be justified by the state's concern for both youth welfare and public health.

Although initial involvement of parents alongside their children ought typically to be encouraged, there are some cases in which children's and parents' interests are so divergent (as in cases of extreme abuse or neglect) or the nature of the decision is so private that either full autonomy or an alternative (non-parental) route of consultation should be recognised. Further, there are instances in which adolescents' avoidance of parental consultation is likely to be so pronounced that in insistence on it will do serious harm to their health and welfare. In such cases, a requirement for parental involvement in decision making may result in gratuitous harm to the child and therefore a violation of due process.

The preceding points illustrate why incompetence is an insufficient rationale for denial of some measure of autonomy for children and youth. Sixth and by contrast, some other factors should enter the equation even when minors can demonstrate decisionmaking skills associated with adults of above-average intelligence. Because of the realities of their economic and social situation, minors' decisions almost always affect their parents, who may bear the financial liability for their children's decisions. In such a context, fairness may dictate parental involvement, even when the children involved are highly competent.

The right question

The degree to which the general focus on competence leads policy in unfortunate directions can be shown by considering the question that such an emphasis implies – the identification of the 'right' age for self-determination. As already noted, primary attention to this question almost inevitably results in a symbolic argument about the nature of childhood and parenthood, often to the neglect of issues that are more directly relevant to the dignity and well-being of both children and parents, as well as other parties.

Moreover, the preoccupation with whether parents or their children of a particular age (or cognitive competence) will triumph misses the central question embodied in Article 12 of the Convention on the Rights of the Child (1989).[2] The Convention requires governments ratifying it to 'assure to the child who is capable of forming his or her own views the right to express those views freely in all matters affecting the child, the view of the child being given due weight in accordance with the age and maturity of the child'. Article 12 further requires that children be provided 'the opportunity to be heard' in formal government proceedings affecting them.

Several points are relevant in understanding Article 12 and other related provisions. First and most fundamentally, the Convention does not establish a game between parents and children in which one side wins and the other loses. (Regardless, the Convention regulates ratifying governments, not families directly.) Article 12 requires that children be given opportunities for participation, not necessarily or even ordinarily self-determination.

The drafters of the Convention, like drafters of other human rights documents, envisioned a world governed by the Golden Rule – i.e., a world in which people, regardless of their circumstances, would be treated with respect for their dignity. Such a vision requires that everyone be taken seriously; at a minimum, the concerns of both children and adults who are likely to be centrally affected by a particular decision ought to be heard and thoughtfully considered. The overarching model is one of *partners*, not competitors in the expression of power.

Second, such an experience does not require a high level of skill. Note that the Convention expects involvement by any child 'who is capable of forming his or her own views'. All that is required is the ability to express a preference. By implication, the Convention demands a norm for relevant government officials (e.g., public-sector health professionals; teachers) of conversations with even relatively young children.

An analogue may be the evolution in health law and ethics toward a requirement of informed consent – a norm that not so long ago was unknown even by adult patients. Although that level of involvement is unrealistic for many children, it *is* realistic to have conversations with children in developmentally appropriate language about what is happening to them and perhaps to try to preserve some domains of choice.

Third, as the last example illustrates, the nature of children's participation properly evolves developmentally. The Convention on the Rights of the Child (1989) presumes gradually increasing participation so that 'the child should be fully prepared to live an individual life in society' (preamble).

The primary focus on the standard for children's independent decision making thus misses the point. The initial and typical focus on the question of who will decide (or the age of the child at which the decision maker will change) not only pits parents against children unnecessarily (indeed erroneously), it diverts attention from the underlying principle. The need is for legal structures to promote and protect children's increasing participation in decision making. To accomplish that end, children often will need preparation for decision making, and the settings of which they are a part often will need to be restructured so that children can be active participants.

Consider the difference in policy responses to the following two questions:

(a) At what age should minors be able to consent independently to health care?

(b) How can law be used to increase children's sense that they are partners in their health care? Not only is the latter question more likely to result in answers leading to meaningful participation by children, but it also is more apt to lead to plans to address practical obstacles to children's participation.

Such barriers often remain even when the law on the books ostensibly recognises self-determination for minors (see, for example, Melton, 1981).

The need for 'Learner's Permits'

When policy makers shift from being *wordsmiths* primarily concerned with nuances in legal standards, more for their symbolic than their practical value, to being *architects* building new structures for children's participation, then practical constraints on legal standards become obvious. As epidemiological research on accidental injuries to children and adolescents makes clear, the entry age for a new task – whether crawling around the house, running about the neighbourhood, or driving down the road – is a time of risk (see, e.g., Li, Baker, & Frattaroli, 1995; Paulson, 1988; Rivara, Alexander, Johnston, & Soderberg, 1993; Schwarz, 1993; Soderstrom & Dearing-Stuck, 1993). The specific age that is chosen to permit exercise of new freedom is much less important than legislators typically believe; whatever the age is, it will be problematic.

Therefore, the practical policy problem is not selection of a magic threshold age carefully aligned with developmental competence. Instead, the general problem is to increase autonomy while minimising risk. The learner's permit may be the optimal model. In such an approach, the child or adolescent gradually assumes independence so that full autonomy is not exercised until he or she has some experience with the decision or task.

The paradigmatic example of such an approach in the United States (as in New Zealand) is in regard to driving. In the simplest form of such a law, a state sets one age (typically, sixteen) as the minimum for *driving* but an earlier age as the minimum for *learning to drive*. A teenager who has a learner's permit may legally get behind the steering wheel, but he or she cannot operate the car without a licensed driver in the passenger's seat.

Increasingly, American states (e.g., South Carolina, 1998) are further graduating this rule. Hence, the characteristics of the responsible licensed driver (e.g., age; relationship) are often specified, and they may change as the driver in training becomes more experienced. Similarly, states now often specify the times of day that a youthful licensed driver may drive independently and even the destinations to which he or she may go. These conditions also may change with experience and sometimes with formal driver's training. The period of various restrictions may be increased if the young driver has a traffic violation or the parents do not give permission to graduate to the next level of independent driving. (New Zealand law incorporates some but not all of these graduated restrictions on youthful drivers.)

As far as I am aware, this approach is systematically applied in US law only in regard to driving. However, the model could be applied to most other tasks, so that parents and other adults gradually shift from being instructors to 'co-pilots' to supervisors to limited supervisors (supervisors only under certain especially risky conditions). It is not difficult to imagine ways that policy could support such an approach through graduated decision making. The school curriculum is an example. Thus, we might permit fourth graders to make some choices about the subjects that they study but only if their decisions are made jointly with their parents or counsellors. Alternatively, the full decision making authority might be vested in parents or school officials but with the proviso that the students themselves have an opportunity to give their opinions. In the same vein, we might limit the fourth graders' choice to the selection of an art medium for study. Older students might be permitted to make some curricular choices on their own but be permitted to make others only with adult involvement and still others not at all. The same principles might apply to school governance.

Note that the theory underlying the learner's-permit model is dualistic. On the one hand, gradually increasing *participation* is necessary to respect for children's dignity, because a society respectful of children as persons enables and indeed encourages an ever-expanding role for children in the community. On the other hand, *practice*, which as a practical matter means participation, is required for protection of children's welfare. Seen in that light, thoughtful 'child liberation' and thoughtful paternalism lead to the same policies.

In that regard, the learner's-permit approach offers means of regulating risky behaviour that we cannot or will not prohibit. By structuring opportunities for supervised and perhaps modelled practice and for taking small steps toward behavior that may require considerable skill and judgement to control, the learner's-permit approach comports well with cognitive-behavioural principles for mastery of complex tasks (cf. Bandura, 1977; Ericcson, Krampe, & Tesch-Römer, 1993; Ohlsson, 1996). Whatever one's age, being 'mature' takes practice.

Some policy alternatives

Avoiding conflicts of interest

To a large extent, the participation requirement of the Convention on the Rights of the Child (1989) is simply an injunction to state-employed or state-directed professionals to remember to involve the affected parties, including children, in decision making. In that regard, one of the attractive elements of the participation requirement is that it avoids clashes of interests among family members. In noting the relevance of the requirement to confidentiality problems in child mental health services, for example, I described the positive side effects of the discussions that should result:

> Following such a framework [of child participation and shared decision making], the clinician should negotiate the limits of privacy. In most circumstances, both the parents and the child should be informed about requests to share or seek personal information. Although the parents may have the ultimate legal authority to give or deny consent, the clinician can establish a norm of consultation so that the child has an opportunity to have a say before a decision is made. Similarly the parents (or the

child in instances in which the child has decisionmaking authority) may partially waive their right of access so that the child (or the parents) retains most control over particular kinds of information; certain exceptions may be agreed upon in advance.

In short, although real quandaries involving real conflicts of interest do occur, the fact that privacy rights are typically waivable leaves the door open for negotiation of arrangements in which the various interests can be accommodated. Such a process could provide a model for mutually respectful resolution of family conflicts. It also could provide a model for resolution of conflicts between, on the one side, parties outside the family and, on the other, the whole family or individual family members. In short, although problems of privacy, especially those involving children, are difficult, they are typically tractable when a humane approach is taken to identification and accommodation of the interests at stake (Melton, 1997, pp. 26-27).

Procedures and structures for shared decision making

To build such an ethic for children's participation – and, for that matter, respectful consideration of the interests of other family members – settings often will need to be restructured so that such conversations occur 'naturally'. Similarly, children may need training so that they will recognise the opportunity for meaningful participation and that their skill in identifying the alternatives and weighing their risks and benefits is maximised. By the same token, at least initially, prompts may be needed so that the relevant adults (e.g., parents; teachers; health professionals) 'get it' and that they learn to listen to children (see, e.g., Melton et al., 1992, showing that prosecutors often knowingly – but unthinkingly – used developmentally inappropriate vocabulary in their conversations with child witnesses).

The only legal context of which I am aware in US law in which there is an explicit provision for shared decision making by parents and children is consent to children's participation in research (see Melton & Stanley, 1996). Research that is not for the participants' own benefit seems on its face to violate the theory of parental consent to interventions in the lives of their children (i.e., that parents have such authority because they are presumed to act in their children's interests). Therefore, federal regulators require informed parental *permission* (not *consent*) and child *assent* for children's participation in nontherapeutic research. Parents' permission is required to avoid unwelcome intrusions on family privacy and undue exposure of children to risk, but the children themselves possess a veto so that they are not required to subject themselves to exploitation, even in the interest of the search for truth.

It probably is more accurate to say that the law on children's participation in research *recognises* both the roles of both parent and child than to say that it actively *encourages* shared decision making. Note that the requirement is effectively for two decisions, not one. Moreover, the law does not establish a process to promote discussion among the parents, the child, and the investigator.

Further, there is substantial evidence that the assent requirement is often effectively abrogated by researchers' or parents' zeal or by children's perception of a lack of a real choice (Abramovitch et al., 1991; Keith-Spiegel, 1983).

It is not difficult, however, to imagine ways that the law could foster more active collaboration and consultation in research as well as other contexts. For example, just as negligence doctrine in tort law was used to establish a duty of health professionals to disclose material information to patients, the standard of care could be expanded to include a reasonable effort to enlist participation by pediatric patients old enough to express a preference in decisions about their care. Such a standard could also be established administratively through licensing requirements for the professionals themselves and the institutions with which they are affiliated. (Analogous provisions might be applied to shape professional conduct in contexts outside the health care system.)

Further, legislatures and regulatory bodies might require or encourage (through financial support, for example) professional societies, licensing boards, and universities to develop guidelines or protocols for children's participation in specific settings or in regard to particular decisions and to conduct related pre-professional or continuing education. Such protocols might identify the processes that might be used, and they might also suggest ways that decisions might be parsed into graduated, increasingly complex, difficult, or independent steps.

Relevant administrative bodies might also sponsor research to evaluate the effectiveness of the protocols in fostering children's participation while minimising risk. Furthermore agencies might undertake or encourage education of parents and children in ways that they might participate more actively in various contexts.

The legal recognition of mentors

The learner's-permit model not only presumes that public authorities will permit and indeed encourage some level of child involvement in key decisions, but it also presumes that trusted adults will be available to supervise children's decisions, to prepare children for decision making, or to serve them as consultants. Time, logistics, weaknesses in motivation and skills, or even conflicts of interest may be barriers to such adult involvement.

It also should be recognised that parents cannot – and, to some extent, should not – be everywhere. Sometimes other adults might be better situated to provide guidance or consultation to a child in a given context (cf. Cochran & Brassard, 1979). Not only can such other adults offer direct support to parents, but they may also offer some measure of independence for children while ensuring adult supervision.

The law might recognise such mentors. For example, parents and children might jointly designate adults who could act as consultants to children or who might share decision-making responsibility in particular contexts. There are existing models for more extensive surrogate roles for adults other than parents. For example, some states (e.g., New York, 1996) have permitted parents to designate standby guardians who would assume parental responsibility if the parents themselves became incapacitated. (Such laws arose as a means of strengthening family environments for children of parents with AIDS.) More limited guardianship (or consultancy or supervision) also could be recognised. Such roles are already present in some cultures through godparenthood or a similar status that might be given legal recognition.

Although the existing legal applications of this model have been in regard to parents of limited competence, the model could be applied more broadly, as the example of godparents illustrates. By recognising parentally approved adults who could serve as mentors for children in shared decision making in particular contexts, the law could strengthen community and extended-family support for parents and children. Specifically, such an approach might increase children's supervised participation in various settings. However, care should be taken in crafting the necessary legal structures to avoid undue intrusions into the privacy of parents or children. The mentors also should be partners in decision making.

New forums for collective decision making

Although some circumstances (reproductive decision making being the prime example) may be so intensely private that group decision making would be difficult to defend, shared decision making need not be dyadic. Particularly in cultures where the extended family or a tribal group shares responsibility for child-rearing, there may be reason to consider the creation of structures that permit direct participation by the child but that also provide a voice to multiple other family members.

An example of such an approach that has received extensive international attention is the family group conference used to establish dispositions in juvenile justice and child protection cases in New Zealand (see Swain, 1995). Combining traditional Maori disputing and reconciliation processes with Western due process norms, the family group conference offers a legally sanctioned means to bring together the extended family and the community members most important to them to reach a collective decision. (In juvenile justice matters, the victim and the police also participate in the initial discussion.) The children in the family participate in the conferences, which appear to have the potential not only to enable everyone to have a say but also to foster community responsibility.

New structures for youth involvement

By the same token, it may be useful to create legal structures to facilitate children's participation in community affairs. Consideration should be given, for example, to ways to increase the meaning of children's participation in school governance, already a powerful institution in democratic socialisation (Sigel & Hoskin, 1981), notwithstanding the trivial authority that student governments typically have. In keeping with the learner's-permit model, opportunities should be available for student involvement in decision making about matters of increasingly serious import, even if adult authorities have the ultimate decision making authority.

Pursuant to legislation initially advocated by the ombudsman for children (Ministry of Environmental Affairs, 1989), Norway has adopted a particularly interesting structure that might serve as a model for youth participation in community affairs in the United States. An adult representative of children's interests is a member of each municipal planning council. Children's interests must be taken into account in every planning (e.g., zoning variance) decision. Accordingly, many Norwegian counties have established elaborate procedures for children's involvement in land use planning and for educational activities to facilitate such involvement.

The framework: Parents and children; teachers and students, etc.

In the end, it is useful to return to the point made at the beginning of this paper. The interests of many parties are at stake in everyday situations involving children. To quote a cliché, 'we're all in this together', regardless of our generation. One of the strengths of the Convention on the Rights of the Child (1989) is that the drafters recognised the compatibility of interests of children and parents (and other family and community members), even if the circumstances and therefore the interests of children and adults are not identical.

Regardless of citizens' age, the law should preserve those aspects of our lives that are most fundamental to personal integrity – to being taken seriously as persons. Children, like parents, have a fundamental interest in protection of family relationships (see Melton, 1996, on children's right to a family environment). In that regard, parents' interest in preservation of their authority in the family, children's interest in autonomy, and all family members' interest in preservation of family options generally push toward the same policies and personal options. Further, all parties, regardless of their age, have an interest in promoting the availability of support for the child and family by extended family and other community members who are important to them.

In short, society as a whole, not only the younger generation, has a compelling interest in the promotion of children's early and frequent participation in shared decision making. The strategy of intergenerational decision making can serve as the foundation for a new communitarian ethic in the various settings of which children are a part. In that regard, creative legal architecture to fulfil the vision in the Convention on the Rights of the Child (1989) may ultimately have a broader effect. With the behavioural commitment to the fact that 'we're all in this together', the model of sharing and participation may help to build or maintain a strong civil society in the face of extraordinary social change and ethnic diversity.

References

Abramovitch, R., Freedman, J.L., Thoden, K., & Nikolich, C. (1991). Children's capacity to consent to participation in psychological research: Empirical findings. *Child Development, 62,* 1100-109.

Ala. Code § 22-8-4 (Repl. Vol. 1998).

Bandura, A. (1977). *Social learning theory.* Englewood Cliffs, NJ: Prentice-Hall.

Belter, R., & Grisso, T. (1984). Children's recognition of rights violations in counseling. *Professional Psychology: Research and Practice, 15,* 899-910.

Cochran, M.M., & Brassard, J.A. (1979). Child development and personal social networks. *Child Development, 50,* 601-616.

Convention on the Rights of the Child, G.A. Res. 44/25, U.N. GAOR Supp. 49 at 165, U.N. Doc. A/44 736 (1989).

Ericsson, K.A., Krampe, R.T., & Tesch-Römer, C. (1993). The role of deliberate practice in the acquisition of expert performance. *Psychological Review, 100,* 363-406.

Gardner, W., Scherer, D., & Tester, M. (1989). Asserting scientific authority: Cognitive development and adolescent legal rights. *American Psychologist, 44,* 895-902.

Ginsburg, K.R., Slap, G.B., Cnaan, A., Forke, C.M., Balsley, C.M., & Rouselle, D.M. (1995). Adolescents' perceptions of factors affecting their decisions to seek health care. *Journal of the American Medical Association, 273,* 1913-18.

Hodgson v. Minnesota, 497 U.S. 417 (1990).

Kahneman, D., & Tversky, A. (1984). Choices, values, and frames. *American Psychologist, 39,* 341-350.

Katz, J. (1984). *The silent world of doctor and patient.* New York: Free Press.

Keith-Spiegel, P. (1983). Children and consent to participate in research. In G.B. Melton, G.P. Koocher, & M.J. Saks (Eds), *Children's competence to consent.* New York: Plenum, pp. 179-211.

Lewis, C.E. (1983). Decision making related to health: When could/should children act responsibly? In G.B. Melton, G.P. Koocher, & M.J. Saks (Eds), *Children's competence to consent.* New York: Plenum, pp. 75-91.

Li, G., Baker, S.P., & Frattaroli, S. (1995). Epidemiology and prevention of traffic-related injuries among adolescents. *Adolescent Medicine, 6,* 135-52.

Lind, E.A., & Tyler, T.R. (1988). *The social psychology of procedural justice.* New York: Plenum.

Lidz, C.W., Meisel, A., Zerubavel, E., Carter, E., Sestak, R.M., & Roth, L. (1984). *Informed consent: A study of decisionmaking in psychiatry.* New York: Guilford.

Melton, G.B. (1980). Children's concepts of their rights. *Journal of Clinical Child Psychology, 9,* 186-90.

Melton, G.B. (1981). Effects of a state law permitting minors to consent to psychotherapy. *Professional Psychology, 12,* 647-54.

Melton, G.B. (1983). Decision making by children: Psychological risks and benefits. In G. B. Melton, G.P. Koocher, & M.J. Saks (Eds), *Children's competence to consent.* New York: Plenum, pp. 21-40.

Melton, G.B. (1987). The clashing of symbols: Prelude to child and family policy. *American Psychologist, 42,* 345-54.

Melton, G.B. (1996). The child's right to a family environment: Why children's rights and family values are compatible. *American Psychologist, 42,* 1234-8.

Melton, G.B. (1997, November). *Privacy issues in child mental health services.* Paper prepared for discussion at the annual Rosalynn Carter Symposium on Mental Health Policy, Carter Center, Atlanta.

Melton, G.B., Berliner, L., Limber, S.P., Jacobs, J.E., Oberlander, L.B., & Yamamoto, M. (1992). *Preparing sexually abused children for testimony: Children's perceptions of the legal process* (Final report to the National Center on Child Abuse and Neglect, Grant No. 90-CA-1274). Lincoln: University of Nebraska-Lincoln, Center on Children, Families, and the Law.

Melton, G.B., Koocher, G.P., & Saks, M.J. (Eds). (1983). *Children's competence to consent.* New York: Plenum.

Melton, G.B., & Limber, S.P. (1992). What rights mean to children: Children's own views. In M. Freeman & P. Veerman (Eds), *Ideologies of children's rights.* Dordrecht, Netherlands: Martinus Nijhoff, pp. 167-87.

Melton, G.B., Lyons, P.M., Jr., & Spaulding, W.J. (1998). *No place to go: Civil commitment of minors.* Lincoln: University of Nebraska Press.

Melton, G.B., & Stanley, B. (1996). The psychology of research involving special populations. In B.H. Stanley, J.E. Sieber, & G.B. Melton (Eds), *Research ethics: A psychological approach.* Lincoln: University of Nebraska Press, pp. 177-202.

Ministry of Environmental Affairs. (1989). *Må barns lek ha voksnes spilleregler? [Must children's games have adult rules?]* Oslo.

Neb. Rev. Stat. § 71-504 (Cum. Supp. 1998).

N.Y. Surr. Ct. Proc. Act § 1726 (Consol. 1996).

Nisbett, R., & Ross, L. (1980). *Human inference: Strategies and shortcomings of social judgment.* Englewood Cliffs, NJ: Prentice-Hall.

Ohlsson, S. (1996). Learning from performance errors. *Psychological Review, 103,* 241-62.

Parham v J.R., 442 US 584 (1979).

Paulson, J.A. (1988). The epidemiology of injuries in adolescents. *Pediatric Annals, 17,* 84-6, 89-96.

Rivara, F.P., Alexander, B., Johnston, B., & Soderberg, R. (1993). Population-based study of fall injuries in children and adolescents resulting in hospitalization or death. *Pediatrics, 92,* 61-3.

S.C. Code Ann. §§ 56.1-40 & 56.1-50 (Law. Co-op. Cum. Supp. 1998).

Scherer, D. (1991). The capacities of minors to exercise voluntariness in medical treatment decisions. *Law and Human Behavior, 15,* 431-49.

Scherer, D., & Gardner, W. (1990). Reasserting the authority of science. *American Psychologist, 45,* 1173-4.

Scherer, D., & Reppucci, N.D. (1988). Adolescents' capacities to provide voluntary informed consent: The effects of parental influence and medical dilemmas. *Law and Human Behavior, 12,* 123-41.

Schneider, M.D., Bersoff, D.N., & Podolsky, S.R. (1989). *Brief for amici curiae American Psychological Association, National Association of Social Workers, and the American Jewish Committee in* Ohio v. Akron Center for Reproductive Health *and* Hodgson v. Minnesota. Washington, DC: Jenner & Block.

Schwarz, D. (1993). Adolescent trauma: Epidemiologic approach. *Adolescent Medicine, 4,* 11-22.

Scott, E.S. (1992). Judgment and reasoning in adolescent decision making. *Vanderbilt Law Review, 37,* 1607-69.

Scott, E.S., Reppucci, N.D., & Woolard, J.L. (1995). Evaluating adolescent decision making in legal contexts. *Law and Human Behavior, 19,* 221-44.

Sigel, R.S., & Hoskin, M.B. (1981). *The political involvement of adolescents*. New Brunswick, NJ: Rutgers University Press.

Soderstrom, C.A., & Dearing-Stuck, B.A. (1993). Substance misuse and trauma: Clinical issues and injury prevention in adolescents. *Adolescent Medicine, 4,* 423-38.

Swain, D. (1995). Family group conferences in child care and protection and in youth justice in Aotearoa/New Zealand. *International Journal of Law and the Family, 9,* 155-207.

Tversky, A., & Kahneman, D. (1974). Judgment under uncertainty: Heuristics and biases. *Science, 185,* 1124-31.

Tversky, A., & Kahneman, D. (1981). The framing of decisions and the psychology of choice. *Science, 211,* 453-8.

Tyler, T.R., & Degoey, P. (1995). Community, family, and the social good: The psychological dynamics of procedural justice and social identification. In G.B. Melton (Ed.), *Nebraska Symposium on Motivation: Vol. 42. The individual, the family, and social good: Personal fulfillment in times of change.* Lincoln: University of Nebraska Press, pp. 53-91.

Va. Code § 54.1-2969(D) (Repl. Vol. 1998).

Vienna Convention on the Law of Treaties, 1155 U.N.T.S. 331 (1969).

Wadlington, W.J. (1973). Minors and health care: The age of consent. *Osgoode Hall Law Journal, 11,* 115-25.

Zimring, F.N. (1982). *The changing legal world of adolescence*. New York: Free Press.

Notes

1 This paper originally appeared in slightly different form as an article in *American Psychologist.* The article, which is reprinted with permission, was based on the author's address at the meeting of the American Psychological Association in Boston in August 1999 on receiving the APA Award for Distinguished Contributions to Public Service. A substantially briefer, non-technical version appeared earlier in *Family Futures*, a magazine formerly edited by the author, produced by the Institute for Families in Society at the University of South Carolina (which the author formerly directed), and published by Lawrence Erlbaum Associates, which provided permission to reprint the expanded article in *American Psychologist.*

The preparation of the report from which this article was initially derived was undertaken when the author was a consultant to the Public Committee (appointed by the Israeli Minister of Justice) for the Reexamination, in the Light of the UN Convention on the Rights of the Child, of Legislative Principles Pertaining to Children and the Law. This blue-ribbon panel is chaired by Judge Saviona Rotlevy, with principal staff support by Tamar Morag of the (Israeli) National Council for the Child. A symposium on the report was held in Jerusalem in June 1998.

2 The United States is the only country with a functioning government that has not ratified or acceded to the Convention. However, as a signatory to the Convention, the United States government is obligated by the Vienna Convention on the Law of Treaties (1969, art. 18[a]) not to take action contrary to the Convention on the Rights of the Child. Further, the Convention on the Rights of the Child has been so nearly universally adopted that it can be argued to have assumed the status of customary international law and thus to be legally binding on American authorities.

Children's democratic rights: Are we ready? What we can learn from young workers

PER MILJETEIG

Abstract

The United Nations Convention on the Rights of the Child firmly states that persons below the age of eighteen should also enjoy important civil and political rights. These rights include the right to freedom of expression; the right to freedom of thought, conscience and religion; protection of privacy; and freedom of association. In common parlance these rights are often referred to as the participation rights of children, and have been the subject of much interest as well as controversy since the adoption of the Convention. In most societies children are normally not thought of as independent citizens, or as subjects in their own right.

With reference to examples where working children and youth have organised themselves and spoken out on their rights as children and workers, this paper presents some thoughts about how the notion of children's participation or protagonism could be integrated into mainstream policy and programming for children. It also raises issues related to the changed roles of children and adults vis-à-vis each other. The concluding part contains a discussion of pressing challenges for adult society in general, and for those who work professionally with and for children in particular: how to alter our attitudes and behaviour if the principles of the Convention are to be fully observed with respect to children's participation rights, or rather, their democratic rights?

Addressing child labour from a child rights perspective

The world-wide implementation of the United Nations Convention on the Rights of the Child (UNCROC) as well as the process to establish a new International Labour Organisation (ILO) Convention against 'the worst forms of child labour' have created a climate that is conducive to viewing child labour and work-related exploitation of children in new ways. UNCROC includes Article 32 especially devoted to the right of the child to be protected from economic exploitation and work that is hazardous or interferes with the child's development or education. Indeed, the whole text of the UNCROC and the spirit behind it establishes an exhaustive framework for protecting children from *any kind of exploitation*. In addition to stating the unalienable rights of the child to survival and development, and to the full development of every child's potential, UNCROC offers several principles that promote the child's well-being and integration into society.

UNCROC also reiterates that persons *below* the age of eighteen enjoy civil and political rights previously laid out by other UN human rights treaties such as the International Covenant on Civil and Political Rights. The right to *freedom of expression* (Articles 12 and 13), the right to freedom *of thought, conscience and religion* (Article 14), the right to *freedom of association* (Article 15), the right to *protection of privacy* (Article 16), and the right to *access to information* (Article 17) are all included in UNCROC. An important innovation included in UNCROC is the right to be *informed about the rights* established by the Convention (Article 42).

If we want to address issues concerning the situation of working children and youth from a child rights perspective, it is crucial to keep in mind that 'participation rights' include all of the above rights. That means accepting that children are capable of having opinions, that these should be listened to and taken into serious consideration. It also implies that children can act on their own, take action to protect their own interests, and act as *stakeholders* in efforts to address their situation. In several countries around the world working children and youth have actively made use of their rights to form organisations and demand to be heard in child labour discourse. The question is: are we ready to take them seriously as *partners* in further efforts to address the problems connected with child labour?

'Participation rights' have been the subject of much interest as well as controversy since the adoption of UNCROC in 1989 (Miljeteig, 1992; 1994). In most societies children are normally not thought of as independent citizens, or as subjects in their own right. Even in societies that – at least in principle – are favourable towards children's participation, there has been discussion about how *genuine* participation could take place in practical terms (see for example, Flekkøy & Kaufman, 1997; Franklin, 1998; Kjørholt, 1998; West, 1997).

In my view, it is only when understood as *civil and political rights* or as *democratic rights,* that those participation rights gain full meaning and become possible to implement. I will raise issues related to the changed roles of children and adults vis-à-vis each other and discuss some pressing challenges both for adult society in general, and for those who work professionally with and for children. The question is: how to alter our (adult) attitudes and behaviour if the principles of the Convention are to be fully observed with respect to children's participation rights or – as I would prefer – their democratic rights? My paper is, to a large extent, based on a review I recently completed for the World Bank, examining the involvement of working children and youth in efforts to improve their own situation and to address issues of economic exploitation (Miljeteig, in press). I will use examples where working children and youth have organised themselves and spoken out for their rights as children and workers to demonstrate what 'participation rights' could mean, and some of the challenges that we encounter when children actively make use of their rights.

Influenced by UNCROC, the child labour discussion has become more focused on the aspect of *exploitation*, how to prevent such exploitation through, for instance education, social mobilisation, and poverty reduction initiatives. Furthermore, it has become accepted that it is necessary to include the perspective of working children and youth as well as that of their families properly if we are to fully understand child labour situations (Miljeteig, 1999; Woodhead, 1999). Working children have tuned in with statements such as: 'We are against exploitation at work but we are for work with dignity with hours adapted so that we have time for education and leisure' (*Kundapur Declaration*, 1996). Taken together, these developments have brought us a significant step further in understanding the complexities and realities of child labour. But we will not see a genuine child rights approach emerge until working children and youth are allowed to influence policies and programmes through active participation and partnership, and until we have fully realised the important resource they represent.

KUNDAPUR DECLARATION

1. We want recognition of our problems, our initiatives, proposals and our process of organisation.
2. We are against the boycott of products made by children.
3. We want respect and security for ourselves and the work that we do.
4. We want an education system whose methodology and content are adapted to our reality.
5. We want professional training adapted to our reality and capabilities.
6. We want access to good health care for working children.
7. We want to be consulted in all decisions concerning us, at local, national or international level.
8. We want the root causes of our situation, primarily poverty, to be addressed and tackled.
9. We want more activities in rural areas and decentralisation in decision making, so that children will no longer be forced to migrate.
10. We are against exploitation at work but we are for work with dignity with hours adapted so that we have time for education and leisure.

First International Meeting of Working Children, Kundapur, India
27 November–9 December 1996.

Working children and youth organising themselves

The very vocal and visible entry onto the scene of working children and youth, who speak out on their rights, including their right to be heard in the debate, has created several reactions. It has taken most of the other adult participants in 'child labour discourse' by surprise, and it has created some uneasiness because they are not really used to dealing with young people and their direct language. In some cases, young workers have caused particularly strong reactions, because they have made claims for their 'right to work' and the right to be respected as workers. Statements from international gatherings of working children and youth are very straightforward in their language and not easy to respond to with clear answers (*Dakar Declaration*, 1998; *Kundapur Declaration*, 1996).

In general, however, the public appearance of working children and youth has helped to give child labour 'a face' and contributed to a more nuanced and diversified understanding of what 'child labour' is. They have demonstrated that, despite being in extremely vulnerable situations, they have resources to make informed decisions about their lives, and that they are not passive *victims* of exploitation.

As an aside, it should be mentioned that working children organising themselves is not a 'modern' phenomenon. Actually one hundred years ago, in 1899, the newspaper boys in New York – the 'newsies' – organised themselves to fight for increased wages, and succeeded (Reddy, 1998). Another example is the Young Christian Workers movement, which originated in Belgium in 1925. It was a Catholic activist movement of workers aged fifteen to twenty-five that later inspired some of the pioneers in Latin America (Swift, 1999). Working children's organisations as we see them today, originate back to the 1970s and emerged simultaneously in different parts of the world. However, it is only during the last few years that the existence of such groups has reached the awareness of main stream 'child labour discourse'. Torres (1994) gives one of the first accounts of such organisations in her descriptions about the birth in Peru of Manthoc[1]. Manthoc is very much inspired by the Young Christian Workers movement and has become known as one of the most vocal proponents of working children's participation (Swift, 1999; Tolfree, 1998).

Overviews of organisations of working children and youth show that they have many things in common.[2] Firstly, they share a strong foundation in an activist approach that primarily aims to support empowerment of poor or otherwise marginalised and disadvantaged people. They are focusing on workers' rights and poverty reduction. They furthermore have in common a strong grassroots nature, with little trust in government and formal structures. They have all grown gradually and spontaneously from small initiatives. Even if they have large numbers of members, their main organisational units are small local groups. It would probably be more appropriate to label them as *movements* rather than organisations in the strict sense. This is also how they seem to perceive themselves, and is consistent with the way they grow to include several communities, states and countries in a region. They share important characteristics of democratic organisations in terms of the importance paid to election to offices and to representativity of those who speak on behalf of the organisations. Some of them have introduced membership identification as a means to identify and protect their members, and to gain acceptance as workers. Particularly, we have seen a rapid growth of groups of organised working children and youth in West African and Latin American countries. Another remarkable thing is the effective international networking among working children's organisations globally, with several, international gatherings of representatives from the various movements.

Achievements of working children and youth

Local level

In order to describe the achievements, so far, of organised working children and youth, it makes sense to distinguish between the local and international levels. Let us first take a look at the local level where the main focus of activity is, and also where the members have their daily lives and work. It is not easy to establish exactly how many members these organisations have. However, they all seem to grow, and to attract new members and supporters. As mentioned before, they tend to spread gradually from country to country within a geographical region. They seem to appeal to those working children who have the energy and the resources to participate in causes of collective concern. It is a clear impression that the members who join become activated and energised. Many of them decide to stay on, even after they technically are too old for the organisations, and become supporters in some capacity or another.

A common goal for the organisations is to support the members in their daily lives. This is typically done through small focused discussion groups, inspired by the PRA approach[3] used by many Non-Government Organisations (NGOs) in developmental work. Here they share their thoughts about the situation they are in, what kind of problems they meet in their work situations, and how to deal with daily hassles. Joining others who are in the same situation creates a sense of belonging, self esteem, and group solidarity. Many of the members are young people who work in the informal sector – for example as domestics – and work in isolation from others of their age. These young people are particularly prone to exploitation, and need to learn about their rights and possibilities. Particularly Manthoc – in the Latin American context – has attached great importance to supporting young workers in gaining a sense of dignity associated with their work and with making a living from decent work. It is assumed that those who achieve better understanding about their situation as children or adolescents, as workers and as citizens will also be better able to protect themselves from exploitation and seek less harmful types of work. For that reason Manthoc has made it a specific part of its philosophy to promote what they call *formación*, an educational approach focused on giving information about the society within which the young workers live and skills that are useful in their particular situation. For the same reason, most of them have paid great importance to disseminating information widely among their members and externally. The African Movement and Bhima Sangha both have newsletters with wide circulation, and have started using electronic communication (e-mail and the worldwide web) to disseminate their information. The Bhima Sangha newsletter has a format that allows it to be used as a poster as well.

In some cases, informal training in literacy and vocational skills is organised within the smaller units of the organisations. Sometimes it is as basic – and effective – as those who have reading and writing skills sharing them with those who do not. The Senegalese Movement of Working Children and Youth has given importance to teaching their members French, the official language of the country, to enable them to extend their linguistic capabilities beyond their local language and better understand what is going on in their society. Working children's groups in West Africa have also successfully negotiated access to classrooms for literacy classes after hours (Mali); or, on a more systematic level, organised literacy courses outside of working hours for their members (Côte d'Ivoire). To address health concerns, they have collaborated with local health services to set up a scheme whereby working children can seek consultation at the hospital at the same price as school children (Côte d'Ivoire), won access to the same services as public servants at the same price (Côte d'Ivoire) and set up a mutual savings scheme for health care (Senegal). In Senegal, young workers have also organised joint purchases of material they need for their work, for instance as shoe shiners.

Both at the community and the national level, the organisations have worked to influence legislation relating to children and youth in general, or more specifically to child labour. Examples of this can be found in Peru and India. The most striking and well-publicised example is probably how the National Movement of Street Boys and Girls in Brazil significantly influenced the inclusion of a reference to children's rights in the new constitution and the drafting of national legislation on children and youth in the late 1980s (Gomes da Costa & Schmidt-Rahmer, 1991). Working children's organisations have participated in local child rights campaigns and established partnerships for instance with local NGOs and trade unions. In Senegal and Mali, for instance, the local movements of working children and youth have become official partners in the local IPEC[4] programmes. In Mali it is represented in the local IPEC governing body.

International level

The young workers who gathered for instance at Kundapur[5] or in Dakar,[6] or sent their representatives to large international conferences in Amsterdam,[7] Trondheim,[8] Oslo[9] or Geneva[10] presented themselves as quite different from what is usually expected of 'child labourers'. These young workers were an effective contrast to the picture of working children as sad and suffering victims, unable to protect themselves. They gave coherent presentations of their own situations, what led them into the work they are doing, the problems and hassles they face on a daily basis, and how they are trying to relate to all of this. Furthermore, they presented ideas and opinions about what needs to be done, and gave warnings about well intended, but not carefully thought out efforts from the international community to 'solve' the 'child labour problem'. The essence of their messages is reflected for instance in the declarations from their meetings in Kundapur and Dakar.[11] Their clear message is that child workers can no longer be perceived exclusively as passive recipients of protection and special services. They are able to take action to improve their situation, and should consequently be consulted and involved in the development of measures to assist them.

At international meetings and conferences, the awkwardness around including young representatives in the regular proceedings of such meetings has been very obvious. The young people are not familiar with the usual formal setting and protocol. The other participants are not used to dealing directly with young people in this setting. Nor do they seem to be comfortable with the language and impatience of the young people. Maybe this will change as the novelty of the situation disappears. There has been some uncertainty about what 'status' the working children and youth have at such events. At the child labour conference in Amsterdam, a panel of young workers was included in the programme. At the Oslo conference, some working children's organisations were invited to participate as part of the NGO caucus. They were invited to make prepared interventions, for instance in the session on 'social mobilisation'. In other words, in Amsterdam, they were treated as 'working children' and given a special place in the conference in the form of a 'working children's panel'. In Oslo, they were 'regular NGO participants' in the conference. Of these two approaches, it is difficult to say which was most efficient or appropriate. It is significant to note that in both cases there were separate children's meetings on the side, to serve as support (among other things) for the young people participating actively in the respective conferences.

One of the critical views against such participation states that these children and youngsters are not representative of working children. 'How can they represent all working children?' 'Some of them are not even children any longer!' are among the most typical comments. In response to the first comment on representativity, technically they cannot speak on behalf of *all* working children.

However, the organisations they come from have been through very careful processes to identify who should represent them in the various meetings. If they sometimes use generalised phrases when they talk, this should not be judged more harshly than in other instances when people make general statements. On the question of age, it is correct that some of the spokespersons for working children are over eighteen years old. Again, it should be noted that they have been elected by the organisations to speak on behalf of them. Some of them have a history as child workers, and have continued to work for the issue. That should be seen as positive and not be used against them. The age issue has also been used the other way around. At the Oslo conference, one of the government delegates publicly accused the representative of the African Movement of Working Children and Youth to be lying about her age. He was making the point that a thirteen-year-old would not be able to speak at an international conference the way she did.[12]

Another point that has not been raised so often – but is probably the most relevant if one wants to be critical about representativity – is that the young workers who speak at international conferences or to the media are probably the most resourceful among the young workers. In that respect, they might not be representing all their fellow workers. This should be borne in mind so that one does not go to the other extreme and expect that same involvement from all working children and youth.

Spontaneous vs planned participation

What makes the experience of organised working children so fascinating to observe is that these young people have not waited for an invitation to 'participate'. They have just acted on their own, and implemented their own rights in their own way, in some cases as a response to information about these rights. Also, they have exercised their right to freedom of association, a right that one normally does not attribute to children. Organisations of working children and youth have typically developed slowly and organically, according to the needs of the people involved as defined by themselves. That makes these organisations difficult to describe in organisational terms, and sometimes difficult for the surrounding world to relate to. They do not always have formalised structures as many adult organisations have. It is characteristic that they, both locally and internationally, tend to describe themselves as movements. It is also interesting that labour organisations, both locally and internationally, have been quite negative about the notion of recognising these organisations as labour unions. This is a discussion that cannot be taken further here but it is interesting that the International Confederation of Free Trade Unions (ICFTU) is now launching a 'youth campaign' where they are encouraging labour unions around the world to recruit young workers as members and to look after their interests.[13]

DAKAR DECLARATION

Debate on the new convention:

- We will ask the ILO to give us a chance to speak during its coming Conference in Geneva so that we can express ourselves on the convention on 'intolerable forms' of child labour.
- We are against prostitution, slavery and drug trafficking by children. These are CRIMES and not WORK. The decision-makers should distinguish between work and crime.
- We are fighting every day against hazardous work and against exploitation of child work. We are also fighting for the improvement of life and working conditions of all children in the world.
- We want all the children in the world to have, one day, the right to make a choice between working and not working.
- Work should be in accordance with the capacity and development of each and every child and not depend on his/her age.

1. Initiatives and politics on child labour

- The Working Child and Youth Movements should always be consulted in decisions on child work. If a decision has to be taken, we should take it all together.
- We will not participate in the Global March Against Child Labour because its organisers refused to involve us and because we cannot march against our own work

2. Our Movements

We have decided to create an International Co-ordination of Working Children Movements so as to:

- reinforce our solidarity;
- make known our ten points decided upon in Kundapur against poverty, to address the basic causes which force us to work and for the improvement of our life and working conditions;
- always make clear our point of view in debates on child work.

We are sending this appeal to all Movements of Working Children so that they all can join us.

Adopted by representatives of the Movements of Working Children and Youth of Africa, Latin America and Asia, at their meeting in Dakar, Senegal, March 1998.

The way these young people act fits very well with the definition Hart (1992) introduced when he tried to specify what children's participation means in the light of UNCROC, and what qualifies as *genuine child participation*. He defines 'participation' as:

> … the process of sharing decisions which affect one's life and the life of the community in which one lives. It is the means by which a democracy is built and it is a standard against which democracies should be measured. Participation is the fundamental right of citizenship (Hart, 1992, p. 5).

To stress the interactive and responsibility-taking aspects of participation, Manthoc introduced the term *protagonism*.[14] The word is now being increasingly used in English, with the meaning it carries in Spanish, to underscore some of the associations normally not linked with participation, such as a capacity to actively take part in the definition of the choices of a given community (see also Cussianovich, 1997; Sanz, 1997; Swift, 1999; Tolfree, 1998; Torres, 1994). To take this further, one could say that a protagonist is a partner.

Tolfree (1998) studied the role of children in various programmes and organisations for working children, and concluded that the direct involvement of children in the running of the organisations creates a sense of responsibility:

> … it is through the collaborative work with others – children and adults – that young people learn to exercise responsibilities. It is in this context that concepts such as protagonism … are important, for they emphasise that the exercise of active participation goes hand-in-hand with the exercise of responsibility. Evidence from the case studies suggests that it is this more active exercise of responsibility which tends to promote positive changes in working children rather than mere participation (Tolfree, 1998, p. 47).

In addition to taking responsibility for themselves and others, members of the working children's organisations also exercise actively their right to access information (UNCROC Article 17). Seeking and promoting information about issues relevant to their situation, such as legislation or health care services, plays an important role in the activities of organisations of working children. Manthoc has, from its inception, used *formación* (creating knowledge and awareness beyond regular education) as a key conceptual tool in its work alongside *protagonism*. The philosophy is that without sufficient and relevant knowledge about their situation and the society in which they live, the working children and their families will not be able to improve their situation. If they are to have impact on policies and programmes developed by local and national governments or international organisations they also need access to information about how such agencies work. Particularly, international collaboration is regulated by a set of intricate formal and informal rules. Without in-depth knowledge of these rules and the procedures for decision making, it is difficult to gain any direct influence.

Furthermore, organised working children and youth make a creative interpretation of Articles 12 and 13 when they insist that information they present *as a group* must be taken into consideration. Taken literally, the text of UNCROC undercommunicates the right of children to *provide* information. In the case of exploitation of working children and youth, it should be obvious that the information they could give us about their working conditions would be a very important input to the planning of interventions aimed at improving their situation. Such information would be crucial to ensure that interventions are effective and actually help the children they are aimed at.

Discussion

The road forward

The organisations of working children and youth are like living laboratories for participation rights and democracy. In the further theorising about how to facilitate and arrange for children's participation, it might be worth taking a closer look at how these organisations work, what strategies they develop and their actual achievements. It would be a falsification of the history not to mention the important role of adults in these organisations. They have often been the key sources of inspiration. In many cases, these adults come from the same background as the working children and have genuine insight into their situation. These adults have, as far as I can see, been very conscious about their role as facilitators, and made great efforts to establish the principle that the organisations are to be led by children and youth, and that they as adults should have only an advisory or supportive role. Most of the organisations have organised – or been involved in organising – training courses for adults working with children. They all have continuous internal debates on the relationship between adults and children, and what the roles of the adults should be vis-à-vis the children. In several cases, the 'adults' are actually young people who have joined the organisation at an earlier age, and who want to continue to support their younger 'colleagues'. Here is a lot of experience to be analysed further, in order to learn more about how children and adults can collaborate towards common goals, and about what kind of adult support is conducive for child-led activities.

The reason behind the apparent success at local level must be found in the fact that the organisations of working children and youth use the actual needs of their members as the entry point for their activities. Thus, they focus on very concrete and real issues or problems that need urgent attention and where the results might be of immediate importance in their daily lives. There is no need to 'construct' themes for collaboration between the young people, or between young people and adults.

The success at local level has not been matched with the same success internationally. There seems to be a large gap between the ability to take responsibility for each other and negotiate solutions to local problems on the one hand, and to participate in and make an impact on international proceedings on the other hand. The main reason is probably a clash between languages and methods of work. But as the examples above show, there is also scepticism and lack of empathy from adults. For example: when some of the working children claim they have 'the right to work', many adults and their organisations react negatively and refuse to talk with them. They have already taken the non-negotiable position that children and work are incompatible. They do not ask why some working children take that position, or try to understand why it is important for them and their families that they work. If they had listened, they would also have heard the majority of working children say that they want education, and that they want time for play, recreation and cultural activities. But they may have a different opinion about what kind of education serves them best or the optimal combination between work and school. In many cases, working children know full well that if they do not work, their families will starve. In that kind of situation, there is little time or energy to attend to ideals. I am not saying that working children necessarily are right and that one should follow all their suggestions. But the least that one should do, in the spirit of UNCROC, is to try and listen in order to establish a dialogue.

Working children who have participated in international conferences report back that they feel there is a big distance between themselves and the adult participants. Two typical reactions from young people were: 'They said they want to abolish child labour, put children in schools because children have to go to school, have to play, and that if a child works then he or she is no more a child. While we have organised ourselves to fight against poverty and improvement of our working conditions.'[15] 'Several researchers presented the results of their studies. They talked a lot and we understood very little of what they were saying.'[16] We should listen very carefully to what such statements actually tell us.

At the local level, there are already initiatives under way to include working children and youth in programmes and operations that are aimed at improving their situation or assisting them in various ways (see for example, Johnson, Ivan-Smith, Gordon, Pridmore, & Scott, 1998; Tolfree, 1998). Local organisations such as Manthoc, Enda, FUNPRONOP[17] and CWC[18] are pioneering, giving working children great influence in their work, and supporting groups or organisations of working children. International NGOs such as members of the Save the Children Alliance have followed suit, particularly in making measures to include – in their own working methods – children when relevant and appropriate by taking a 'child-centred approach'. Organisations that work both at local and international levels, such as Save the Children and UNICEF could play an important role in two ways: (1) by using their resources to develop models for genuine and culturally sensitive participation of working children in planning and programming which relate to their situation; and (2) by serving as advocates for working children and youth by helping to convey their views and opinions from the local level into relevant international fora.

As mentioned before, there is a need to examine already accumulated experience and, based on that knowledge, develop more comprehensive approaches. Since the organisations mentioned above for the main part operate at the local level, it is a particular challenge to develop strategies for partnerships with international organisations of working children and youth, where such exist. Other organisations that operate internationally, such as the World Bank, have included participation of their beneficiaries as an important principle in their operations. They should be challenged to apply the principles they have developed for working with disadvantaged groups, such as poor people or women, to working with young exploited workers as well.

Here it should be mentioned very briefly that there are exciting initiatives to include children in designing, implementing and evaluating programmes within the fields of community and environmental development (for example, see Hart, Espinosa, Iltus, & Lorenzo, 1997; Johnson *et al.*, 1998) and urban planning (for example, see Chawla, in press; Swart-Kruger & Chawla, 1998). So far this process has not included programmes aimed at children and work in any significant way. It is to be hoped that these processes could merge and create synergies.

Challenges

Looking at the experience gained by organisations of working children and youth and their encounters with the 'adult world', the following challenges should be addressed urgently, if we mean to take children's civil and political rights seriously. In order to show respect to children and young people and prove that we take their rights seriously, we need to *establish a culture of listening to children*. As Roger Hart has put it: 'Children's participation is often promoted as a "children's voices" movement, but it should equally be an "adult ears" movement' (Hart, 1998, p. 147). This means that we are obliged to respect young people's right to have different opinions from our own, and that we are willing to examine them without prejudice. We cannot reject statements we do not like without trying to understand the reasoning behind such statements.

The next challenge follows almost automatically if we take the first one seriously. There is a need to *establish a dialogue* with young workers, a two-way communication based on respect. At the local level, where children and adults work very closely together in the movements, this seems to function. Let us study how they have managed to establish this mode of collaboration and partnership. Further, we need to examine the *language* we use. Well-intended adults and their organisations talk about abolishing child labour, making work below certain ages forbidden by the law, rehabilitating child workers. Many working children and youth find this language offensive because they feel that such phrases do not reflect respect for them as individual human beings. In a joint statement addressed to the 1999 International Labour Conference, some of the movements commented on the language in the new convention on the worst forms of child labour: 'Instead of talking about "rehabilitation"... we prefer the phrase "the necessary attention and assistance" and instead of "return into society" we prefer "active participation" in the community and in society.'[19] No wonder that young people who contribute actively to the economy of their societies and families feel provoked by indications that they are outside of society! Such statements should serve as an important reminder that we need to pay more attention to language. Trying to establish a common language that avoids the unnecessary confrontations and misunderstandings should be the ultimate goal. Where a common language is not possible, or desirable, one should at least establish an understanding of what is meant by words and phrases used, and the reasoning behind them.

If there was a willingness to establish a dialogue, using the appropriate language, there might also be a willingness to find *ways to include representatives for working children and youth* in such international proceedings as those leading up to the new ILO convention. The regional movements of working children and youth have had several international gatherings with difficult negotiations among themselves, and have managed to reach agreements. Why should they not be able to take part in negotiations with adults? I would suggest it has more to do with willingness from adults than with young people's ability.

Working children and youth can provide valuable information and insights about their work, what brings them into working situations, and how they can improve their working conditions or find ways to combine earning a necessary income with relevant and future oriented education. They can also tell us something about what works and what does not work in interventions to help them. Some programmes for working children have started to include the 'beneficiaries' as partners in the design, implementation and evaluation of the interventions. Some researchers have tried to develop ways to seek information directly from working children about how they experience their work and the impact it has on their situation (for example, see Johnson et al., 1998; Tolfree, 1998; Woodhead, 1998). I see a great challenge in finding ways to collect such information on a systematic basis, and make use of and value it as an important tool to improve the situation of working children and to eliminate exploitative work.

There are many different *roles of adults* vis-à-vis working children: those of parents, employers, facilitators in working children's programmes, local authorities, representatives of local and international organisations. One central question relates to all: how far are they/we willing to regard children and young people as partners worth listening to, and people to include in our reasoning and planning? The young people are reaching out to meet us – are we ready to meet them on equal terms?

This leads us to the ultimate and unavoidable question of whether we are willing to revise (or even change) our *understandings of democracy*. Are we willing to change our perceptions about who defines the 'reality' in such issues as child labour, and who makes the decisions? Are we willing to give up power and admit that sometimes young people come up with better explanations and better solutions than we do? Cockburn (1998) has suggested a new model for democracy that is based on the fact that children and adults are interdependent. Such a model might provide theoretical grounds for arguing that all children carry some responsibilities and duties. This is the case that working children and youth are making. If we expect that even the youngest members of society have responsibilities and duties, it is only fitting they are awarded rights and citizenship. The youngest children might be more 'dependent' upon some adults. This should not necessarily exclude them from citizenship, as we are all in some sense or another dependent upon others (Cockburn, 1998).

References

A letter from the street. (1998). No. 17. Dakar: Enda Tiers Monde.

Chawla, L. (in press). Toward better cities for children and youth. In L. Chawla (Ed.), *Growing up in an urbanising world.* London: Earthscan.

Cockburn, T. (1998). Children and citizenship in Britain. A case for a socially interdependent model of citizenship. *Childhood*, *5*(1), 99-117.

Cussianovich, A. (1997, June). *The 'out of place': Paradigm of a new society.* Paper presented at Urban Childhood conference, Trondheim, Norway.

Dakar Declaration. (1998). Adopted by representatives of the Movements of Working Children and Youth of Africa, Latin America and Asia, at their meeting in Dakar, Senegal, March 1998.

Flekkøy, M.G., & Kaufman, N.H. (1997). *The participation rights of the child. Rights and responsibilities in family and society.* London: Jessica Kingsley Publishers.

Franklin, B. (1998). Children's political rights. In E. Verhellen (Ed.), *Understanding children's rights. Ghent papers on children's rights – No. 3.* Ghent: Children's Rights Centre, University of Ghent, pp. 157-73.

Gomes da Costa, A.C., & Schmidt-Rahmer, B. (1991). Brazil: Children spearhead a movement for change. In *The Convention: Child rights and the UNICEF experience at the country level.* Florence: UNICEF International Child Development Centre (Innocenti Studies).

Hart, R.A. (1992). *Children's participation: From tokenism to citizenship.* Florence: UNICEF International Child Development Centre (Innocenti Essay No. 4).

Hart, R.A. (1998). Children's right to participate: Some tools to stimulate discussion on the issue in different cultures. In E. Verhellen (Ed.), *Understanding children's rights. Ghent papers on children's rights – No. 3.* Ghent: Children's Rights Centre, University of Ghent, pp. 141-56.

Hart, R.A., Espinosa, M.F., Iltus, S., & Lorenzo, R. (1997). *Children's participation. The theory and practice of involving young citizens in the community development and environmental care.* London: UNICEF, Earthscan.

Johnson, V., Ivan-Smith, E., Gordon, G., Pridmore, P., & Scott, P. (Eds). (1998). *Stepping forward. Children and young people's participation in the development process.* London:

Intermediate Technology Publications.

Kjørholt, A.T. (1998, November). *Children as active citizens: Perspectives on Norwegian Child Policy and the implementation of the UN Convention on the Rights of the Child.* Paper presented at Children's Rights and Wrongs Conference, Nicosia, Cyprus: Centre for World Dialogue and UNICEF.

Kundapur Declaration. (1996). Adopted at First International Meeting of Working Children, Kundapur, India, 27 November 9 December, 1996.

Miljeteig(-Olssen), P. (1992). Children's participation: Giving children the opportunity to develop into active and responsible members of society. *Social Education, 56*(4), 4.

Miljeteig, P. (1994, June–July). *Children's involvement in the implementation of their own rights – present and future perspectives.* Paper presented at International Society for the Study of Behavioural Development, XIIIth Biennial Meeting, Amsterdam, the Netherlands.

Miljeteig, P. (1999). Understanding child labour. *Childhood, 6*(1), 5-12.

Miljeteig, P. (in press). *Creating partnerships with working children and youth.* Washington, DC: The World Bank.

Reddy, N. (1998, September). *Child labour and the value of children's decisions: The child's place in policy and practice.* Paper presented at the ISPCAN congress, Auckland, New Zealand.

Sanz, A. (1997). From Kundapur to Geneva. The international coordination of working children. *NATs Working Children and Adolescents International Review, 3*(3-4), 11-23.

Save the Children. (1998). *Report on the working children's forum. Oslo, Norway 21st October – 2nd November 1997 and the international conference on child labour 27th – 30th October 1997.* Geneva: The International Save the Children Alliance.

Swart-Kruger, J., & Chawla, L. (1998, November). *Children show the way: Participatory programs for children of South African streets and squatter camps.* Paper prepared for the Conference on Youth in Cities: Successful Mediators of Normative Development. Marbach Castle, Lake Constance, Germany.

Swift, A. (1999). *Working children get organised: An introduction to working children's organisations.* London: International Save the Children Alliance.

Tolfree, D. (1998). *Old enough to work, old enough to have a say.* Stockholm: Rädda Barnen.

Torres, N. (1994). Working children, leading the struggle to obtain and defend their own rights. In E. Verhellen & F. Spiesschaert (Eds), *Children's rights: Monitoring issues.* Ghent: Mys & Breesch Publishers.

West, A. (1997). Children and political participation. In E. Verhellen (Ed.), *Understanding children's rights. Ghent papers on children's rights – No. 2.* Ghent: Children's Rights Centre, University of Ghent, pp. 243-57.

Woodhead, M. (1998). *Children's perspectives on their working lives. A participatory study in Bangladesh, Ethiopia, The Philippines, Guatemala, El Salvador and Nicaragua.* Stockholm: Rädda Barnen.

Woodhead, M. (1999). Combatting child labour. Listen to what the children say. *Childhood, 6*(1), 27-49.

Notes

1. Movimiento de Niños y Adolescentes Hijos de Obreros Christianos. In English: Movement of Working Children and Adolescents form Christian Working Class Families.
2. For more detailed accounts of the individual organisations and their histories see for instance: Swift (1999); Tolfree (1998). The organisations which I have drawn my examples from are Manthoc and the Latin-American movement of working children and youth;

Enda-Jeunesse Action and the African Movement of Working Children and Youth; MNMMR - The National Movement of Street Boys and Girls (Brazil); Bhima Sangha (India). To a large extent I have also made use of their newsletters and other information material, as well as personal communications as sources for my work.

3 Participatory Rural Appraisal, a method that was originally developed to empower local communities, and increasingly used with children and youth.

4 The International Programme for the Elimination of Child Labour (IPEC) is a special programme under the International Labour Organisation (ILO). It is implemented through a series of national programmes based on an agreement between ILO and the national government with multiple local partners.

5 First International Meeting of Working Children, Kundapur, India, 27 November–9 December 1996.

6 International Movement of Working Children, meeting in Dakar, Senegal, March 1998.

7 Conference on the elimination of the most intolerable forms of child labour. Amsterdam, 26–27 February 1997.

8 Urban Childhood conference, Trondheim, Norway, 9–12 June 1997.

9 Working Children's Forum, Oslo, Norway, 21 October–2 November 1997 and International Conference on Child Labour, Oslo, Norway, 27–30 October 1997.

10 Forum of working children and youth held in connection with the International Labour Conference, Geneva, June 1997.

11 See boxes with full text of *Kundapur Declaration* and *Dakar Declaration*.

12 This incident was duly underlined and commented upon in the children's debriefing after the conference. See Save the Children, 1998; *A letter from the street*, 1998.

13 ICFTU has made a strict limit at the age of fourteen to fifteen (depending on type of country) to comply with international standards as expressed in ILO Convention No. 138 concerning Minimum Age for Admission to Employment.

14 From Spanish: 'Protagonísmo'.

15 Dibou Faye, African Movement of Working Children and Youth, about the International Conference on Child Labour, Oslo 27–30 October 1997 (*A letter from the street*, 1998).

16 Representatives from Dakar Working Children's Association, about the Child Labour Section, Urban Childhood Conference, Trondheim, 9–12 June 1997. *A letter from the street*, 1998.

17 Fundaciòn Olof Palme (The Olof Palme Foundation) in El Salvador.

18 The Concerned for Working Children, Bangalore, India.

19 Declaration addressed to the 87th Assembly of the ILO, (June 1999) from the NAT's movements of Asia, Africa, Latin America and the Caribbean on the new ILO Convention and Recommendation on child labour.

Urban children and families in distress: Global trends and concerns

Irene Rizzini

Thoughts on globalisation and global trends

Over the past few years there has been a growing interest in discussing globalisation as well as values, morals and ethics in a globalised world. This is a debate that extends to many topics and is far larger than the effect of globalisation on domestic economies.

Because the term 'globalisation' has become popular, there is much overgeneralization, confusion and oversimplification of its meaning. Phenomena that confuse us or make us anxious are often laid at the door of globalisation. It has been pointed out, however, that globalisation is neither a new concept nor a recent phenomenon (Soares, 1996, Wilson, 1998, Moore, 1998).

What differentiates us then in present times? I would agree with the sociologist Roland Robertson, who argues that 'we in the late twentieth century live increasingly in a condition of conscious globality'. According to Robertson's argument, however, globalisation is not to be seen '... as a consequence of modernity' rather it is 'a condition that facilitates modernization and promotes divergent modernities' (Robertson, 1996, pp. 74–75).

The impact on people's lives of a growing globalised world is certainly far from understood. The emphasis on the globalisation of the economy has left many other topics out of the debate, particularly those related to social and psychological changes in the everyday lives of people in general. Of special interest to us is the lack of debate about the effect of globilization on children and youth. The condition of childhood is connected to the future of any given society since the young ones are the main transmitters of moral values (Myers, 1992). However obvious this may seem, the fact is that in the current literature on global issues, children have not been considered (Kaufman, Rizzini, & Wilson, 1999).

In the next pages, I will focus on some of the global trends most directly related to urban families and children. In doing so, it is important to keep in mind the following considerations:

- The multidimensionality of the phenomenon. Beyond the commonly addressed political and economic dimensions, there are a multitude of human issues at stake.

- I will use a global/local as well as global/individual perspective with the understanding that no matter how global and universal certain trends seem to be, they affect different countries and people differently both in individual and collective ways.
- I will be highlighting and discussing mostly trends which reflect distress. According to recent world reports on social indicators, there has been progress in most countries – for example, in infant mortality, life expectancy and educational attainment. Nevertheless, human deprivation and a broad range of inequalities continue to be great challenges worldwide.
- In the presentation of indicators, tables and figures, people are portrayed solely as the subjects or victims of a global system against which there is nothing to be done. The general sense of impotence in living in a 'global village or community' may or may not be stronger than a peasant living under feudal regimes centuries ago, nevertheless it certainly characterises our present lives. Global trends are helpful in giving us a broader sense as well as a comparative perspective of where we are heading as collectives. I would add that they can be most helpful in assisting governments to shape their policies to improve people's lives if they wish to.
- Let us not forget that behind each of the facts, thoughts and figures, that there are real people who are targets of devastating consequences because of the lack of commitment of insensitive transnational corporations. It is important to remember that such corporations would not be allowed to freely act if it were not for the consent of public authorities who, in the name of democracy, ought to represent their nations and peoples, but act on behalf of a privileged minority who always profit, no matter what.

Urban children and families in distress: Global trends and concerns

Change and crisis. There is a growing consensus that the world is undergoing major and accelerated changes. The twentieth century has been a period of extraordinary human advancement and profound contradictions which gives us all a sense of deepening crisis. It is hard to say whether we are living in a specially critical time as compared to other moments in the history of humankind. Apparently, our ancestors, at different times, faced a similar sense of fear and chaos when confronted with a rapidly changing political, economic and social order, which forced them to reorganise their life styles and adapt to a new reality. For example, in the nineteenth century the same kind of perplexities and concerns we are experiencing today about the escalating growth of cities and urban population, and the increase in crime, were reported as one of the most important problems. Louis Chevalier, referring to the city of Paris, spoke of 'Laboring classes and dangerous classes', a rather common topic in the literature at the time:

> And in the central quarters themselves, where the capital's complex and disordered growth had engendered a tangle of lanes, passageways, courts and blind alleys and had ranged cheek by jowl sunny street and cesspool, the affluent mansion and slum, areas of light and shade in a landscape we can now barely make out, and had almost everywhere left nooks and corners ideally suited to robbery with violence by day or night and, indeed, in some places day hardly differed from night (Chevalier, 1973, p. 2).

At the turn of the last century, the German sociologist Simmel (1902–76), published a series of articles analysing what he called 'the metropolitan life-style'. This new and fashionable urban lifestyle, which so rapidly influenced the habits of people used to the rural life, came to symbolise progress and modernity at the time – not, however, without a fantastic dose of confusion! The new life style was, according to Simmel, characterised by speed, discontinuity, unexpected images and impressions, along with a complex and diverse social and economic life, based on monetary negotiations. All of this was in deep contrast to the experience of life in rural villages and small towns. As a product of the new psychological conditions that the metropolis creates, emerges a new type of man – metropolitan man – centred on his own individuality, governed by the 'sophisticated character of the metropolitan psychic life' (Rizzini, 1997, p. 41).

The dramatic change from rural to urban life has affected people worldwide over the twentieth century, with great impact on family, community structures, and organisation. The impact seems to be even more dramatic at present. What makes this time seem to be one of deepening crisis? With no intention of fully answering this question, I will discuss some of the global issues, indicators, and trends of direct relevance to urban families and children. My main focus will be on what seems to be an unsolved contradiction between globalisation and the economic, social and political inequalities which lead the world towards deepening segregation and increasing gaps between the wealthy and the poor. This is one of our most difficult challenges for the third millennium.

Global trends: significant local impact. Despite the efforts of international organisations, such as UNICEF and the World Bank, to advertise the progress achieved by the developing countries in improving some of their social indicators, the brutal reality is that '... currently, more than 1.3 billion people in the developing world still struggle to survive on less than a dollar a day' (World Bank, 1997, p. 17). The contrasts are so staggering in different parts of the world that it suggests the coexistence of entirely different universes. For example:

> Life expectancy in Sub-Saharan Africa is just 50 years; in Japan it is almost 80. Mortality among children under 5 in South Asia exceeds 170 deaths per thousand; in Sweden it is fewer than 10. More than 110 million children in the developing world lack access to primary education; in the industrial countries anything less

> than universal enrollment would rightly be regarded as unacceptable. The starkness of these contrasts attests the continuing toll of human deprivation (World Bank, 1990, p. 1).

While there is no simple correlation between poverty and distress, it is reasonable to believe that those who live under constant deprivation are more likely to suffer as they are more vulnerable. This is particularly true for women and children, since it is well known that in poor households women often work longer hours than men and get lower salaries. Children, too, particularly girls, suffer disproportionately, and the future quality of their lives is compromised by poor nutrition, health care, education, and heavy workloads. Young girls are frequently responsible for all the housework and for taking care of their siblings while their parents work long hours. In most countries, this is not considered 'labour' (UNICEF, 1992; Salazar & Glasinovich, 1998).

According to Andrews (1998), the increasing pace and complexity of political, economic and social transformations over the past few decades have coincided with rapid changes in family life. However, it is important to consider that no matter how rapidly and profoundly families have been impacted, human development in the earliest years has changed little. It seems to be universally accepted by psychologists that 'throughout the world, children rely on families for healthy physical, mental, social, moral, and spiritual development' (Bronfenbrenner, 1990, cited in Andrews, 1998, p. 2).

I will now look at some of the recent global trends in family life and relate them to the way they seem to be impacting on children. Note that we are dealing with broad generalisations here, which means we are not taking into account any specific cultural, ethnic, racial or other differences in this discussion. One of the main sources of information for the following section is Andrews (1998).

Families and children

Families are smaller than they have ever been. Some of the important indicators here are that fertility rates are declining, single parent families are increasing, sibling groups and extended kin networks are smaller. Birthrates decrease as women gain access to contraceptives, health care, education and economic opportunities. However, this does not mean better or equal opportunities for all, as 98 per cent of the population growth occurs in the developing world (Zwingle, 1998). On the positive side, smaller families are more likely to provide better care for their children. On the other hand, one of the main drawbacks related to the decreasing numbers of people in family units is that children (as well as parents) are more isolated. Other factors closely related to this are the rapidly changing patterns of work, family and community life (Kovarik, 1994).

Mobility tends to be higher these days. Migration and migratory distances are increasing due to several factors, such as: search for employment opportunities, forced migration due to war, civil conflict, and disaster. Parents separate and connect with new partners. Family members often live geographically apart. Recent painful examples display cases of massive migration in Latin America (Nicaragua, Colombia, Mexico), the former USSR., Yugoslavia, Central Africa, and Palestine. Demographers point out that migration occurs mainly because of two factors: to search for better job opportunities or to escape from the negative impact of life at home, such as political unrest and natural disaster. These migrations have taken place for a long time, and do not constitute a new trend, except that because unskilled labour is less in demand, this mass of displaced people are not welcome anywhere. When families break apart and travel long distances with little hope of reconnection, there is a great impact on children as they feel their parents are often out of place and vulnerable, unable to provide for their protection and well being. A number of other cultural, ethnic and racial factors are at stake here as growing numbers of children live in environments where they feel hostility and prejudice towards their families (see Stephens, 1995; 1997).

The diminished spatial autonomy of children in urban settings is another aspect. Take the example of California, where it is estimated that one quarter of the residents are immigrants from Mexico, other parts of Central and Latin America, China, Hong Kong, and Korea. According to a study carried out in the inner city of Los Angeles, most of the families are transnational, moving back and forth between the US and their home town or village. But while they live in two worlds, their new life has new constraints. According to Thorne, 'in the US kids have more material objects and perhaps better long-range opportunities, but they are often confined in spaces because of the dangers of street violence, gangs and drugs' (Thorne, 1998, p. 3).

Families are together for less time. There are growing numbers of parents at work, women are more likely to work outside the home, and balancing work and home is becoming more stressful. As for the children, they are at child-care centres or schools for increasingly extended periods, there is less adult-child interaction with independent leisure choices, more peer groups interaction with no participation of family members, children are increasingly likely to care for themselves, and children have few or no adults nearby. One effect of the world-wide intense urbanisation process is that the community is larger and less cohesive, affecting parent–child relationships and family life as a whole.

In the industrialised world, increased labour force participation of women results in the growth of women's dual work role (labour force and domestic). In the United States, for example, the burden on poorer women is made greater by the fact that job growth in metro regions has been in areas where poor families do not live. This means long travel times (adding to the length of the day) even for families with cars, and impossible commutes for people relying on public transportation. One of the consequences is the scattering of the family, with the children having a lot less adult attention than they used. Hence, peer influences are even more important in their lives.

Families tend to be less socially stable. Births to mothers without committed partners or husbands seem to be increasing; marriage is declining, divorce and redivorce is high. Remarriage is more likely to happen. The consequence is that children are more likely to be in blended family networks.

The patterns of cross-generational dependencies have changed. According to Andrews, historically, in rural/agrarian cultures, interdependency among generations prevailed, with children being valued for their ability to contribute to the family economy and provide security to family members in old age. Due to several changes related to urbanisation and education, material interdependency across age has decreased, however the need for emotional interdependencies has not changed much (Andrews, 1998).

While needs have not changed, the realities have. Family units are more individualistic and nuclear, separated from other family members and by generation. Changes in family structures related to other broader changes in society have weakened many of the supports and informal controls for guiding children that were once taken for granted in most families and neighbourhoods (Chapin Hall Center For Children, 1997).

Diversity is one important characteristic of modern societies. Families are far more blended by race, religion and ethnicity. There is more tolerance for single-gender families and gay/lesbian parents. Grandparent caregiving is another growing trend, which includes, for example, grandparents routinely preparing grandchildren for school, providing full-time daycare for preschool grandchildren, and raising grandchildren with no assistance from the parents of the children (Hirshorn, 1998).

Families are more female-influenced. Particularly among vulnerable populations, women are assuming most family responsibilities. Historically, female-headed families were mainly due to death of the father or distance by migration. In just one generation, the rate of absent fathers by choice has increased dramatically across the world. Also, births to mothers without committed partners or husbands are increasing. There are growing numbers of matrifocal families: mothers change partners and normally keep the children; across generations, children have mothers and grandmothers as the most stable influences in their lives.

The dynamics of parental and gender roles is changing dramatically in different cultural contexts. There have been significant changes in parental roles and gender relations within the family unit. Men and women are increasingly faced with demands in roles and functions which were once clearly specified as 'the father's' or 'the mother's'. Yet the central role of mothers in nurturing their children remains unchanged.

A survey was carried out this year by CESPI at the University of Santa

Ursula in which a thousand families from different social and economic segments of Rio de Janeiro were interviewed. A preliminary analysis of the survey revealed that the mother is the main figure in most families; she is the one who is present in practically all of the child's daily activities, be they at home, at school, or at any other of the child's social space (Rizzini, 1999).

Another survey recently carried out in Brazil showed that :

> The mother fuses loving care with authority. She is the one who talks to and punishes the children; she is the one who takes care of the house, but she is also the provider; in short, she play in all positions. 'The mother is everything', it is said. For 74 per cent of Brazilians at age 16 and over, the mother is considered 'very important' while for the same group, only 50 per cent consider the father 'very important'. The man shares the provider role with the woman, however, he does not expand his duties at home (*Família*, 1998, pp. 8–9).

Parenting tends to be more permissive. One of the most frequent complaints by parents is their difficulty in disciplining and setting clear limits for their children. Parents show signs of being scared, and allow their children to become real tyrants in their family relations. One of the most-read magazines in Brazil recently published an article on this subject, with the following heading on the cover: 'Experts say that parents need to set limits in order to bring up their children' (*Veja*, June 1999).

There are several broader political, economic, social, environmental and gender interrelated forces directly affecting family life and values with great variations in different cultures and within cultures. Among them, some are especially crucial as they promote disruption and distress, such as increasing urban populations, higher incidence of poverty, unemployment rates, cutback in basic social programmes; urban violence, migration and displacement of masses of people, accelerated alteration and degradation of the planetary ecology, to mention a few. In essence, what all these indicators suggest is that increasing global inequality and impoverishment are major trends which are absolutely crucial to the issue of children's rights.

Consensus on global values

One of the first objective conclusions that emerged from the debate on globalisation was that despite the sense of greater closeness it gave through technologies which facilitated rapid information exchange, the world was becoming increasingly segregated. We seem to be living a time of especially visible contradictions; a time for transcending boundaries and borders in the realm of virtual reality, whereas in the context of our everyday lives it is clearly a time for fixing territories and intolerance towards the 'Other'. Episodes of violence involving ethnic and religious differences in different corners of the world are a manifestation of such intolerance.

On the other hand, there seems to be a quest for a consensus on values.

(Rapoport, 1997; Kaufman, 1998). The concern for global citizenship and ethics, peace, human rights and environmental treaties are some good examples. There is a general and somewhat unquestioned consensus that we all should be fighting for democracy, for a healthy environment and defending human rights. The question is: how much of that is more than a consensual ideal, something that is so distant from our everyday realities that it is used as simple rhetoric?

Let us use the concept of democracy to illustrate this point. It is a fact that the world has become more democratic than it was a few decades ago, if one defines democracy by the number of countries ruled by elected civilian leaders. However, that has not guaranteed a substantial change in democratic practices in most parts of the world. What seems to happen in societies with historic anti-democratic traditions is that individuals are called citizens but in reality have no grounds for political participation and no guarantee of human rights protection. Human rights violations and unequal opportunities for citizen participation occur in all democratic countries, but newly democratic countries have a particular problem in throwing off totalitarian practices. This is part of their political culture which is not likely to change quickly. The appearance and reality are certainly much more complex than what is often accepted as the case (Ahnen, 1999).

The situation is even more complicated when it comes to countries with a long tradition of authoritarian and corrupt government. Take the case of Latin America, for example – today considered a democratic continent. The truth is that many countries are very far from practising what could be considered as democratic governance. Corruption and authoritarian political practices continue to characterise the continent.

In relating these thoughts to child rights violations, there is much to be said and a long way to go. Perhaps the most dramatic example lies in the assassination of children and youths. Unfortunately Brazil appears as the most well known violator of the most basic human right: the right to life. The culture of impunity, through which the élite historically managed to put themselves above the law, is still very strong (Da Matta, 1998). Thousands of young people have been the victims of such impunity.

Despite the scope of contemporary human rights problems, this mentality is still the prevailing one today in many parts of the world. This is certainly true for Latin America. From a historical perspective, our testimony is that a deep vein of violence is entangled in the history of our continent and resides in our collective unconscious. Our forerunners, the indigenous peoples, were decimated by the colonisers. Slaves coming from Africa and born in the new continent passed on to us, together with their heroism and resistance, memories of the violence inflicted upon them by the colonisers. We are united by threads of violence that were woven into our rulers' strategies so they could conquer, dominate, and maintain their power. The historical heroes of our countries did not leave us worthy examples of how to build nations for the good of all citizens (Rizzini, 1994).

The history of our continent is marked by some of the most brutal forms of violations of human rights, ranging from disrespect of local cultures, resource exploitation, and the imposition of foreign values, beliefs and customs to physical brutality and murder. Every child and youth whose potential is wasted in our countries reflects this history of profound inhumanity.

Yet, no one would question that Latin America now lives mostly under democratic governments; that Brazil has gone through an impressive process of re-democratisation, after twenty years of military dictatorship. And despite all the children's rights violations, Brazil has been considered a paradigmatic example of intense popular mobilisation in defence of children's rights. The rights of children have received particular emphasis as part of the process of the country's recent political transition.

Starting in the mid-1980s, a number of Non-Governmental Organizations (NGOs), university-based researchers, advocates, and grassroots groups, including some that were linked to the Catholic Church, together with some progressive factions within the government, began collaborating to improve children's policies and programmes. Media reports on the often abysmal conditions in existing children's institutions and the treatment of street children by police, plus advocacy efforts by NGOs, resulted in a considerable national outcry on behalf of street children and low income children.

One of the results of this advocacy and social mobilisation movement on behalf of poor children was a Federal Constitution, approved in 1988, specifically pertaining to children's rights. This was the first such provision in Brazil's history. Brazil's Children's Act (known officially as the statute on the Child and the Adolescent) was also born out of this national movement. Inspired in part by the United Nations Convention on the Rights of the Child, the statute went through numerous revisions during the 1980s, and with constant organisation, advocacy and public pronouncements by broad sectors of Brazilian society, eventually became law in its current form in October 1990. The statute, in terms of its level of detail and scope in the protection and promotion of children's rights and participation, and its decentralised implementation, is considered a model for Latin America.

Nevertheless, the marks of historical violence, inequality and social injustice are still present in current practices. The same conclusion, though inspired by Latin American history, could well be applied to many other people and places in their own colonising experiences. These continuing signs tell us about dominant powers' struggles to conquer and control by annihilating local cultures and differences through the use of oppressive power and cruelty. Most important of all, the example tells us about identity constructions, and of people's constant search for establishing a sense of both collective and self identities within the global arena.

In our present historical place as citizens of the world, a challenge in advocating for children's rights is how to make the best possible use of our global awareness, and the fantastic technological and human resources available, to fight for a better world. In this context, to advocate effectively for children's rights requires major changes in the paradigms and values that have existed in our societies. Conscious of the fact that there are deep-seated interests in some sectors of society against notions of equality and rights, our aim is to find where collaboration and collective efforts can maximise our effectiveness (Rizzini, Barker & Cassaniga, 1998a, 1998b).

International and local/regional agendas

What follows is not by any means an attempt to propose a 'global agenda for the third millennium' but rather to encourage people to go beyond their local laws and conventions. The experience of those involved in building Agenda 21 as a resolution from the Earth Summit in Rio in 1992 provides a valuable example. Agenda 21 urges all countries to adopt national strategies towards a common agreement of environmental preservation based on principles of sustainable development (Gallopin, 1997).[1]

Green plans are an example of such strategies. They are comprehensive, integrated and large-scale programmes, involving partnerships between government and the private sector, aimed at dealing with the negative impact of environmental problems. New Zealand has recently enacted a green plan called the Resource Management Act (RMA), which has made the country one of the world's leaders in environmental policy.

The idea of sustainability implies careful planning to avoid ongoing deterioration which puts the planet's life at risk. In other words, it anticipates needs; it cares for future generations. This is closely related to our concerns about children's lives and futures. There is nothing more tragic than to leave as a legacy to our children the sense of hopelessness in the face of the possibility of a totally devastated environment (Korten, 1998). Korten (1998) places environmental issues as crucial challenges to be faced in a world of just and sustainable human societies. He states that:

> ... each addition to economic output results in a comparable increase in the stress that humans place on the earth's ecosystem, deepens the poverty of those who have been expropriated and labor exploited to fuel the engines of growth, and accelerates the destruction of non human species. The terrible costs fall on those who are denied a political voice – the poor, the young, and generations yet unborn (p. 10).

Agenda 21 is based on the principles of justice and equity, and envisions practical ways of preserving what we have got. Children usually love and care for nature and animals. It is a simple matter of stimulating what they already know. Furthermore, children are the main victims of environmental carelessness with a lifetime ahead of them to deal with the consequences; but they would also be, together with other generations to come, the main beneficiaries of sustainable development. Children should therefore be more included in the process of consciously caring for the planet and solidifying the idea of sustainability as opposed to economic growth only.

World-wide children's agendas, as part of a well structured global movement, could be a fruitful venture. In addition to helping children develop new knowledge and perspectives about natural resources, such a movement would stimulate children's participation in key public debates and processes. Children would be given the opportunity to fulfil their potential as citizens of the globe and to create the necessary conditions for what environmentalists call a 'planetary solidarity'. Let us stop repeating the cliché that 'children are the future' and instead give them simple tools to dream about the future and build it accordingly.

Priorities for global/local agendas

It is important to recognise that although people's aspirations for better living standards can be considered universal, local situations vary considerably, so priorities should differ. One key to successful globalisation of the economy should be ways to respect and respond to those different priorities.

Some of the priorities for global/local agendas that would promote children's rights would be:

- **The end of child labour:** According to statistics by the International Labour Organisation (ILO, 1998) there are 250 million child labourers in the world, 30 million of whom live in Latin America and the Caribbean. A large body of research has shown that labour has a negative effect on children's development as a whole. In Guatemala, for example, approximately one quarter of children and teenagers in the work force do not attend school, and work is their main reason for dropping out of school when they reach the sixth grade.
- **Sustainable development:** We should expand and intensify efforts to address a sustainable development agenda as a basic step towards more economic and social equality. Since the end of the Cold War, the world economy has grown explosively. Nonetheless, nearly 1.5 billion people experienced declining or stagnant per capita incomes and GDP throughout the 1990s. Several organisations involved in environmental issues have pointed out that this expansion has caused tremendous social and ecological problems that threaten continuing improvements in the standard of living worldwide (Myers & Brown, 1997).
- **Third world debt:** International renegotiation of Third World debt should be undertaken. There are many examples of what such debts mean to poor countries. Tanzania, half of whose population is illiterate, spends a third of its budget on international debt payments and spends more on repaying debt

than it does for primary education. Nigeria, where life expectancy is only forty-seven years, spends more on debt payments than it does on health and education combined. The 700 million people living in the forty-one poorest, most indebted countries live on average on $4 a day. Combined, these countries owe the IMF, the World Bank and Western countries $130 billion. There are some discussions going on about debt forgiveness, but it is not clear what will happen. In some powerful quarters there is not much support for helping the poorest countries emerge from the burden of international debt. Recently the *Wall Street Journal* reported that:

> The Group of Seven Nations proposed to reduce by up to 70 per cent the $127 billion in debt owed by 33 poor countries, mostly in Africa, and endorsed ways of heading off financial crises. The plan must be approved by the IMF, the World Bank, whose support is likely, and also by the US Congress, where backing is less certain (*Wall Street Journal*, 27 June 1999).

As an example of the consequences of such an initiative, White House economic adviser Gene Sperling said that Mozambique now devotes 30 per cent of its government revenue to pay off debt. Under a debt forgiveness programme, that could be reduced to 15 per cent. Such a change would allow their health budget, for example, to be increased by 50 per cent. This is not going to be as easy as it sounds, but it gives space for negotiation and calls attention to the need for a solution that would force countries to reallocate their investments (*Wall Street Journal*, 27 June 1999).

- **Basic health and education rights:** High priority needs to be given to basic health and education rights. I believe that no arguments are needed to prove the obvious importance of providing decent health and education services for all children, though in so many countries children do not get such care. Effective public services should be provided worldwide for children, more attention should be given to failing urban schools, and the increasing commercialisation and privatisation of health and education services should be stopped.

The advantages of a world-wide agenda is that we can see the extent of our shared problems. The challenge is to grasp some opportunity and make a difference for the poorest of the rising generation.

In Memory of Sharon Stephens

Sharon Stephens was a North American anthropologist dedicated to children's issues. She was one of the international voices in defence of children's rights that inspired many others. Unfortunately, Sharon left us much too early. For a number of years Sharon Stephens had much to contribute with her acute sensitivity and deep knowledge as a member of Childwatch International, a global research network which aims at strengthening child research world-wide.

Acknowledgements

I would like to thank Malcolm Bush, from the Woodstock Institute, Chicago, for all the support over many years of dialogue and exchange between North and South America. Also, Marco Alajmo, from the European Union, El Salvador, for debating with me some of the ideas explored in this paper. Rogeria Itaboray Cunningham and Jerry Cunningham helped me with the language; I am very grateful to them for their kind support in several of my writings. And finally, I am thankful to all the CESPI members who have been working with me in the Elos Project (Family Ties Project).

References

Ahnen, R.E. (1999). *Defending human rights under democracy: The case of minors in Brazil.* Unpublished doctoral dissertation, University of North Carolina at Chapel Hill.

Andrews, A.B. (1998). *Trends in everyday lives of children: Family life.* Childwatch International Study Group on the Effects of Political and Economic Transformations on Children. Columbia, SC: Institute for Families in Society at the University of South Carolina.

Chapin Hall Centre for Children. (1997). *Primary supports working group. Research framework.* Chicago: Chapin Hall Centre for Children, University of Chicago.

Chevalier, L. (1973). *Labouring classes and dangerous classes in Paris during the first half of the nineteenth century.* Princeton, New Jersey: Princeton University Press.

Da Matta, R. (1996). Globalisation and national identity. Considerations based on the Brazilian experience. In L. Soares (Ed.), *Cultural pluralism, identity, and globalisation* (pp. 174-186). Rio de Janeiro: UNESCO, ISSC, EDUCAM.

Família [Family]. (1998, September 20). São Paulo: *Folha de São Paulo.*

Gallopin, G.C. (1997, March). *Planetary solidarity: Premises, values and principles for sustainable development.* Paper prepared for the Earth Chapter Project.

Hirshorn, B.A. (1998). Grandparents as caregivers. In M.E. Szinovacz (Ed.), *Handbook on grandparenthood.* London: Greenwood Press, pp. 200-14.

International Labour Organisation. (1998). *ILO declaration of fundamental principles and rights at work and its follow-up.* Geneva: ILO.

Kaufman, N. (1998). *The impact of political and economic transformations on the everyday lives of children: status in international law.* Childwatch International Study Group on the Effects of Political and Economic Transformations on Children. Columbia, SC: Institute for Families in Society at the University of South Carolina.

Kaufman, N., Rizzini, I., & Wilson, K. (1999). *The impact of political and economic transformations on the every day lives of children: Status in international law.* Childwatch International Study Group on the Effects of Political and Economic Transformations on Children. Columbia, SC: Institute for Families in Society at the University of South Carolina.

Korten, D. (1998). *Globalising civil society.* New York: A Seven Stories Press.

Kovarik, J. (1994). The space and time of children at the interface of psychology and sociology. In J. Qvortrup, M. Bardy, G. Sgritta, & H. Wintersberger (Eds), *Childhood matters: Social theory, practice and politics* pp. 101-22. Aldershot: Avebury Press.

Moore, B. Jr. (1998). *Moral aspects of economic growth, and other essays.* Ithaca: Cornell University Press.

Myers, R. (1992). *The twelve who survive. Strengthening programs of early childhood development in the third world.* London: Routledge.

Myers, N., & Brown, N. (1997). *The role of major U.S. Foundations in the implementation of Agenda 21. The five-year follow up to the Earth Summit*. Report to the Earth Council.

Rapoport, R.N. (1997). *Families, children and the quest for a global ethic*. Hants, Vermont: Ashgate.

Rizzini, I. (1994). Children in the city of violence: The case of Brasil. In K. Rupesinghe & M. Rubio (Eds), *The culture of violence* (pp. 257-75). New York: United Nations University Press.

Rizzini, I. (1997). *O século perdido: raízes históricas das políticas públicas para a infância no Brasil* [The lost century: The historical roots of public policies on children in Brazil]. Rio de Janeiro: Editora Universitária Santa Ursula/Amais Livraria e Editora.

Rizzini, I. (1999). *The Elos Project. Family Ties: Parents in society – Family survey in Rio de Janeiro*. Rio de Janeiro: University of Santa Ursula Center for Research on Childhood.

Rizzini, I., Barker, G., & Cassaniga, N. (1998a). Children, participation and democracy: A case study of the Statute of the Child and Adolescent in Brazil. *Family Futures, 2*(1), 35-42.

Rizzini, I., Barker, G., & Cassaniga, N. (1998b, October). *From street children to all children. Improving the opportunities of low income urban children and youth in Brazil.* Paper presented at the Johann Jacobs Foundation Conference, Marbach, Germany.

Robertson, R. (1996). Values and globalisation: Communitarism and globality. In L. Soares (Ed.), *Cultural pluralism, identity, and globalisation* Rio de Janeiro: UNESCO, ISSC, EDUCAM, pp. 73-93.

Salazar, C.M., & Glasinovich, W.A. (1998). *Child work and education. Five case studies from Latin America*. Hants/UK: UNICEF, Ashgate.

Simmel, G. (1976). A metrópole e a vida mental. In O.G. Velho (Ed.), *O fenômeno urbano* (pp. 26-34). Rio de Janeiro: zahar. (Original work published 1902).

Soares, L. (Ed.). (1996). *Cultural pluralism, identity, and globalisation*. Rio de Janeiro: UNESCO, ISSC, EDUCAM.

Stephens, S. (Ed.). (1995). *Children and the politics of culture*. Princeton, NJ: Princeton University Press.

Stephens, S. (Ed.). (1997). Children and nationalism. *Childhood, 4*.

Thorne, B. (1998). *Global economic restructuring and social relations among children*. Childwatch International Study Group on the Effects of Political and Economic Transformations on Children. Columbia, SC: Institute for Families in Society at the University of South Carolina.

UNICEF. (1992). *Educating girls and women: A moral imperative*. New York: UNICEF.

Wilson, K.K. (1998). *Globalisation: emerging theoretical perspectives*. Childwatch International Study Group on the Effects of Political and Economic Transformations on Children. Columbia, SC: Institute for Families in Society at the University of South Carolina.

World Bank. (1990). *World development indicators. Overview. World Development Report 1990. Poverty*. Washington DC: World Bank.

World Bank. (1997). *Advancing sustainable development. The World Bank and Agenda 21 since the Rio Earth Summit*. Washington DC: World Bank.

Veja [magazine]. Especialistas afirmam que os pais precisam estabelecer limites para criar seus filhos [Experts say that parents need to set limits in order to bring up their children]. São Paulo: Revista Veja, junho de 1999 [June 1999].

Zwingle, E. (1998). *Women and population*. Millennium supplement: Population. Washington: National Geographic.

Note

1 I was recently introduced to the Brazilian advocacy movement around Agenda 21

Children's rights and early childhood education: The rights of babies and young children[1]

ANNE B. SMITH

Introduction

Children and children's rights have been argued about for centuries. 'Rights are entitlements, valuable commodities' which we 'do not have to grovel or beg to get', according to Freeman (1996, p. 70). Children's rights are not greeted with huge enthusiasm by people generally in New Zealand, and I have not heard politicians giving children's rights any prominence. The idea of children having rights tends to be interpreted as being permissive and giving them too much power and control, while at the same time taking power and control away from parents (or others in authority over children, such as teachers). Yet in the work that we at the Children's Issues Centre do in promoting children's rights, we have come to the view that the rights of children in New Zealand are very much at risk, and that there is an ever increasing need for everyone to be vigilant about them. In this paper I argue that we should be advocating for children's rights much more strongly, using the United Nations Convention on the Rights of the Child where possible, and showing how it is relevant to the rights of babies and young children. In particular children should have access to high quality early childhood education, and to have their rights met within early childhood services.

Child advocacy involves taking a proactive approach towards recognising the rights of all children, and responding by changing systems, policies and individuals to ensure that they are given the opportunity to reach their potential and improve the processes which affect their daily lives. It is NOT about undermining the role of parents and families nor is it about denying children their childhood.

Things are not very rosy for children and young people currently in New Zealand, and there is a great need to advocate for better conditions of childhood in this country. There has been, in recent years, a major increase in the number of children who experience poverty; we have high rates of suicide amongst young people; basic health care is not being delivered to many children; there is a serious problem with the exposure of children to violence; child care and protection systems are not functioning adequately; and clearly there is not equal access to high quality education for children from different backgrounds. Lack of equal access to good quality education is a reality at the school level where there are increasingly schools for the 'haves' and the 'have nots'. It is also true at the early childhood level, as I explain later in this paper.

I have been an advocate for children for many years, and I have always argued from my knowledge as a researcher in child development to advocate for better environments for children. Recently I have come to realise that there are also legal and ethical grounds on which to argue for changes to policy in favour of children, and I would like to expand on these in this paper. Child advocacy is very much needed, but as much as possible it must be carried out with humility, without seeking personal glory or for one's own political ends, and in partnership with children. Adults for centuries have made assumptions about what is best for children, but recently we have come to question this perspective, and to argue that to be an effective child advocate it is necessary to listen to children's voices and be sensitive to children's perspectives. Melton (1987) argues that if children are involved in setting the agenda for child advocacy, there is much less danger that it will be dominated by adult ideology. Listening to children and viewing the world from their perspective is an important ingredient in child advocacy, even when it concerns young children.

The United Nations Convention on the Rights of the Child

We have one very useful tool to promote children's rights, the United Nations Convention on the Rights of the Child, which I believe we in the early childhood sector (as well as other professionals working with children) should be using much more proactively in persuading governments to support better policies for children. The Convention provides an internationally accepted standard to be applied to basic human rights affecting children. We can learn a lesson from the Mäori people and the prominence of the Treaty of Waitangi in New Zealand, about how helpful a legal document can be in raising awareness and changing policies. Many New Zealand policies, programmes and legislation can be measured against the UNCROC in terms of their impact on children. This process is only just beginning in New Zealand. According to Michael Freeman:

> It [the UNCROC] can be used in a number of ways: to make children aware of their rights, to put pressure on the legislature, on governments and policy makers, to measure practices and policies against, to make the case for child impact statements, to be used in committee discussion and commissions of inquiry, and as an advocacy tool. As such it can be used by ministries, by institutions, such as the Commissioner for Children and, most importantly, in litigation, by lawyers arguing cases and by Judges by reasoning their judgements (Freeman, 1996, p. 84).

Freeman argues that it is becoming accepted in New Zealand that the language of legislation must be consistent with the principles of the Treaty of Waitangi, so the same standards could be applicable to the use of other international treaties or conventions. Hence the UNCROC can be used in constructing legislation and policy which affects children's lives directly. Freeman (1996) says that everyone concerned with children's issues and concerned to advocate for children should be thoroughly familiar with the UNCROC and also with the literature on childhood. Child advocates 'should be committed to a rights based ideology and will be able to use this knowledge and commitment as advocacy tools', according to Freeman (1996, p. 69).

The United Nations Convention on the Rights of the Child was adopted by the United Nations General Assembly in 1989 and ratified by New Zealand in 1993, subject to reservations relating to the children of illegal immigrants, employment law and criminal custody rules. Only two countries in the world, the United States and Somalia, have not ratified the Convention. The beginnings of international concern with children's rights emerged in 1924 when the League of Nations adopted a declaration relating to the rights of children affected by the Great War and its aftermath. It was focused on children's basic material needs – food, shelter, health care and care for orphans. In 1959 the UN adopted the United Nations Declaration of the Rights of the Children, which emphasised duties to children and set out ten rather vague principles. Between 1959 and 1989, there was a rapid growth in consciousness of the plight of children in the world, culminating in 1979 with the International Year of the Child, which caught public imagination very effectively. Ten years later these developments resulted in the drafting and adoption of the UNCROC. It took many years of discussion and negotiation to achieve a document which was acceptable to the UN and the international community.

The Convention consists of fifty-four articles which have been divided into three main types of rights (the three 'P's') by Lansdown (1994, p. 36):

- **Provision Rights**. Rights to minimum standards of health, education, social security, physical care, family life, play, recreation, culture and leisure.
- **Protection Rights**. Rights to be safe from discrimination, physical and sexual abuse, exploitation, substance abuse, injustice and conflict.
- **Participation or Autonomy Rights**. Civil and political rights such as the right to a name and identity, to be consulted and to be taken into account, to physical integrity, to information, to freedom of speech and opinion and to challenge decisions made on their behalf.

New Zealand was required to make a report to the United Nations within two years of ratification and that document was submitted by the Ministry of Youth Affairs on behalf of the government in 1995. A report was also prepared by Non-Governmental Agencies and three delegates from New Zealand – Alison Blaiklock, Alistair Paterson and Moana Sinclair (representing indigenous people) – met with the UN Committee on the Rights of the Child in Geneva to present the report on behalf of the NGO group, Action for Children In Aotearoa. The Committee reported back in 1997 to the New Zealand government, giving its judgement of how well New Zealand had met its obligations under the Convention. They had several major criticisms of New Zealand's performance, including our fragmented approach to children's rights and lack of co-ordination between different government departments, the lack of a global plan of action on children's rights and the effect of the economic reforms on support services for children and families.

The context of economic rationalism

The last point raises an important issue, that the state is not fulfilling its responsibility towards children and that New Right economic polices have worsened the situation for them. Henaghan (1996) talks about the importance of three basic concepts of children's rights embedded in the UN Convention: first, the autonomy of the child to express views and receive information; second, the primary responsibility of the family to nurture, care for and educate children; and third, the state's responsibility to protect, educate and enhance the development of children. There is currently a struggle in achieving that third emphasis, state support for children's rights. This has become very difficult in a climate where:

> More and more responsibility is being placed on individual family members to care for and provide for children … Consequently it depends on the capacities and capabilities of the family into which the child is born as to what chances and opportunities the child will have in life (Henaghan, 1996, p. 167).

In New Zealand this discourse of private responsibility was illustrated in attempts to introduce a Code of Social and Family Responsibility, a draft of which was sent to every household early in 1998. This Code was aimed particularly at beneficiaries, and set out ten key assumptions and responsibilities for parents, such as keeping children healthy, helping five-year-olds learn, preparing children for school, loving and caring for children, managing money, and getting a job. The draft Code adopted a punitive approach to families suggesting punishments for those who did not meet its expectations, such as removal of benefits for families where children were not attending school. The naive assumptions behind the Code were that the parents who it was aimed at were sufficiently in control of their own lives and free from immediate stressful events to be capable of complying with the code. Considerable research (e.g. Fergusson, Horwood & Lynskey, 1994) suggests that the families who have difficulties meeting their responsibilities have themselves been subjected to multiple disadvantages in their own childhoods – for example, poor educational achievement, poverty, unemployment, and poor parenting.

The Code side-stepped the issue of the State's responsibility not to expose children and families to stresses such as poverty, a growing gap between rich and poor, unemployment, market rentals for public housing, increased user charges for health and education (but poorer access), and a struggling child care and protection system. Fortunately, it was announced later that the Code would be quietly dropped, which is likely the result of the force of public submissions against the idea. This was an expensive and pointless public relations exercise but one which illustrates the very strong ideology driving the policies of the previous government.

The philosophy that families should fit the picture of a traditional thrifty and self-reliant family who are responsible for their own welfare is part of the New Right discourse (Winter & Connolly, 1996). The New Right argues that the state should retreat from 'interfering' in the family and remove it from a 'dependency culture'. This has been the main rationale for running down the welfare state and the public sector and the introduction of such schemes as 'work for the dole'. In this discourse there is no recognition of changes in the nature of the family or the existence of a variety of different family forms, and little consideration for the effects of such changes on the most vulnerable members of the family, children.

Children's rights and early childhood education

There is no direct mention of early childhood education in the UNCROC, probably because of the uneven distribution of early childhood educational opportunities throughout the world. The Convention preamble, however, makes two important points, first, that the family is of prime importance and needs to be supported and second, that the child (and, it is implied, including the very young child) 'needs special safeguards and care, including appropriate legal protection, before as well as after birth' (Preamble, p. 1):

> The family, as the fundamental group of society and the natural environment for the growth and wellbeing of all of its members and particularly children, should be afforded the necessary protection and assistance so that it can fully assume its responsibilities within the community.

Articles 28 and 29 deal with the rights of a child to education. Article 28 says that 'State parties recognise the right of the child to education' but the rest of the Article refers specifically to primary and secondary education. It argues for compulsory primary education, accessibility of secondary and higher education, elimination of ignorance and illiteracy and regular attendance at school. Tapp (personal communication) argues that article 28 gives all children the right to an education, and that the items stipulated are seen as a minimum, taking into account the difficulties that developing countries have in meeting these. Hence countries like New Zealand are expected to provide more than the minimum, and this should include Early Childhood Education.

Article 29 is more directly applicable to early childhood education.

Article 29

1. State parties agree that the education of the child should be directed to:
   (a) The development of the child's personality, talents and mental and physical abilities to their fullest potential.
   (b) The development of respect for human rights and fundamental freedoms, and for the principles enshrined in the Charter of the United Nations;
   (c) The development of respect for the child's parents, his or her own cultural identity, language and values, for the national values of the country in which the child is living, the country from which he or she may originate, and for civilizations different from his or her own;
   (d) The preparation of the child for life in a free society, peace, tolerance, equality of sexes, and friendship among all peoples, ethnic, national and religious groups and persons of indigenous origin;
   (e) The development of respect for the natural environment.

Reaching Full Potential and Early Experience

Although the UNCROC does not deal specifically with early childhood, many of the articles have strong implications for improving the early experiences of children under five. Article 29 on Education suggests that education should be directed towards children reaching their fullest potential. To fulfil article 29 adequately we need to pay much more attention to the most formative years of a child's life and to offering children a good beginning. If children are to attain the highest standards of educational achievement, it is essential that we provide a good environment for them in infancy and early childhood, since these early years are the most important in influencing future development.

Deborah Phillips (1995, p. 6) talks about the 'quiet crisis' for young children in the United States. She explains the term 'quiet crisis':

> 'Quiet' because babies rarely make the news: they are not terrorising neighbourhoods, and they are not contributing to unemployment or the deficit or crime statistics – the noisy problems of today's society. 'Quiet' because parents of infants and toddlers deal silently and often alone with their anguish at having to return to work within weeks of the birth of their baby, with the worries about finding affordable and decent child care, and their fears about their patchwork health care coverage that may well not cover their medical costs should their child become seriously ill. 'Quiet' because the lives of policy makers and other national leaders are usually far removed from the crises that face our youngest citizens.

The conditions Phillips describes in the United States, a huge increase in children living below the poverty level, an increase in single parents, a rise in family breakups, a lack of high quality child care and increasing levels of child abuse are all factors which are also problems in New Zealand. The number of households in poverty more than doubled between 1984 and 1993. All households have been affected, but those which have been hardest hit are single parents (an issue which was mentioned in the United Nations Committee on the Rights of the Child's response to the New Zealand government report). According to Stephens, Waldegrave and Frater (1996), about a quarter of families with children were living below the poverty line in 1993. Mortality rates for young children, a very sensitive indicator of poverty, show that New Zealand currently ranks 15th out of 21 OECD countries while in 1960 we were ranked sixth (Ministry of Health, 1998).

Phillips (1995, p. 9) also argues that:

> Recent decades have brought a reversal in the economic fortunes of children and the elderly, such that improvements for the elderly have coincided with a deterioration in the economic well being of families with children.

Again there are a parallels in New Zealand. Massey University historian, David Thomson (1998) provides overwhelming evidence of how the fortunes of children and younger people have declined dramatically since the 1960s, when many government policies were designed to enhance the opportunities for families with children, towards a marked downturn in their economic well being in the nineties. Currently the young bear the brunt of lower incomes for families – for example, through fewer tax concessions for families with children, removal of child benefits and tertiary allowances, lack of funding for cheap housing, emphasis on low inflation rather than full employment, and so on.

There is, however, strong evidence to show that exposure to high quality early childhood education is a factor which can ameliorate poverty (Barnett, 1998; Frede, 1998). Barnett (1999) reviewed thirty-eight different early childhood education programmes (based in many countries) for children in disadvantaged environments. He found substantial evidence to show that in the overwhelming majority of studies there were positive effects on learning and school success, which generalised across a wide range of communities and programmes. Only a small number of studies followed children until high school, but long-term effects of early childhood programmes, well beyond the early childhood years were established. We have recently completed a comprehensive review of early childhood education research for the Ministry of Education, and have found international evidence to support the effectiveness of high quality early childhood programmes for children who are experiencing poverty.

> In general, research has shown that poor students who attend large scale (e.g. Head Start) and small model early childhood intervention programs have superior academic readiness skills or show greater gains in these skills than their peers. These programs have also been found to result in lower rates of grade retention and assignment to special education and enhance performance. The same effects have been replicated in experimental studies and in quasi-experimental studies that carefully controlled for pre-existing differences in children's cognitive functioning and background characteristics such as maternal education and parental presence (Smith, Grima, Gaffney & Powell, 1999, p. 23).

Supporting children and families during the first few years of life helps set the stage for their life course. Although later intervention can be effective, it is much more expensive, time-consuming and requires greater intensity (Barnett, 1998; Hertzman, 1997; Phillips, 1995; Smith, 1998). The first three years of life (and most especially the first year) are crucial, so we need policies to protect and support early development.

In my view, in order to be fulfilling its obligations under article 29, children and families in New Zealand need access to affordable and good quality early childhood education programmes to allow children to achieve their fullest potential educationally. Parents are also important agents in supporting their children to achieve their educational potential and the ability to invest time in children is greatly affected by social and economic circumstances. The provision of paid parental leave is an area where we have a very poor record compared to most of the rest of the industrialised world. Parents need to be able to take time off paid work to be with their babies during these crucial early years, and they also need to receive support in the form of access to high quality early childhood programmes and family-friendly work environments. We also should be providing ready access to families from all income, ethnic and class groups to family-friendly and non judgmental systems of family support. However, governments seem to be placing more and more responsibility and pressure on parents to solve their own problems, something that many are powerless to do. I think that they need to be reminded that the State also has a role and responsibility in helping children achieve their educational potential and that putting resources into the early childhood sector is one highly effective way of achieving equality of opportunity.

Other UNCROC Articles relevant to ECE

There are some other articles, only some of which I have selected, which are particularly relevant for ECE. I invite you to reflect on whether these articles are being met or not in early childhood provisions.

Article 2 says that children's rights are for all children 'irrespective of the child's or his or her parent's or legal guardian's race, colour, sex, language, religion, political or other opinion, national, ethnic or social origin, property, disability, birth or other status.'

Article 3 says that in all matters concerning children the 'best interests of the child' are a primary consideration. It also says that the State should provide adequate care and protection for children and 'shall ensure that the institutions, services and facilities responsible for the care or protection of children shall conform with the standards established by competent authorities, particularly in the areas of safety, health, in the number and suitability of their staff, as well as competent supervision.'

Article 6 says that the State has a responsibility to ensure that the child has a right to development.

Article 12 says that the views of children should be taken into account in decisions affecting them, according to age and maturity. This means listening to children's voices respectfully.

Article 13 says that children have the right to express their views and to be given information.

Article 18 says that parents have a responsibility for raising their child and that the State will 'render appropriate assistance' to parents in performing these responsibilities.

Article 19 says that children must be protected from all forms of maltreatment by parents or others responsible for their care.

Article 23 says that disabled children have a right to special care, education and training.

Article 30 says that indigenous children have the right to enjoy their own culture, religion and language.

Article 31 says that the child has the right to leisure, play and participation in cultural and artistic activities.

There are three issues arising out of the provisions of the United Nations Convention on the Rights of the Child which I would like to discuss: Access, Quality, and Sensitivity to Children's Perspectives.

1. Access

In order to meet Article 2, which states that all children should have the same rights, regardless of ethnicity, socio-economic status or other differences, children from different backgrounds should have equal access to early childhood education. It is also important for families to have access to sufficient intensity of ECE to make a difference to children's educational potential. This does not seem to be the case currently in New Zealand. A recent Department of Labour survey shows clearly that some ethnic and socio-economic groups are participating less in early childhood education (Department of Labour, 1999). Maori and Pacific Island families are less likely to have their child in an early childhood centre, and lower income families have less chance of their children participating. 66 per cent of European, 53 per cent of Maori, 48 per cent of Pacific Island and 42 per cent of children in other ethnic groups have their child in early childhood arrangements. Participation in early childhood services is related to income, with 74 per cent of children from higher income families, 61 per cent of children from middle income families and 52 per cent of children from lower income families participating in early childhood services. Mara (2000) points out that only 40 per cent of Pacific Island children attend a recognised early childhood provision, which is disturbing evidence of unequal access to the benefits of early childhood education for these children.

I am also concerned about the lack of intensity of New Zealand children's exposure to ECE programmes. The importance of length of time in early childhood education is highlighted by the New Zealand Competent Child study. Wylie, Thomson & Lythe (1999) found that length of time in early childhood education had a positive effect on later competencies. Children who started early childhood education before two years of age generally scored 6–7 percentage points more than those who started later, in five competency areas – motor skills, communication, logical problem-solving, literacy and curiosity. Frede (1998) argues that the most effective programmes (especially for children from low income families) are those with the most intense and long-lasting interventions.

According to the recent DOL survey, just under half (46 per cent) of the pre-school children participating in an early childhood setting were doing so for less than ten hours a week, while 29 per cent attended for between eleven and twenty hours a week, 19 per cent attended for between twenty-one and forty hours a week, while 6 per cent used more than forty hours a week. Most children are, therefore, in early childhood settings for quite small amounts of time, and they are also in very low cost care, since the DOL study showed that most parents paid $10 or less per week. About a third of all families were dissatisfied with their child's early childhood education, usually because of the lack of flexible hours provided by the centre (e.g. in half-day programmes), the long waiting lists, or inability to pay for more hours.

2. Quality

Articles 29, 3 and 19 have implications which suggest that the state has a responsibility to ensure high quality in early childhood centres. Perhaps we could agree that minimum standards are more or less being achieved through the Child Care Centre Regulations and Desirable Objectives and Practices. There may be questions, however, about the extent to which regulations are actually enforced and whether a safe and healthy environment for all children in early childhood centres is achieved. Minimum standards are not enough, in my view. The research literature on ECE emphasises, again and again, that quality is the most important aspect of ECE and that it has an effect on children's emotional, social, physical and cognitive development. The positive impact of high quality care is strongest for children who would otherwise experience an unstimulating and unresponsive environment at home. Moreover, the quality of children's early childhood education is not independent of family background. There is evidence that families with low risk backgrounds tend to use higher quality care and families with high risk backgrounds tend to use lower quality care. This is probably not the place to go into detail about what constitutes quality (see Smith, 1998 and Smith, 1999), but the 'iron triangle' of ratios, group size and training as well as the equally powerful variable of staff wages are some of the important structural aspects; while process quality includes teacher/child relationships and interactions (such as joint attention), peer harmony, and curriculum models which allow children to initiate, participate in meaningful activities, and explore, and teachers to scaffold their developing skills (Smith et al., 1999).

An Auckland friend recently told me that she is paying NZ$200 a week for childcare, admittedly very good quality childcare, but not something that more than a minority of families can afford. While the government does provide subsidies for childcare, there is still a high cost to families. Some centres offer very high quality, but in order to do so they charge high fees. In order to maintain profits and compete in the market place to attract parents, many centres (and not just private ones) have to lower their fees and the only way that they can do this is to increase the ratio of children to staff and employ untrained or poorly trained staff. Hence in too many childcare centres for young children, at the time in their development when quality is most crucial, many centres (around a third in my estimation) barely meet the minimum requirements (Smith, 1996; Smith, 1999). In contrast to countries like France, Sweden, or Israel, the burden of cost in New Zealand is placed on parents, who are still expected to pay most of the cost of early childhood education for children under three years of age.

3. Sensitivity to children's perspectives

Articles 12 and 13 are about giving children a more active role in society and are perhaps the most controversial in the UNCROC. Historically, we have been much more comfortable with advocating protection and provision rights than with participation rights. I have been working with colleagues on a book (Smith, Taylor & Gollop, 2000) about children's participation rights in society. In the book we argue that too often children's viewpoints have been ignored because of their presumed incompetence. What different cultures think children can or cannot do varies a lot. Almost everything that young children have ever been assumed to be incapable of doing, such as seeing things from other people's perspectives or being reliable witnesses, have been challenged by research. Sociocultural theory suggests that allowing children to participate to the fullest extent of their ability, with support and guidance, actually helps them learn. Children need the opportunity and space to practice decision-making or they will remain unskilled. The opportunities offered by their early childhood setting to participate, will have a major effect on the skills and abilities children develop, and whether they become responsible citizens.

Listening to children and hearing children's 'voice' does not depend on them being able to talk. There are a few people now writing about the relevance of

Articles 12 and 13 for very young children (Alderson, 2000; Alexander, 1995; Pugh and Selleck, 1996)

> 'Listening' to very young children does not necessarily mean taking all their utterances at face value, but it does mean observing the nuances of how they exhibit stress, or curiosity or anxiety, or pleasure in a manner which is congruent to their maturity. It does not imply that their views carry more weight than the powers of wise or loving adults over the outcome of any decision-making process, but it does require that their views are respected (Pugh & Selleck, 1996, pp. 121-2).

Pugh and Selleck argue that in the context of close relationships, adults can 'read' children's perspectives from birth. Early communications between mother and child illustrate joint action and intense mutual sensitivity. Playing with infants, for example cradling, rocking, or playing peek-a-boo, gives them a chance to control others as well as offering intimacy and closeness. Alderson (2000) argues that children are born with abilities to communicate, for example using tiny head movements in time with the movements and sounds other people make when talking to them. Babies watch intently and read other people's moods, imitate others from an early age, and initiate interactions. Babies show that they can form views by responding differently to objects and events, showing interest and pleasure in activities, and through developing relationships with other people, for example copying, playing, greeting and sensitively responding.

Babies develop trust (or mistrust) in their carers and willingness to co-operate with them (or not), through their experiences of being treated gently or roughly. They respond to reassuring explanations before they understand words, and they learn to talk by being spoken to for months beforehand, as if they can already talk. 'Information' includes physical contact and other body language, games, pointing and holding objects and pictures, feeding and playing, and many other means of supplementing or replacing words (Alderson, p. 22).

If children have opportunities in an early childhood centre 'to think, choose, plan, challenge and feel valued' then their participation rights are being respected (Pugh & Selleck, 1996, p. 125). In Reggio Emilio centres in Italy a great deal of attention is given to the design and arrangement of equipment and furniture to allow small children a say in decisions. For example there are small cots or 'nests' made like baskets at floor level, which allow babies as soon as they can crawl, to choose the comfort of their personal nest rather than being lifted by adults into a cot. Babies can also collect their own clean nappies from low cupboards and climb onto a little ramp with changing mats where adults can be invited to change them.

A well-known Danish study (Langsted, 1994) describes a project where staff working with pre-schoolers attempted to review the rules and give children more of a say in what happened in an early childhood centre. They used teenagers to talk to the younger children and found that children had many fewer opportunities to decide for themselves in their early childhood centre than they did at home. It was relatively easy to modify the environment to allow children more choice about issues like when they could have a drink, participate in an activity or go outside to play.

Alice Gallaway is an early childhood teacher who did a major project on the perspectives of twenty-eight four-year-old children about kindergarten (Gallaway, 1999). She found that most of the children (twenty-five) were happy with kindergarten and about half of this group said that having friends and playing with friends was the reason that they liked kindergarten. All of the three children who did not like kindergarten said that this was because of other children 'being mean' or teasing them. The interview asked the twenty-five children who did like kindergarten if there was anything that they did not like about kindergarten. Twenty-one of the twenty-five children said that what they did not like was being hurt by other children (punched, whacked, hit, kicked and scratched). Gallaway reports that the project has made her realise the importance of peers in children's lives and to respect and listen to the children's views in a different way. For example, if there is to be a kindergarten outing, the children are consulted about where they would like to go. For adults listening to these young children's perspectives suggests that bullying can be an issue even for very young children, and that we need to be vigilant about children's safety and physical integrity in early childhood settings.

Conclusions

It is vital that we pay more attention to promoting and sustaining children's rights to quality early childhood education, and making sure that these rights are respected within early childhood settings. I believe that we can make better use of the United Nations Convention on the Rights of the Child to achieve these goals. We should be working to:

- Strengthen systems of child advocacy and focus them on the needs of babies and young children;
- Provide affordable, accessible high quality early childhood services;
- Provide paid parental leave, good family support services, and improved workplace conditions for parents with young children;
- Be more sensitive to children's perspectives in early childhood services and give children practice in participation and making decisions from an early age.

A children's rights perspective on early childhood education forces us to look on children not merely as the passive recipients of efforts to educate them or to look after them while their parents work, but as active competent citizens who have their own understanding of the world, and who can make an active contribution to their own education if they are given the opportunity.

References

Alderson, P. (2000), *Young Children's Rights: Beliefs and Practices.* London: Jessica Kingsley.

Alexander, G. (1995). Children's rights in their early years: From plaiting fog to knitting treacle. In B. Franklin (Ed.) *The Handbook of Children's Rights*. London: Routledge, pp. 131-46.

Barnett, W.S. (1998). Long-term cognitive and academic effects of early childhood education on children in poverty. *Preventive Medicine,* 1-4.

Barnett, W.S. (1999). Long-term effects on cognitive development and school success. In W.S. Barnett and S.S. Boocock (Eds), *Early care and education for children in poverty: Promises, Programs and Long-term Results*. Albany, NY: State University of New York Press, pp. 11-44.

Department of Labour and National Advisory Council on the Employment of Women (1999). *Childcare, Families and Work: The New Zealand Childcare Survey 1998: A Survey of Early Childhood Education and Care Arrangements for Children.* Wellington: Labour Market Policy Group.

Freeman, M.D.A. (1996). The importance of a children's rights perspective in litigation. *Butterworths Family Law Journal.* December, 165-96.

Gallaway, A. (1999). *Children's Perspectives on Kindergarten.* Research paper for CHIC 401 (Advocating for Children), Children's Issues Centre, Dunedin.

Fergusson, D., Horwood, L.J. & Lynskey, M. (1994). The childhood of multiple problem adolescents: A 15-year longitudinal study. *Journal of Child Psychology and Psychiatry, 35*(6), 1123-40.

Frede, E.C. (1998). Preschool program quality in programs for children in poverty. In W.S. Barnett & S.S. Boocock (Eds), *Early Care and Education for Children in Poverty: Promises, Programs, and Long-term Results*. Albany, NY: State University of New York Press, pp. 77-98.

Henaghan, M. (1996). *New Zealand the United Nations Convention on the Rights of the Child: A Lack of Balance.* Chapter 9 in M. Freeman (Ed.) Children's Rights: A Comparative Perspective. England: Dartmouth Publishing Company Ltd, pp. 165-96.

Hertzman, C. (1998). Population health and human development. In N.J. Taylor & A.B. Smith (Eds), *Enhancing Children's Potential: Minimising Risk and Maximising Resiliency.* Children's Issues Centre, University of Otago, pp. 53-72.

Langsted, O. (1994). Quality in childcare – from the child's perspective. In P. Moss & A. Pence (Eds), *Valuing Quality in Early Childhood.* London: Paul Chapman Publishing Ltd, pp. 28-42.

Lansdown, G. (1994). Children's Rights. In B. Mayall, (Ed), *Children's Childhoods: Observed and Experienced.* London: Falmer Press, pp. 33-44.

Mara, D. (2000). Response to Professsor Miriam K. Rosenthal: A Pacific Islander's perspective. *Childrenz Issues*, *4*(1), 18-20.

Melton, G. (1987). Children, politics and morality: The ethics of child advocacy. *Journal of Clinical Child Psychology*, *16*(4), 357-67.

Ministry of Health (1998). *Our Children's Health: Key Findings on the Health of New Zealand Children.* Wellington.

O'Brien, M. (1998). *Economic and Social Changes and their Impact on Children and Families.* Paper presented at 12th International Congress of International Society for Prevention of Child Abuse and Neglect. Auckland, September 6-9.

Phillips, D. (1995). Giving voice to young children. *European Early Childhood Education Research Journal, 3*(2), 5-14.

Pugh, G. & Selleck, D.R. Listening to and communicating with young children. In R. Davie, G. Upton, V. Varma (Eds) *The Voice of the Child: A Handbook for Professionals.* London: Falmer Press, pp. 120-36.

Silva, P. & Stanton, W. (1996). *From Child to Adult: The Dunedin Multidisciplinary Health and Development Study.* Oxford: Oxford University Press.

Smith, A.B. (1996). The quality of child care centres for children in New Zealand. *New Zealand Association for Research in Education 'State-of-the-Art' Monograph 4*, pp. 1-63.

Smith, A.B. (1998). *Understanding Children's Development: A New Zealand Perspective.* 4th Edition, Wellington: Bridget Williams Books.

Smith, Anne B. (1999). Quality childcare and joint attention. *International Journal of Early Years Education, 7*(1), 85-98.

Smith, A.B., Taylor, N.J. & Gollop, M.M. (Eds). (2000). *Children's voices: Research, policy and practice.* Auckland: Pearson Education.

Smith, A.B., Grima, G., Gaffney, M. & Powell, K. (1999). *Early Childhood Education: Literature Review Report to the Ministry of Education.* Dunedin: Ministry of Education.

Stephens, R., Waldegrave, C. & Frater, P. (1996). Measuring poverty in New Zealand. *Social Policy Journal of New Zealand 5,* 88-112.

Tapp, P. (1999). Personal Communication. September 1999.

Thomson, D. (1998). *How History is Failing our Families.* Keynote address to Australian Institute of Family Studies Conference, Melbourne, November 25-27.

Tuohy, P. (1997). Child health in New Zealand – the end of the golden weather. Guest Editorial. *Childrenz Issues, 1*(2), 5-6.

United Nations Convention on the Rights of the Child. Adopted by the United Nations General Assembly, 20 November 1989, ratified by New Zealand 1993.

United Nations Committee on the Rights of the Child (1997). Concluding Observations of the Committee, 24 January 1997.

Winter, K. & Connolly, P. (1996). 'Keeping it in the family': Thatcherism and the Children Act 1989. In J. Pilcher & S. Wagg (Eds) *Thatcher's Children? Politics, Childhood and Society in the 1980s and 1990s.* London: Falmer Press, pp. 29-42.

Wylie, C., Thompson, J. & Lythe, C. (1999). *Competent Children at 8: Families, Early Education and Schools.* Wellington, New Zealand Council for Educational Research.

Note

1 This paper was originally presented at the Seventh Early Childhood Convention in Nelson, New Zealand, 29 September 1999.

Consent in child health: Upholding the participation rights of children and young people

BETH WOOD AND PAT TUOHY

Abstract

Consent is a fundamental concept in the provision of health care services. It is based on practitioners' ethical obligations to uphold and enhance their patients' autonomy. It is supported in part by legal provisions. Where children are concerned, consent to health care is a complex issue. In order to uphold the participation and self-determination rights of children and young people, health care practitioners must address questions of the competency of a particular child, their parent's views and attitudes, cultural factors, a range of inconsistent legislation and their own prejudices and beliefs. Decisions sometimes need to be made in emergency situations, in busy settings, and when the patient and their families are distressed.

Article 12 of the United Nations Convention on the Rights of the Child requires that children be assured of the right to express their views in all matters which affect them, and that those views be given due weight in accordance with the age and maturity of the child. Other articles also have some relevance to issues of consent to health care.

In 1998 the Ministry of Health completed a project to examine legislation in regard to children and young people and consent to health care in New Zealand, to identify relevant practice issues and to develop information for child health practitioners of all disciplines. This is an important step in ensuring compliance with New Zealand's obligations under the Convention.

This paper identifies the relevant legislation, discusses the inconsistencies, examines some of the beliefs which have potential to interfere with children's participation rights and suggests some 'best practice' approaches which will address potential difficulties.

Introduction

In European society, children have traditionally been regarded as the property of their parents and have had little or no personal autonomy. More recently society has acknowledged children's vulnerability, and the fact that those who care for them do not always respect their safety and interests. State action to intervene and protect children and promote their development is likewise a relatively recent development. Society has not entirely resolved its ambivalence about intervening to promote children's rights when these seem to be at variance with the wishes of their parents.

Children are more vulnerable than adults but their vulnerability reduces as they grow up and they develop the capacity to think and care for themselves. As a society we have been slow to respect children's developing capacities and to afford them the involvement they deserve. Such respect and involvement improves the way we regard children and children's rights and it also contributes to their development.

These issues of children's rights versus parents wishes, and children's developing capacity to be involved in decision making, are key aspects of consent to medical treatment. Despite the fact that the medical profession has an ethical tradition going back at least as far as Hippocrates, the health sector has not always done well in respecting the autonomy and self-determination of its consumers. At a time when we are slowly, but surely, taking children's rights more seriously, it is very apt to consider the complex issues of consent as they relate to children.

Consent is a fundamental concept in the provision of health care services. The ethical obligations, which underlie it, are backed to a large extent by legal provisions. Seeking informed consent is an external expression of a health care practitioner's pivotal duty to uphold and enhance their patient's autonomy – their ability to think, decide and act on their own deliberation freely and without coercion. Informed consent respects the personal integrity of the patient by affirming their right to determine what is done to him or her. It has physical, spiritual, mental and emotional aspects.

Consent is a process, not a single act. It involves both being informed and making a decision free of coercion. Where children are concerned there are additional complexities brought about by their developing capacity to understand complex issues. Children's developing sense of identity is intricately bound up with the dependent and interdependent relationships they have with their family, extended family and wider community. It is therefore within the parameters of children's developing capacities, the family and culture they belong in, legal and ethical obligations and the often highly stressful settings of health care, that issues of consent to health care have to be considered.

United Nations Convention on the Rights of the Child

The United Nations Convention on the Rights of the Child emphasises that children have a special need for protection, but at the same time a special need to be regarded and treated as individuals. It recognises both their autonomy and the fact that they belong within families whose right to guide them is to be respected unless the child is at risk of harm. The Convention itself demonstrates that a balance between children's rights and parents' rights is possible, as is a balance between individual rights and collective rights. Of particular interest are:

- Article 12 requires that all children be assured the right to express their views on matters that affect them, and that those views be given due weight in accordance with the age and maturity of the child.
- Article 12 is complemented by the provisions of Article 13 (freedom to seek, receive and impart information and ideas of all kinds) and Article 17 (assuring access to appropriate information).
- Article 3 requires that, in all actions concerning children, the best interests of the child shall be the primary consideration. This is not incompatible with the provisions of Articles 12 and 13, but care must be taken to ensure that the best interests principle is not used by adults to override the wishes and interests of the child. A balance can be achieved by ensuring that children are well informed to their level of understanding and that their views are taken seriously.
- Article 5 requires respect for the responsibilities, rights and duties of parents and, when applicable, members of the extended family or community. Parents and family have a right to provide (in a manner consistent with the evolving capacities of the child) appropriate direction and guidance in the exercise by the child of rights recognised in the Convention.

Confusion in the child health community

In 1998 we received many reports of confusion and lack of confidence in matters of consent to medical treatment from the child health community. Our response was to organise a workshop and develop a publication aimed at informing practitioners. These activities promoted children's rights by encouraging practitioners to inform and involve children and young people in decision making and to maximise their chances of receiving the health care they need. The basic advice of a Ministry of Health publication for child and youth health care practitioners is that children should be well informed in a way in which they understand, and that their views should be taken seriously (Ministry of Health, 1998). We acknowledged that, for many children and young people, their family and cultural settings are the ones in which they belong and are supported.

The legislation

It is hardly surprising that there is confusion and uncertainty around legislation on consent. A range of legislation, some not particularly specific, touches on issues of consent and children. McDowell (1997) comments:

> ... despite increased legal clarity pertaining to consent by adults to medical treatment (and increased recognition by medical professionals as to their obligations relating to issues of adult consent), the law is not so clear in respect of the capacity of children

> to consent to their own medical treatment. Orthodox medical practice, formulated on many years' reliance on outdated and inconsistent statutory provisions and common law, fails to recognise the ability of 'mature' minors to consent to medical treatment (p. 81).

There is lack of case law in regard to capacity. Case law does exist in regard to some of the other dilemmas that arise for health care practitioners. This gives some guidance but it does not prevent some practitioners having to struggle with very difficult decisions on occasions and it does not replace some of the good practice principles we will touch on shortly.

We have identified at least twelve pieces of legislation which have some relevance to children and consent to health care. In this paper, our particular focus is children's rights to participation and their best interests, in particular their right to treatment and survival. The legislation of most relevance with respect to these issues are the Code of Health and Disability Services Consumer Rights 1996 and the Guardianship Act 1968.

Code of Health and Disability Services Consumer Rights 1996. This is a regulation under the Health and Disability Commissioner Act 1994 and places obligations on people and organisations providing health and disability support services. Children are entitled to all rights under this code.

The code provides that no health or disability service can be provided to a consumer without his or her informed consent (Right 7 (1)). The elements of consent are effective communication, full information and that consent is freely given by a competent person. The code makes a presumption of competence – that is, that every consumer is competent to give consent unless there are reasonable grounds for believing that they are not competent. A practitioner must therefore judge whether any child is competent depending on their understanding, maturity, and the gravity of the condition or procedure being considered. Even when a child is not judged competent to give consent they have a right under the code to information at a level they will understand. This seems clear. The code is, however, subject to other legislation and to common law. For example, the Guardianship Act 1968 might be interpreted by a court as meaning that age, rather than competence, is the criteria for giving consent.

Guardianship Act 1968. Under the provisions of this Act (sections 25 (1) and (2)) any person over sixteen, or any married person under sixteen, may consent (or refuse consent) to any medical, surgical or dental procedure (including blood transfusion) to be carried out on him or her. The Act does not specifically refer to the right of other people under sixteen to consent to health care and there has been a presumption that parental consent is necessary. This presumption is not consistent with the Code of Health and Disability Services Consumers' Rights or with common law. The common law rule as to the ability of children under sixteen to give effective consent to health care received careful consideration by the House of Lords in the United Kingdom in 1985. In *Gillick v West Norfolk and Wisbech AHA*, the court decided that whether or not a child can give effective consent to medical treatment depends on the child's individual capacity to make an informed decision.

This decision is relevant in New Zealand. Under the Guardianship Act an application can be made to the Family Court or the High Court for guardianship orders to be made in favour of the Court and allow an identified person to act as agent for the court. This section is used from time to time when parents refuse to consent to treatment essential to saving a child's life.

In a very public case in New Zealand in 1998, a successful application was made to the High Court to have the court made guardian when parents were not willing to consent to termination of treatment, in this case life support, without which the child was unable to survive. The court balanced the severely disabled baby's right to life with her right to be free from discomfort and pain, and took into account her parents' wish for her life to be prolonged as long as possible. However, the judges said the child's welfare was the first and paramount consideration and that prolonging her life was not in her interests. The court made the child's medical specialist its agent and a decision to discontinue life support was made.

An alternative approach, which might be used when parental refusal to give consent places a child's life or health in serious danger, is making an application for a declaration that the child is in need of protection under the Children, Young Persons and their Families Act 1989.

Consent paradigms

The ways in which we conceptualise consent can themselves restrain or promote good practice. Alderson and Goodley (1998) suggest that consent is understood differently by different disciplines and professions. They describe a number of different theoretical models.

Positivism

Positivism assumes that there is real consent implicit in the factual exchange of health care information. In this model, information, including information about risks, is given as a tangible 'thing' to patients, and it is assessed by checking understanding and recall. Problems in consent are attributed to patients' and doctors' limited knowledge and communication skills and are addressed by efforts to improve these elements. Surveys have shown that this is the usual model used within the health arena. The benefits we see accompanying this model include:

- It encourages health professionals to be accountable and to know and explain clearly what they plan to do and why.
- Basic information standards are agreed and are achieved partly through research, audit and education.

- Respect for patients' consent acknowledges their physical and mental integrity.
- It defends patients from unwanted intervention and coercion.

However, the authors argue that the standards this model sets are too high, making them unrealistic for both patients and clinicians and leading to disillusionment about consent. It ultimately leads to unrealistic and unachievable expectations on the part of the practitioner and the patient.

Social construction theories

Social construction theories are based on the premise that it is the individual's subjective experience of an event which ultimately matters. With respect to consent, social constructionists assert that making decisions involve a process of working through a journey – say, from fear of treatment, to greater fear of not having the condition untreated, to a growing trust in their health carers. This theory does not see personal abilities as fixed, but partly as responses to relationships. It acknowledges the number of social and personal matters, which influence choice. This is particularly relevant when thinking about children. Alderson and Goodley (1998) give a poignant example. A fourteen-year-old boy with cystic fibrosis, whose brother died of the disease, was asked if he wanted to have the recommended heart-lung transplant. He replied: 'My mother would be sad if I did not have it.'

Functionalist theory

Functionalist consent is described as a polite ceremony, a convenient means of transferring risk from the practitioner to the informed patient. While most practitioners would not explicitly support this view of consent, it must be acknowledged that in busy settings consent can be a simple formality.

Dilemmas and issues

Some of the following dilemmas have been addressed in the courts in relation to specific cases. Others are dilemmas not tested in court. Discomfort with attempting to resolve them can restrain good practice.

When should the consent of a child or young person be sought? The Guardianship Act is not specific about the rights of young people under sixteen years to consent to health care. In general, practitioners have presumed that parental consent is required and there is a dearth of case law associated with this issue. It is therefore not surprising that, despite *Gillick* (1986) and the provisions of the Code of Health and Disability Services Consumers' Rights, health care providers feel cautious and confused. The best advice we can give health practitioners under these circumstances, and considering our wish to promote the rights of children and young people to have their views heard and taken into consideration, is to seek the consent of competent children and their parents.

The issue of a child or young person's rights to refuse treatment is very unclear – for a well-developed discussion paper on the topic we refer you to Austin (1992). Our practice advice refers to the *Gillick* case and the Code of Health and Disability Services Consumers' Rights. However, we rely on the suggestion that if a child or young person is informed in the right way and at the right time and with the involvement of a supportive family, the chances of the child agreeing to treatment are enhanced.

How does one judge competence? As with many issues practitioners face, this is not as simple as it seems. Not only is there the issue of judging the developmental maturity of the child or young person, but there are situational issues to take into consideration. Children, and others, may not process advice and information well when they are unwell, afraid and in pain. They are influenced by the needs and feelings of other people who are important to them. Clearly good practice can help alleviate the impact of some of these factors. The advice we give practitioners is that it is not acceptable to presume children are automatically incompetent. Children should be assumed competent unless assessed otherwise. Determining competence is a process that is situation and treatment specific and must be assessed in each situation. Some criteria to be taken into account are:

- does the child understand why the treatment or procedure is needed?
- does the child understand what it is for and what is involved?
- does the child understand the probable benefits, risks and alternatives?

A child or young person seeks medical treatment and does not want their parent involved. This is an issue that arises regularly for some practitioners. In some situations, for example, contraception and abortion, the child or young person can clearly consent without a parent being informed. Our advice beyond this is that:

> Although the situation has not been tested in court, it is likely that the child/young person's treatment and consent rights under the Code of Health and Disability Services Consumer's Rights and common law and their privacy rights under the Health Information Privacy Code enable them to be advised and treated without their parents being involved (Ministry of Health, 1998, p. 14).

We also advise:

> This situation must be judged on a case by case basis, and where it is clearly appropriate (in terms of the individual's safety and support needs) the practitioner should discuss the matter with the child/young person and encourage the child/young person to involve their parents. In some situations it may be important to disclose the child's condition to others in order to keep the child safe (for example, suicide attempt or child abuse) (Ministry of Health, 1998, p. 14).

The parents refuse treatment regarded by practitioners as essential. There are a range of reasons why parents sometimes refuse to take the advice offered them by their health-care practitioner. If the matter is not one of life or death or serious threat to the child's well-being, the parents' right to consent or not consent to the medical care of a very young child can only be addressed in informal ways through the provision of good information, advice and support. It is a different issue when the child's chances of survival are severely compromised by specific treatment being refused. Parents sometimes refuse to give consent because of strongly held cultural or religious beliefs, faith in alternative medicine, or for 'quality of life' reasons. Case law is relevant.

For example: *Norma* (1992) was a young child suffering from Ewing sarcoma. The recommended treatment involved limb amputation and chemotherapy. After six weeks of chemotherapy her parents removed her from hospital and treated her at home with traditional Samoan medicine. The parents ultimately refused to allow the child to return to hospital for further investigation. The Department of Social Welfare applied to have Norma made a ward of the court, with orders to be made that the Director General of Social Welfare be authorised to consent to any medical or surgical procedure advised by her clinicians.

The judge acknowledged that the court had jurisdiction to place the child under the guardianship of the court for purposes of giving consent. He also recognised that in applying the 'best interests of the child test', that a child's welfare is bound up with his or her family and that any factor which might cause serious distress and disruption within a family was a factor to be taken into account. However, he accepted the advice of doctors that the child still had cancer and authorised the court as her guardian so that she could receive the benefit of modern treatment.

In the case of *J* (1996), a three-year-old boy, whom doctors considered in need of a blood transfusion after a severe nose bleed, was made a ward of the court with a medical specialist appointed to act as agent to consent to any medical treatment involving blood transfusion. This overrode the objection of the boy's Jehovah's Witness parents.

In the case of *T* (1997), parents of a child born with a liver defect refused to consent to a transplant operation. The child and his parents had gone to live overseas. The English Court of Appeal set aside the original judge's decision (that the child must return to the United Kingdom to undergo surgery) on the grounds that the best interests of the child went beyond clinical interests and must include broader issues relating to the child's well-being and quality of life within his own family.

Cultural issues

The final dilemma we want to refer to in this paper is that of culture. Our laws, regulations and practices do not address the different values and traditions of Maori, Pacific Island and other cultural groups in our society. The values of personal autonomy and self-determination and privacy have different meanings in different cultures. Individual independence is highly valued in European society, but in some other cultures the value of personhood is something realised more completely through collectivity. Within the discourse of child abuse there is a term: 'cultural stand-off', meaning that members of one culture, anxious to do the right thing in relation to the values of any other culture, but lacking confidence and fearing offending, do nothing. This also applies in the context of consent and we believe that health-care organisations can adjust policies and protocols to pro-actively plan for the needs of all cultures by ensuring that opportunities are made for parents and children to discuss consent issues with wider family and community.

Attitudes and values. A number of cases, made public in the media in recent months, have highlighted issues of attitude and values which exist where children and young people's rights to self determination and to treatment are concerned. We do not want to judge and discuss the rights and wrongs of the decisions and behaviours of people and agencies involved in these cases. However, we would like to reflect on some of the dilemmas and difficulties associated with these cases.

A young person's rights to privacy and self-determination vs parents' right to know. Last year a thirteen-year-old girl was referred, by her school counsellor, to a GP for emergency contraception. The referral was, we believe, within the law under the Contraception, Sterilisation and Abortion Act 1997. Public outcry centred on the fact that it was not compulsory to inform parents in such circumstances. We hope that counsellors and practitioners assisting younger teenagers with contraception, or in fact any other medical intervention or advice, will encourage them to involve their parents. However, we believe that where the young person is unwilling, for whatever reason, to do this, their rights to treatment, self-determination and privacy must be upheld.

The other view that some people hold in cases such as this one is that young people are not developmentally mature enough, or perhaps emotionally stable enough, to make important decisions for themselves. Our view is that if a young person understands the consequences of her behaviour, in this case having sexual relations and risking pregnancy, understands the risks of intervention or non-intervention and is making a choice freely, she is quite mature enough to give consent to the intervention involved. We also believe that the young person has the right to choose who the information is shared with – a view supported by privacy provisions. She also has a right to choose whom she will have support and guide her. In this case she turned to a school counsellor.

A young child's right to treatment based on the best clinical evidence available vs their parents' rights to determine what is best for the child. The other case attracting public attention was a three-year-old child with cancer whose parents refused to give consent to chemotherapy treatment. The parents chose instead to go into hiding and have the child receive 'alternative' treatment despite a court order placing the child in the state's care.

The public issue most commented on by the media, in the huge volume of letters to papers and on many hours of talk-back discussion, was that of parents' rights. Debate centred on whether professionals should have recourse to statutory protection for children whose parents refuse medical treatment. We like the model of parenthood suggested by Dingwall, Eekelar and Murray (1983). They suggest that the best legal model for analysing the relationship between parents and children is that of a 'trust'. Trustees have rights over the property which they can defend against third parties but which they must use in the interests of the beneficiary. This leads naturally to the need for provisions that allow third parties – for example, judges, mediators or advocates – to protect the interests of the beneficiary on occasions.

Despite the fact that society does place limitations on parents' rights to determine how their children are managed – in care and protection and education, for example – the issue of choice of treatment stirs up strong feelings of ownership. This may well differ with the particular condition which a child suffers and the same outcry would be unlikely in the case of a Jehovah's Witness child requiring a blood transfusion. Cancer is a frightening condition, conventional treatment not always successful and non-invasive alternatives offer attractive opportunities to parents.

A requirement of consent to medical treatment is that the decision maker is 'informed'. The matter of informing patients, or the parents of young patients, is far more difficult than it appears superficially. The degree to which people are able to access, process and accept the information they are given is affected by values, beliefs, ability and feelings. How can we expect parents of critically ill children to objectively weigh up the balance of complex, evidence-based research against simpler more attractive possibilities, which appear to offer hope?

Finally we do not have difficulty with the notion of the child's interests being the paramount consideration in a case such as this one. However, it must be acknowledged that for anyone in a position to seek or grant protection of those interests, the best interests of the child go beyond clinical interests and include broader issues relating to the child's well-being and quality of life within his or her own family. Family beliefs and values are relevant to the child's quality of life and acceptability within the family. Defining or prioritising a child's 'best interests', particularly where prognosis is uncertain, is an unenviable responsibility.

Practice advice

Thankfully other issues inhibiting good practice around children and young people and consent to health care are more practical. Some of these occur because of the settings in which the need to obtain consent are very busy ones and it is difficult to find the time necessary to work through issues well. Emergency situations require rapid responses and the child and the family are distressed. They increase the risk of practitioners taking a very functionalist approach. Such situations are confounded when practitioners lack good information, are confused and lack confidence about consent requirements. It was in an effort to improve awareness of consent issues and give guidance about practice that we developed the Ministry of Health (1998) publication.

We identified four principles that we believe, if used as the basis for practice, will assist in avoiding some of the dilemmas arising and at least partially cut through any uncertainties which accompany legislation. They assist in assuring that the participation rights of children and young people are respected. They respect the rights of both children and their parents and attend to the fact that it is not helpful to view the child outside the context of their family and their culture.

The principles

Respect each child or young person as an individual, and give them information and opportunity to participate in decision making at a level they are mature enough to cope with. Consider their needs and address them within the context of their particular culture and family.

Effective communication is a key component of good practice. Information may need to be shared more than once and in more than one form. There are a variety of ways in which communication with children can be enhanced. Use of the most culturally appropriate person and the most appropriately skilled person is also important. Time and timing are also crucial elements.

The best interests of the child should guide all action but not override giving opportunities to children and parents to express their views and have these given due weight.

Staff must be well informed and guided by clear policies which encourage practice that both complies with legislation and supports and includes parent and child participation in decision making. Confidence and compliance depend on information and support.

Conclusion

The UNICEF publication the *Implementation Handbook for the Convention on the Rights of the Child* (Hodgkin & Newell, 1998) addresses the issue of consent to medical treatment. The UN Committee monitoring states' compliance with the Convention seeks information under Article 1 in relation to legal and medical counselling without parental consent. The handbook points out that the right to seek advice does not in itself imply a right to make decisions, which would be dependent on the child's evolving capacities. The checklists supplied to assist states with their reporting to the committee ask:

> Do children acquire rights, either at prescribed ages, or in defined circumstances, for:
>
> - getting legal and medical counselling without parental consent?
> - having medical treatment without parental consent?
>
> (Hodgkin & Newell, 1998, p. 16).

Some countries have set an age at which a child can give valid consent to health care, but generally the picture is a very mixed one, combining age-based entitlement and 'sufficient understanding' elements. In considering the implications of Article 12, 'the views of the child being given due weight in accordance with the age and maturity of the child', the handbook advises:

> In deciding how much weight to give the child's views in a particular matter, the twin criteria of age and maturity must be considered. Age in its own right is not the criterion; the Convention on the Rights of the Child rejects specific age barriers to the significant participation of children in decision-making
> (Hodgkin & Newell, 1998, p. 150).

This is the approach taken in the Code of Health and Disability Services Code of Consumer Rights and we believe that it is possible to apply this in practice, within both the law and the child's personal contexts, his or her family and culture.

References

Alderson, P., & Goodley, C. (1998). Theories in healthcare and research: Theories of consent. *British Medical Journal, 317,* 1313-15.

Austin, G. (1992). Righting a child's right to refuse medical treatment: Section 11 of the New Zealand Bill of Rights Act and the Gillick competent child. *Otago Law Review, 7*(4), 578-96.

Dingwall, R., Eekelar, J., & Murray, T. (1983). *The protection of children: State intervention and family life*. U.K: Basil Blackwell.

Hodgkin, R., & Newell, P. (1998). *Implementation handbook for the Convention on the Rights of the Child.* New York: UNICEF.

McDowell, M. (1997). Medical treatment of children: Assessing the scope of a child's capacity to consent or refuse to consent in New Zealand. *Journal of Law and Medicine, 5*, 81-96.

Ministry of Health. (1998). *Consent in child and youth health: Information for practitioners.* Wellington: Ministry of Health.

Cases

Gillick v West Norfolk and Wisbech Area Health Authority [1986] 1 AC 150.

Re J [1996] 2 NZLR 134.

Re Norma [1992] NZFLR 455.

Re T [1997] WRL 242.

· *15* ·

Summary: Where do we go next?

Robert Ludbrook

It was John Wilmot who said more than three hundred years ago: 'Before I married I had six theories about children but no children. Now I have six children and no theories.'

This conference is described as a child and family policy conference and we have been privileged to hear from some of the leading theorists and commentators on children and childhood. For me it has been an exciting and enriching experience. Surely no-one can go away from the conference unstimulated. The only disappointment for me has been that I have often had to choose between three or four papers, all of which I was desperate to hear.

One recurrent theme at this conference has been that theories about children have not always served children well. Theories about children and childhood usually represent adult interests, values and concerns and tend to be imposed on children. We all know of the romantic view of childhood presented by the French philosopher Jean Jacques Rousseau which sees children as innocents of nature untainted by the corrupting influences of the real world. At the other end of the spectrum there are the notions of Martin Luther that children are tainted with original sin and that, in order to save their souls, adults have a Christian duty to drive out their wilfulness and wickedness. What these conflicting theories of 'children as angels' and 'children as devils' have in common is that they express adult preconceptions about children rather than reflect everyday experience of children. These notions are still around today and influence adult attitudes towards children.

Berry Mayall in her paper told us of the Swedish social reformer Ellen Key who, at the dawn of the twentieth century, saw the 1900s as being the Century of the Child. Berry Mayall doubts that this prophesy has been fulfilled. She sees a defining characteristic of the twentieth century as being the massive intervention into the lives of children by whole armies of educators, health experts, psychologists and social workers (and in the New Zealand context I would add lawyers). Instead of the century of the child we got the century of child professionals! Looking around this gathering I must conclude that most of those present fall within one or other of this category. Berry spoke of the unprecedented surveillance and control over the lives of children at home, in school and in public places. She also touched on the artificial extension of childhood (or, as I would call it, the infantilisation of young adults) which is typical of New Right social policies, which require parents to support their children until well past actual dependency.

Berry Mayall made the point that concerned adults making decisions about children based on an adult view of their welfare may, ultimately, deny children their rights. In our protectionist zeal we may fail to elicit their views or to encourage their participation in decision making. We do not ask them to contribute to the development of theories about childhood. Berry argued that the child development industry has cornered the market in knowledge about children. Children are viewed as pre-people, apolitical creatures, and social reactors rather than social actors.

Berry urged child professionals to shift their thinking so that children are perceived not as objects of adult concern, but as competent, contributing social actors, people who interact with and influence the family, the school and the world around them. While we as adults and as professionals have a responsibility to protect and provide for children, we must take great care to avoid patronising them by treating them as objects of concern rather than real people. UNCROC reminds us that children have a right to express their views freely in any decision that affects them and exhorts us that their views should be given serious consideration. Berry touched on a topic about which I feel strongly. She said that children's subordination to adults leads them to adopt whatever tactics they can in order to assert their rights – wheedling, lying, demanding, refusing. Time and time again I hear social workers, psychologists, judges describing children as 'manipulative'. What this means is that, if children do not accept unquestioningly the professionals' views or decisions, they try to influence the outcome through indirect strategies. Denied direct access to decision making they have no choice but to use indirect methods to have their voice heard.

Gary Melton looked closely at what we mean by child autonomy. He used the memorable phrase 'The central issue is not whether we should treat children like adults but whether we should treat them like people.' I suggest we all take these words away from the conference and display them on our desks, notice boards or bedroom mirrors. Gary urged us to beware of simplistic approaches. Autonomy should not be linked with competence and it should not be framed as an issue of children's rights versus parent's rights. We should think in terms of parents and children rather than parents or children, and encourage democratic family-decision making where everyone's point of view is seriously considered and discussed.

In giving children opportunities for increasing independence, one can minimise the risks by promoting opportunities for graduated decision making, which Gary Melton calls 'learners' permits'. Driving laws in New Zealand and liquor laws which allow drinking with a family member or as part of a meal, and which restrict alcohol consumption in public places, are examples of this approach.

In Gary's view, self-determination is less important than participation. 'Nothing is more fundamental to the experience of being taken seriously than simply having a say, being heard politely and having one's perspective considered – in effect being part of a conversation about matters of personal significance.' The question: 'How old should a child be before they have a right to … ?' misses the point. Melton referred to research that indicates that young people aged fourteen and older are no less competent than adults. In assessing autonomy rights, one needs to consider the risk of harm. Even marginally competent children should be encouraged to make decisions where little harm can flow from making an unwise decision. Children may benefit from having opportunities to make their own decisions, even where their skill in giving reasons for their decisions is undeveloped. Participation helps develop democratic values and is a preparation for future civic involvement. This point is made in the Preamble to UNCROC which stresses that one reason for giving children rights is to prepare them 'to live an individual life in society … in the spirit of peace, dignity, tolerance, freedom, equality and solidarity'.

The message we can take from Gary Melton is that 'We should all be architects, building new structures for child participation.' Why do adults find it so hard to accept and encourage participation by children? As a long-term advocate of child involvement in decision making I am often asked, 'How can we communicate with children?' or 'How can one get children to participate in decision making?' as if it was some esoteric secret to which only highly qualified professionals have the key. I usually reply, 'Why not just listen to children' or 'Ask a few children'. We sometimes see children as creatures from another planet. I have found that they usually respond very positively to any adult who is genuinely interested in their views and who will take the time to listen.

I found Pauline Tapp and Mark Henaghan's paper very challenging. They articulate very well ideas I have been grappling with for some time. Is the huge amount of time, effort and public money invested in the process of resolving disputes about children actually of benefit to children themselves? They make the point that 'Adult assumptions about the needs of children dominate the landscape in family law.' They point out that family law procedures can (with minor exceptions) be instigated only by adults and the dispute from the beginning is framed according to adult needs and perceptions.

With illustrations from decided cases, they showed how the views of children are filtered out through a series of attitudinal factors and procedural mechanisms. One judge has described the welfare principle as amounting to little more than unsubstantiated myth, and I have described it elsewhere as just another manifestation of the philosophy that 'adults know best'. Having worked for many years as an advocate for children, I add my voice to the view that the most common complaint from children involved in family law disputes is that 'No-one is listening to me.' Many adults have a particular penchant for listening to children but not hearing what they are saying. Because of a misapprehension of the role of counsel for the child, even the child's lawyer frequently does not listen to the child or does not take the child's views seriously. I have with mixed success encouraged children to write a personal letter to the judge, to ask for an opportunity to speak face to face with the person who is going to make an important decision about their lives. I believe that even quite young children may have a more mature appreciation of the family situation than any of the adults involved. I remember a seven-year-old who knew exactly what his parents' problem was and what was the best solution. Listening to children and encouraging their participation is not just a matter of rights or fairness, it is a matter of reaching a decision which will best serve their needs. Their involvement in decision making will enhance the quality of the decision. Mark and Pauline quoted cases where the court's decision to override a child's wishes has proved wrong. I can give many such cases from my own experience.

Several papers, including Cindy Kiro's and Irene Rizzini's, reminded us that children's rights must be viewed in a cultural context. UNCROC has been criticised for its promotion of values of western democratic societies and there will always be areas of conflict between deeply held cultural values and human rights as conceived by the United Nations.

Dr Le Tagaloa told us about Samoan society and the importance of the aiga, of the indigenous language and the relationship with the land. We are all guilty of ethnocentrism, seeing our own cultural values as the model by which other cultures should be judged. We have never fully grappled with the issue of whether a Samoan child living and being educated in New Zealand should be subject to Samoan values, papalagi values or a synthesis of the two, and the allied question of whether some protections for children are so important as to be universal and not subject to cultural variation.

Dr Le Tagaloa gave an account of an incident when a child in Savaii was fatally injured. Through my palagi eyes I see it as an example of the unintended but dangerous consequences that can flow from the use of harsh punishment. Dr Le Tagaloa explained it as un-Samoan because it happened on the Sabbath. Having spent time in Savaii I can confirm the strict observance of the Sabbath – a real pleasure for those used to the roar of traffic and the graunching of motor mowers which typifies Sunday morning in Auckland. This paper also raised the issue of overseas influences on traditional cultural values (with the global culture purveyed by television, popular music, comics etc) and the problem of children who straddle two cultures. Samoan children growing up in New Zealand or who have lived in this country have picked up values and attitudes which are quite contrary to Samoan life and culture.

It is heartening that Dr Le Tagaloa dismissed as a false notion that physical punishment by parents of children is part of Samoan culture. That claim has been made on frequent occasions to the New Zealand courts and accepted by judges from time to time. It was also put forward by a Samoan speaker at a recent child protection conference.

As a New Zealander I have been particularly impressed by the contributions to this conference made by our overseas guests. Norway has led the world in many aspect of human rights and Per Miljeteig spoke interestingly on young workers speaking out about their rights. We ignore the huge contribution to the workforce and to the tax take of young workers. It was of great interest to me to learn from Dr Claudia Menezes of children's rights in Brazil. Those who enjoyed the films *Pixotte* or *Central Station* will be aware of the importance of children's rights in that country, including the right to life.

Where do we go next? Recommendations and thoughts

The Children's Issues Centre is to be congratulated on organising a youth forum and children's forum. One message we can take away is that whenever we organise a seminar or conference on children's issues we should arrange for children to have real input. It is very important that child participants have support and time enough to get to know each other so that they feel confident in putting forward views which may not necessarily be what the organisers want them to say, and that they are made to feel that they are part of the seminar or conference, not just a side-show.

We should also take heed that when we plan research or prepare a paper for a conference we should ensure that in some way or other we involve children. Otherwise we may be falling into the trap of many adults in the past: claiming to know what is best for children and speaking on their behalf without bothering to check out their views.

Child advocacy

There are three basic types of child advocacy:

Systems or policy advocacy. Many at this conference will consider themselves to be advocates for children at a systems or policy level. This is an honourable and worthwhile role, providing we are not merely foisting our own views about children on children and other adults. Any man who set himself up as a spokesperson for women would be looked at with suspicion or antagonism. Similarly adults who set themselves up as experts on children (and there are many who do) deserve to be treated with scepticism. It is quite proper for adults to advocate for children in the sense of urging decision makers to obtain and take notice of the views of children affected by the decision. And it is quite acceptable to advocate for views expressed by children. But adults have a tendency to make grand overarching generalisations about children in the absence of knowledge about individual childhoods in cultural and everyday environments. By doing so, we will be promoting adult perspectives of childhood, not children's perspéctives. Another pitfall is to become so absorbed in our theories about childhood that we lose sight of children.

Individual child advocacy. Advocating for an individual child avoids the danger outlined above in that the advocate is (or should be) promoting the views of the individual child. Speaking personally I feel most comfortable advocating for individual children because I can then feel confident that I am presenting a child view and not an adult view. Sadly some child advocates fall into the same trap of advocating for the child's welfare based on some theory or generalisation about children. In this way they may be betraying and disempowering the child for whom they are advocating.

Self-advocacy. One of my disappointments about this conference has been the little attention given to the encouragement of children to speak for themselves. It would have been valuable to include participation and perspectives of young people for the entire conference. Not including them in this way seems to defeat the purpose of a conference on children's rights.

Priorities for the future

Some commentators refer to the rights in UNCROC as falling into three categories: Protection, Provision and Participation. I would like all of us to take away from this conference a new set of three Ps: the personal, the professional and the political. On the *personal* level it is important for all of us to put time, money, thought and energy aside to make a difference for children and to work against the 'invisible child syndrome'. On the *professional* level we should approach our fellow professionals and professional bodies and evaluate how child friendly they are and whether they involve children in decision making. I truly believe involving children is not just a question of fairness and rights, it is a question of values about the wisdom of children and the contribution they can make to decisions. On the *political* level we need to draw attention to the fact of the New Zealand government's dismal failure to even start on the process of implementing UNCROC. The baseline requirement of reviewing laws and developing a plan of action with specific goals and time frames has not been undertaken. It is essential that in this election year we remind politicians that ratification of UNCROC and other human rights instruments is a solemn obligation which must be implemented and enforced. It is high time that the New Zealand government embarked on the first faltering steps towards implementing the Convention.

In conclusion, I congratulate the Children's Issues Centre for an exciting, stimulating and challenging conference. I am confident that the ideas expressed in the conference and in this book of conference proceedings will have a positive impact on the well-being of children in New Zealand in the future.